Going Lean

Going Lean

How the Best Companies
Apply Lean Manufacturing Principles
to Shatter Uncertainty, Drive Innovation,
and Maximize Profits

Stephen A. Ruffa

AMACOM

American Management Association
New York ▪ Atlanta ▪ Brussels ▪ Chicago ▪ Mexico City
San Francisco ▪ Shanghai w▪ Tokyo ▪ Toronto ▪ Washington, D.C.

Special discounts on bulk quantities of AMACOM books are available to corporations, professional associations, and other organizations. For details, contact Special Sales Department, AMACOM, a division of American Management Association, 1601 Broadway, New York, NY 10019. Tel: 212-903-8316. Fax: 212-903-8083. E-mail: specialsls@amanet.org • Website: www.amacombooks.org/go/specialsales To view all AMACOM titles go to: www.amacombooks.org

This publication is designed to provide accurate and authoritative information in regard to the subject matter covered. It is sold with the understanding that the publisher is not engaged in rendering legal, accounting, or other professional service. If legal advice or other expert assistance is required, the services of a competent professional person should be sought.

Library of Congress Cataloging-in-Publication Data

Ruffa, Stephen A., 1961–
    Going lean : how the best companies apply lean manufacturing principles to shatter uncertainty, drive innovation, and maximize profits / Stephen A. Ruffa.
        p.   cm.
    Includes bibliographical references and index.
    ISBN-13: 978-0-8144-1057-8
    ISBN-10: 0-8144-1057-X
    1. Business logistics—Management. 2. Production management.
3. Manufacturing processes. 4. Organizational change. I. Title.
    HD38.5.R84 2008
    658.7—dc22
                                                    2008014102

Printing number
10 9 8 7 6 5 4 3 2 1

Table of Contents

Permissions

GRATEFUL ACKNOWLEDGMENTS are made to the following for their permission to print quotations, data, or excerpts:

Garrity Tool Company   Southwest Airlines
Hibbett Sports   The Washington Post
John Wiley & Sons   Ward's Automotive Group
Retailing Today

Acknowledgments

THE PREMISE OF THIS BOOK—that corporations everywhere can innovate and sustain excellence in the midst of severe, dynamic circumstances—might seem hard for some to accept. I, too, was startled when I first stumbled across this phenomenon—a measurable reality within a small but growing number of corporations. Great credit, therefore, must go to the ingenuity and perseverance of those at the Toyota Motor Company, Wal-Mart, and Southwest Airlines—firms whose powerful examples made this book possible. Recognition must also go to Hibbett Sports, and the Garrity Tool Company—two firms whose examples show the principles of lean dynamics in small, growing businesses. Special thanks to Marilee McInnis at Southwest Airlines; Joy McCord, at Hibbett Sports; and Don Garrity, John Entwistle, and Ryan De Anda at Garrity Tool Company for the information and insights they provided into the workings of their companies.

I must recognize those whose research, demonstrations, and writings opened the doors to new ways of thinking about business management and set the stage for this project—from W. Edwards Deming, Peter Drucker, and Genichi Taguchi, to Michael Hammer, Peter Senge, Jack Welch, and many others. Particular credit goes to Alfred Sloan, the brilliant business leader whose writings provided the background and data that supported my method for analyzing corporations' dynamic value creation. I am thankful for the efforts of those who introduced and demonstrated the concepts of lean manufacturing, Six Sigma, Reengineering, system dynamics, and other management disciplines, along with the insights gained from those who applied these methods—both the successes and the failures—which were critical to developing the thesis of this book. Moreover, the insights and infrastructures they have created will go a long way toward ensuring success for those who will implement lean dynamics.

I am truly thankful to those who entrusted me with important roles across a wide range of activities, giving me what might be characterized as a "lean" experience base, spanning end-to-end across the business of aerospace—from the design, test, manufacture, and quality assurance to repair and spare parts support for cutting-edge aircraft. I am grateful to have had the opportunity to work through diverse challenges with talented engineers and dedicated program managers across the Naval Air Systems Command. In particular, I would like to thank Kalmen Leikach, a true leader who taught me the power of rigorous analysis and precise writing—skills on which I have grown to depend.

I would like to thank all of those who took part in my unprecedented study of lean in aerospace—a government-industry collaboration aimed at identifying the means for breaking the cost escalation that stood to make new generations of aircraft unaffordable. I am grateful to the Joint Strike Fighter Program for sponsoring this project, but especially to Jon Schreiber without whose vision, confidence, and support the study would not have taken place. I was fortunate to have led a team of true experts, including Karl Stenberg, a pioneer in aircraft composite structures; Jim Painter, whose insights on jet engines proved invaluable; and Don Garrity, whose manufacturing expertise continues to be visible today in his thriving parts fabrication business—just to name a few. And this study would not have been possible without the tremendous access we were given by such leading firms as Boeing, Lockheed Martin, British Aerospace, Pratt & Whitney, GE Aircraft Engines, Loral Corporation, Rockwell Collins Defense Electronics, Texas Instruments, and others.

I am grateful to those at the Defense Logistics Agency who contributed to SURGE (Supplier Utilization through Responsive Grouped Enterprises), WICAP (World Wide Web Industrial Capabilities Assessment Program), and other projects I led demonstrating lean principles for mitigating risk in obtaining military supplies. I would particularly like to thank Michael Perozziello, whose passion, insights, and hard work helped make these and other efforts a success.

Special thanks go to Reid Boates, my literary agent, for his guidance and enthusiasm, my editor Bob Shuman, whose insights and detailed feedback honed my manuscript, and all those at AMACOM who helped make this book a reality.

Finally, I thank my family and friends whose encouragement helped sustain my efforts. Most of all, I thank my wife, Staci, and my children, Adam and Emily, for their understanding and support throughout the long days, weekends, and vacations I spent working to research and write this book.

Going Lean

Solving the Mystery
of Success

THIS BOOK IS FOUNDED on one simple but enduring truth: Excellence is best seen in a crisis.

In 1973 when oil shortages compromised the profitability and stability of the global automotive industry, the excellence of one corporation stood apart. Its booming operations fueled continued profit and competitive advantage just as others were clinging to survival. Its sustained success ultimately catapulted this firm—the Toyota Motor Company—to market prominence, and has made its unique approach to management the envy of the business world.

This very same phenomenon can be seen again today.

In the wake of disaster—from September 11th and into war, to economic downturn and then hurricane Katrina—American business throughout this decade has been thrust into crisis. Corporations everywhere have been hard hit from lost sales, disrupted by shifting customer demands, sent reeling from new uncertainties rippling from customers to suppliers. Once-unquestioned leaders found themselves in a terrible struggle, one by one driven into financial turmoil or even bankruptcy. But a few firms—Toyota, Wal-Mart, and Southwest Airlines—remained strong, even thriving amid the chaos that crippled their peers.

What makes these corporations different? How do they seemingly defy gravity, extending their edge in a business environment that should have dragged them down?

The answer is simple. While others insist on managing their businesses just as they had done in the past, these companies took a different path. They saw that the world has dramatically changed, that uncertainty and crisis are no longer the exception but are now the rule. And they adopted a set of principles and practices I call *lean dynamics*—thus preparing themselves long beforehand to meet this head on.

Those who read this book will learn what years of success followed by decades of struggle should have taught managers everywhere: What marks excellent companies is not how efficiently they operate when demand is stable and conditions are optimal. Rather, those who apply lean dynamics continue to thrive—sustaining strong profitability, growth, and innovation—even when unpredictability is constant and change is normal.

Lean dynamics goes beyond tweaking existing operations and organizational structures—quick fixes that offer uncertain benefit to the bottom line. It goes further than simply finding and removing today's most visible problems—the focus of so many of today's improvement efforts. Instead, it is *transformational*—a new way of managing that corporations of all types and sizes can put in place to create the tangible, sustainable, bottom-line results they need to compete.

Throughout the last century, corporations struggled to refine a system of management that was never originally intended to accommodate the business needs of today. Founded by Henry Ford as an answer to the unsolved problem of bringing his new innovation—the Model T—to the mass markets, America's management system quickly spread to become the gold standard for much of the world. Its basic premise—that tremendous efficiencies can be derived from managing jobs by their most basic steps—permitted managers to drive out hidden variation and waste, streamlining work and making complex products widely affordable. Yet, their system for keeping such a myriad of independent tasks moving together in lock step brought with it a new problem: Its effectiveness demands stability—a condition that has become increasingly hard to find.

For years, new strategies and techniques arose to hold chaos at bay. As expanding mass markets gave way to fragmented, variable customer demand, managers came to rely on buffers and quick fixes to protect their way of doing business. And with bouts of change increasingly driving disruption and crisis, corporations continued to do what worked so well for them in the past: Struggle harder until conditions once again stabilize.

A few have come to understand the losing proposition of demanding stability from a world that over the last several decades has become increasingly driven by disorder. Advanced technology and heroic effort can no longer overcome the shortfalls of a system that has reached its limits. What was once a manageable gap has grown to a chasm, one that can no longer be bridged through the methods of the past.

The solution is clear. Corporations can no longer thrive on a system that is built on the presumption of stability. Instead, they must prepare for change.

Going Lean challenges how companies have learned to think about the way they do business. It sets aside the notion that efficient operations and innovation are only possible when business is steady and demand is growing; that disruption and loss are the price that must be paid each time change is introduced. Instead, it shows how a new breed of companies has demonstrated a powerful yet unexpected weapon in the battle against uncertainty. Their lessons strike to the core of what is perhaps today's greatest mystery of success: how one firm's adversity can become another's competitive advantage.

This discovery did not come as the result of a single project or event. Rather, it grew from the combined experiences of innovators from diverse industries striving to gain the quality, flexibility, and cost structure they needed to compete.

More than a decade ago I first saw the need to pull these lessons together. Immersed in the furious problem solving that marked the development, production, and fielding of military aircraft, I found that this industry—a beacon of American ingenuity and achievement—was not at all as it seemed. Manufacturing inefficiencies were high, flexibility low, and quality came at a tremendous price. Simply stated, the management of its operations stood in stark contrast to the technological prowess that characterized its products.

How could this be?

This is the question I spent much of the next dozen years exploring. Fortunately, as my passion for gaining this understanding grew, so did my ability to study and report on it.

My first opportunity arrived with my study of seventeen aerospace facilities across a dozen major aerospace firms—from GE to Boeing—who granted me and my team of researchers tremendous access to scrutinize their factories.[1] We traced their improvement initiatives from beginning to end, looking to see what had worked and what had not, across practices ranging from lean manufacturing to statistical process control and Six Sigma.

I quickly found that things were not as I had imagined. As an engineer I had been trained to use a straightforward, logical approach to problem solving. I came to believe that finding a solution lies in isolating those steps where problems are most evident and then targeting them for action. What I found to be true was quite the contrary. While most struggled, those who managed to make substantial gains did not do so by giving greater attention to the disruption they could readily see or those problems already at hand. Instead, these companies had reached beneath the surface, taking steps that addressed the underlying conditions that had led to their occurrence in the first place. In doing so, many of the problems they once faced simply went away.

By taking a range of *internal* actions, these firms had made great strides in overcoming the substantial constraints of their *external* environments. They had been able to mitigate many of the effects of their variability, overcoming huge amounts of waste that had long been seen as a standard and accepted part of doing business.

I searched for the means to study this closer. Could these same methods be extended for even greater advantage? Were the steps they had taken transferable to other industries; and could they be applied across broad enterprises? How could companies avoid risk to their operations as they put them in place?

Then opportunity struck again. As I set out in a different management position, I was immediately confronted head on with many of the very same problems that plagued those whom I had previously studied. Charged with leading efforts aimed at mitigating the Defense Department's risk in obtaining a wide range of critical supplies during sudden demand surges—particularly those seen in times of war—I had to find a way to help overcome the effects of the tremendous uncertainty faced by those who produced them. From aircraft spare parts to medical and pharmaceutical supplies, I searched for ways to demonstrate how the techniques I had discovered could help.

The result? Through a series of initiatives using internal measures for mitigating external conditions, I was able to show tremendous, tangible results. Lead times for critical items dropped by as much as two-thirds; availability of hard-to-get spare parts skyrocketed even during extreme, unforeseen circumstances (including a demand spike to more than one thousand percent of normal levels).[2] In all, these succeeded in driving down the risks of supply disruptions while eliminating the need to hold as much as a billion dollars of inventory.[3]

I had proven that this new way of thinking could quickly achieve what many did not seem to believe was possible. Still, one question remained: With such great potential, why weren't America's leading businesses using this approach already?

Or were they?

To answer this, I looked to retailers, airlines, manufacturers—businesses of all types. I focused my research on those who managed to profit amid the terrible uncertainty and crisis that shook American business since September 11th; on those industries—retailers, manufacturers, and especially airlines—that were the most hard-hit from lost sales, reeling from skyrocketing fuel prices, and then struck by the ill effects of Hurricane Katrina. A few firms had indeed yielded very different results. Had they also applied the tools and practices that I had shown to be so successful?

I was astounded by what I found. As I anticipated, these firms had taken a range of internal measures to overcome tremendous change and uncertainty, but they had gone much farther. Each turned out high-quality, low-cost products and services using a fraction of the effort— but not just when conditions were steady and predictable.[4] They had demonstrated something new—the set of principles and practices of lean dynamics—turning what should have been overwhelming circumstances into tremendous advantage.

And in doing so they were changing the rules of business for all.

For much of the last century, sudden change and uncertainty affected everyone in much the same way. It was widely understood that periodic shifts in the economy would temporarily create disruption, drive down profits, and lead businesses to stagnate. All were impacted; no one was immune. Thus, these dynamic factors did not favor one firm over another—so long as the same management system remained the standard for all.

But this was not to be. The Toyota Motor Company was the first to visibly defy this standard three decades ago.[5] While other automobile manufacturers buckled under the tremendous pressures of a global oil crisis, this company reaped the fruits of a management system it had been honing for years. And with its ability to consistently create value when others could not—across a wide range of expected and unexpected circumstances—Toyota was able to overcome the tremendous advantage once held by the "Big Three," as it was now on the verge of becoming the world's largest automobile producer.

Consider the case of Southwest Airlines. In an industry that found itself at ground-zero in the weeks and months following September 11th, Southwest continued to advance. The company extended its low prices and superior service into new markets—even expanding into competitors' traditional strongholds. It continued as the only major airline to remain profitable, extending a streak now more than thirty years long while its competitors announced multibillion dollar losses and bankruptcy. For Southwest, the rules of business had clearly changed.

How was this possible? The company's founder, Herb Kelleher, had prepared the firm well. He never learned what most corporate leaders have come to accept: that business is generally predictable and stable. Instead, he came to see that "reality is chaotic," and built his system of management around it.[6]

Wal-Mart exhibited much the same phenomenon. During the economic downturn that began after September 11th, this firm pressed forward, posting strong profits just as it had done during downturns before. In fact, Wal-Mart seemed to *thrive* on these downturns, each time expanding into new territories and new markets. Again and again Wal-Mart defeated long-established leaders within the most challenging sectors, taking commanding positions in everything from consumer electronics to toys and even food.

Even more astounding was how Wal-Mart smashed conventional thinking by setting the standard for rapid response in its relief efforts following hurricane Katrina. Rather than exhibiting the sluggishness normally associated with such enormous scale, the company showed tremendous agility, overcoming vast damage to its stores and unprecedented destruction to the region's infrastructure, quickly reopening to hand out truckloads of water and other critical supplies in hurricane-ravished areas. Aaron F. Broussard, president of New Orleans' Jefferson Parish, praised the firm in his captivating "Meet the Press" interview, saying that, if relief efforts ". . . would have responded like Wal-Mart has responded, we wouldn't be in this crisis."[7]

Today, Wal-Mart, Southwest Airlines, and others are reaffirming what Toyota showed years ago: Sudden shifts or unpredictable conditions need not undermine a company's ability to efficiently operate. Instead, these firms continue to thrive despite some of the most severe circumstances, setting the new standard for value.

Moreover, this ability to sustain steady value underlies what is perhaps their greatest strength: their ability to innovate. The same flexibility that lets their operations smoothly adapt to the turmoil around them also streamlines their introduction of new products or services, making possible updates or changes that others might deem too costly and unrealistic. Equally critical is their ability to sustain a low-cost structure no matter what conditions they face. This helps create a stable stream of capital to invest in new development—the kind that offers real value to their customers, inspiring them to buy the company's products or services in the first place.

These companies came from different industries and businesses; each met with different barriers and constraints. Yet each had followed much the same path—letting go of the prevailing methods of management in favor of something very different. Knowingly or not, they adopted a common philosophy and a new set of rules.

And each achieved the same result: excellence in the face of crisis.

Going Lean shows how corporations can make the shift from a system of management that has served America well to one that will serve it better. It lays out the path paved by those who have succeeded despite today's harsh conditions and the hazards uncovered by those who have not. It demonstrates how producers of goods and services alike have abandoned the tried and true and embraced lean dynamics to achieve the seemingly impossible.

But it is not simply about applying such cases directly to other businesses. It is not about chasing anecdotes—a strategy that itself leads to disruption and crisis. Instead, this book shows how companies of all sizes—and across disparate industries—are applying their underlying lessons to achieve sustained excellence.

I began this study by examining an industry steeped in innovation—one whose continued success has depended on its ability to turn advanced technology into new products. As I look again at aerospace and then to other industries I see that even this lead is beginning to decay. What has worked well in the past is no longer enough; corporations must see that only in conjunction with a broader management shift can they preserve the effectiveness of this long-standing advantage.

For managers to succeed, they must begin by rethinking their business right down to the very goals of their organizations. They must cease striving for simply lowering costs or improving quality within the environment in which they prefer to operate. Instead, they must become broadly effective in creating and sustaining value within the one that now exists.

Part I

From Crisis to Excellence

AMERICA'S MANAGEMENT PRACTICES once made its corporations the envy of the world. For most of the last century they became the standard for all. Yet, with uncertainty and crisis striking from every direction—from overseas competition to economic slowdowns and surging oil prices—the time has come to revisit their underlying presumptions that no longer work but continue to serve as the foundation for how companies do business.

Chapter 1 shows how this growing environment of uncertainty, coupled with disconnects in how businesses operate, undermines corporations' ways of doing business. Chapter 2 examines the roots of this breakdown by exploring the basis for America's system of management—from its origins in Henry Ford's Model T line to its heyday during postwar expansion, to its challenges in operating in today's increasingly dynamic marketplace. It shows why this system's inherent dependence on stable conditions—once central to its success—now belies corporations' best efforts to keep chaos under control.

Chapter 3 demonstrates that there is a better way. It shows how a few firms have broken from today's cycle of loss to adopt a system of *lean dynamics* that protects their operations against the ill effects of change and uncertainty others have come to accept. It introduces the concept of the *value curve,* using hard data to illustrate how Toyota, Wal-Mart, and Southwest Airlines consistently sustain greater value to create an overwhelming competitive advantage. Chapter 4 concludes this part by examining the five common characteristics that distinguish this new system of management.

One

Awash in Chaos!

Today's problems come from yesterday's "solutions."
—Peter M. Senge[1]

UNPREDICTABILITY: Corporations everywhere struggle against its devastating effects. For, where there is change and uncertainty, there is crisis.

Yet change is everywhere in their world these days. Increasing competition, shifting customer expectations, and disruptive world events have shattered the marketplace and undermined once-straightforward management techniques. To meet this challenge, companies seek to take on new practices. But instead of making the fundamental shift they need, most insist on simply adding new features to the same foundation with which they are most familiar.

Their lesson is clear: The same system that powered their success for much of the past century now stands in the way of their progress.

Peter Drucker once wrote of the collapse of a diverse group of once-powerhouse corporations who suffered their fate by doing nothing wrong. The world simply changed around them; in each case, they did not see the need to respond until it was too late.[2] Many of today's greatest companies now face this same reality; they must embrace a new vision of the future and act—or concede their industries to those who do.

American managers take pride in their ability to react to the effects of uncertainty, demonstrating time and time again their tremendous capability to overcome adversity. Throughout much of the past century, this basic strength powered their firms to heights in productivity and innovation never before imagined—and made possible their very system of management.

But what happens when these effects extend beyond corporations' abilities to react? Perhaps the economy slows, technology shifts, or customers simply change their tastes. What happens when unforeseen external forces drive the marketplace to shift entirely? The bottom line is disruption and workarounds—chaos that translates to poor quality, missed deliveries, and dissatisfied customers. Sales plummet, efficiencies collapse, and operating costs skyrocket. Corporations frantically search for solutions, blaming their environment—all the while failing to see that much of their problem comes from within. Consider the examples in the following paragraphs.

- US Airways, like most major airlines, creates efficiencies by working to keep its planes fully loaded. Rather than flying its passengers directly to their destinations, the company first shuttles them to a number of *hub* airports—central locations where it concentrates the core of its operations. This way it can reliably fill its fleet of larger, more sophisticated aircraft by bringing together travelers using smaller aircraft from each of these feeder routes (or *spokes*) to complete the long-haul part of their journey.

  For many years this industry standard worked fairly well. Flights generally arrived on time; fare structures drew sufficient passenger volumes for airlines to expand; and corporate profits were large enough to attract no shortage of competitors.

  That is, until conditions abruptly changed.

  After September 11th the entire industry's passenger volume plummeted. US Airways, like its peers, found that keeping flights reasonably full meant dropping others—parking many of its largest aircraft that it no longer could keep busy. Spoke routes were hit hard as well, but their importance in sustaining passenger volumes at the airline's hubs probably meant continuing flights even with very low passenger loads. The company laid off employees in droves; sudden, dramatic changes to planning, staffing, and other activities must have created great turmoil, further impacting the efficiencies of the airline's operations.³

The outcome? Revenues plunged; costs mounted while idle and underutilized planes continued racking up costs. The company faced an unwinnable choice: either charge increased prices to its passengers (further driving down passenger volume and undermining its efficiencies), or absorb the costs directly and suffer financial loss. Either way, the airline faced a deep crisis; like so many others it ultimately fell into bankruptcy.

- How do factory workers respond to shortages of parts and materials that disrupt their operations? Often by keeping more of these items on hand to carry them through the next stock-out. By tucking away as many as possible the next time the parts become available, they assure that their shops can continue to operate without disruption into the future. Or can they?

Consider what happens when the weatherman calls for snow. Shoppers across the region turn out in droves, stocking up on essential groceries. We have all experienced the consequences: By the time you reach the supermarket there are no eggs, milk, bread, or toilet paper anywhere to be found! What causes this to happen? Such widespread reaction to uncertainty overwhelms the supply system. The result? Many cannot get what they need for days, until the system finally recovers from this event.

Just as with the snowstorm, workers who hoard materials to buffer their own shop's needs introduce tremendous variation into their supply system. Not only can such well-intended actions cause initial shortages, but they set the stage for these to occur on a regular basis. Demand patterns no longer match production needs as workers deplete and restock their hidden stores at largely random intervals. Resupply becomes chaotic, no longer based on meaningful consumption forecasts. All of this makes the availability of the items they need even less certain, further increasing workaround activities as others act similarly to prevent shortages.

The bottom line? *Workarounds*—reactive fixes intended to

protect against the effects of uncertainty—often make the problem worse. They themselves create unpredictability, amplifying
the effects of change and setting off crises that spread up and
down the production line, ultimately impacting suppliers and
customers alike.

- Over recent years, major automobile producers have bolstered
  their profitability by selling large trucks and Sport Utility Vehicles, or SUVs. For the Ford Motor Company, profits from
  SUVs became enormous contributors to its revenue; their high
  profitability increasingly offset lagging sales across other product lines. The company focused great attention on product and
  process development, seeking refinements that might sustain or
  further grow the company's SUV market share.

  Then the marketplace suddenly shifted. In September 2005,
  gasoline prices turned sharply upward—rising past the $3-per-
  gallon threshold. Drivers everywhere felt the pinch; they began
  trading in their larger vehicles for smaller cars that consumed
  less gasoline. The impact? Demand for SUVs plummeted by
  more than fifty percent. The company's overall sales sank by
  more than twenty percent—just as other firms who were better known for their fuel-efficient vehicles saw sales increases by
  more than ten percent.[4]

  Clearly, Ford faced no easy answer. Shifting to produce a
  significantly different mix of vehicles would likely drive up costs
  while causing planning and scheduling nightmares. Reducing
  overall production volumes to match customers' much lower
  demands might make matters even worse—perhaps undermining the firm's economies of scale and driving disruption through
  its factories and across its suppliers' activities as well.

  The company clearly faced a difficult situation. Not only
  would it probably have to rethink everything from its product
  mix to its business strategy, an enormous task unto itself, but it
  now had to play catch-up at the same time that it found its revenue stream severely impacted.

- Manufacturers and distributors across the country increasingly
  outsource major functions traditionally performed by their own

workforces. Instead of buying and storing large quantities of parts or components, many now create long-term arrangements for their suppliers to deliver precise quantities of materials just as they are needed to support their operations or those of their customers. This means that rather than tracking and managing supply activities at each step along the way, these corporations might now simply measure their suppliers' outcomes against preset agreements.

Initial results can seem tremendous. Corporations yield great savings by reducing or even eliminating warehoused inventories used to replenish factory bins. Their suppliers instead keep the right quantities on hand. All seems to run like clockwork—just so long as conditions turn out precisely as planned.

But think of what happens when unforeseen changes in demand suddenly emerge. Inventories these suppliers use to offset normal demand fluctuations can quickly dry up, insufficient to buffer spikes that go far beyond levels anticipated at the outset of these arrangements. Unable to draw items from pools of inventory, suppliers' ability to meet their agreed-to commitments can quickly disintegrate. Worse still, with only their outcomes tracked, their diminishing capabilities might be obscured from view until their buffers finally break down, escalating into all-out crisis.

The end result? Those downstream find themselves caught off guard. Deliveries can degrade or stop with no advance warning, creating immediate shortages for shops or factories who, because of these arrangements, have given up protective measures of their own. Work stoppages up and down the line can drive costly expediting and widespread disregard for established procedures. And at the end of the line is the customer who, in one way or another, must deal with the burden created by these failures.

It is not hard to find similar situations that show in real terms the effect that sudden change has on those who continue to manage in the manner they have in the past. We see here just a few examples; many others exist that show how corporations' conventional ways of structuring work, introducing new products or innovations, and implementing improvement initiatives do not work well within the uncertain and dynamic conditions so prevalent today. Too often such actions lead to long-term problems, declining competitiveness, or even bankruptcy. Sadly, despite the near-certainty that today's dynamic environment is here to stay, many firms continue to insist on running their business in this manner.

A Solution That Doesn't Follow the Problem

Michael Hammer, the well-known author and originator of business reengineering, labels as "contemporary myth" the presumption that successful companies operate as "a showcase of efficiency."[5] His critical observation—that American corporations are replete with disruption and crisis—describes what I, too, found during factory visits, making clear to me that this problem extends far beyond only a few firms, or just a single industry.

But if disruption is so widespread, why isn't it fixed? Perhaps because managers remain generally unaware of its lasting effects within their firms' operations. Companies have become adept at managing crises—mobilizing enormous teams and diverting whatever resources they need to quickly stabilize a disruptive situation. Once they conquer a crisis, it is soon forgotten; managers quickly shift their attention to dealing with the next problem. Yet, in its wake they leave behind armies of expeditors, piles of inventories, and extraordinarily long lead times; and these continue to accumulate over time as mountains of waste.

Such waste takes many forms. Companies apply countless resources to purchase and maintain unneeded inventories; they stand up huge workforces for stocking and issuing supplies and enormous warehouses in which to store them; they incur costs in identifying and correcting defects, waiting for late deliveries, or identifying and executing work-arounds to minimize schedule impacts caused by supply shortages. They perform unnecessary processing steps, cause excess movement of people and materials, and extend transportation distances. Each of these creates a negative impact on bottom-line results, drawing time and attention from engineers, managers, and workers—time that could otherwise be spent adding value to the corporation and its customers.

The late Taiichi Ohno, architect of the famed Toyota Production System, targeted seven distinct forms of waste in his quest for operational excellence (waste in overproduction, waiting, transportation, processing, inventory, motion, and defects—most of which were mentioned in previous paragraphs). Ohno set forth a powerful vision: He believed that a firm's production operations should progress smoothly without disruption—a vision demanding the virtual elimination of waste.

Each of Ohno's wastes corresponds to some form of *loss* in value—loss in material, factory, and equipment utilization, time, man-hours, and dollars that companies must ultimately pass to their customers. And each of these losses can be linked to a common underlying condition: *Variation*—deviations from intended objectives.

Variation—A Fundamental Driver of Loss

To understand the effects of variation, consider your drive to work in the morning. Suppose the journey begins twenty miles from your place of employment. On the average your drive may take about thirty minutes—a reasonable commute in many cities. Except your chance of arriving late is substantial; great potential exists across these twenty miles of distance to encounter such disruptive factors as road construction, traffic accidents, increased volume, or the effects of adverse weather.

The result? Frequent, unscheduled delays. On any given day your thirty minute drive could double or even triple without warning. To protect against late arrival, you will need to depart perhaps an hour earlier. The loss here is very clear: You lose precious time to sleep or to spend with your family, only to typically arrive well before your work shift begins!

It is important to see that the primary issue is not your *average* commute, but the *deviations* from this core time. We have all suffered the embarrassment of arriving late to a meeting, the frustration of missing a plane, or the financial loss of late arrival fees, perhaps with a child's day care provider. Since fulfilling these arrangements depends on meeting an expected arrival time, none of these losses would occur if our drive went as planned. Thus, it is the unpredictability caused by deviations from this nominal commute that leads to disruption and loss.

Now suppose that you could shift your work day to begin at a time when few cars are on the road. With this lower traffic volume, you face a dramatically reduced potential for encountering these disruptive factors. Thus, by targeting the true source of your problem—the *variability*, or wide deviations from expected commuting times—your arrival time becomes much more consistent, substantially reducing your loss.

Variation—causing unanticipated swings in processing times or outcomes—extends to each step taken by every organization on the planet; for this reason, they all must have in place some sort of means to deal with its effects. But making a critical distinction—addressing the real impact of these deviations instead of their internal effects or average outcomes—distinguishes those who are most successful in mitigating loss. As noted by Jack Welch, GE's former CEO, this focus was not at first evident as his company rolled out Six Sigma (a program aimed at narrowing process variation to improve quality and reduce costs):

> . . . we were measuring improvement based on an average—a figure that calculated our manufacturing or services cycle without regard to the customer. If we reduced product delivery times from an average of 16 days to 8 days, for example, we saw it as a 50% improvement. . . . Foolishly, we were celebrating. Our customers, however, felt nothing but variance and unpredictability.[7]

Three years after beginning Six Sigma, GE finally "got it."[8] After taking a step back and asking a different set of questions, it became clear that the company's initial aim, reducing *average* lead-times, made no sense. Filling some orders early by five days and others five days late showed up as overall on-time performance—but it did nothing to help the customer. Real improvement instead comes about by shifting focus to addressing the impact of this variability on the customer and the corporation.

Seeing the problem, however, represents only the first step; implementing effective solutions is where most firms fall short. Depending on how managers address them, they may end up simply replacing one form of waste with another. Worse yet, it can cause problems to actually worsen.

The Risk of "Tampering"

A classic experiment used by the late Dr. Deming, perhaps the twentieth century's greatest authority on business variability, illustrates the hazards of such a disconnect: [9]

> Find a table, a set of 50 marbles, and an ordinary funnel with an opening just large enough for them to roll through freely.
>
> Begin by placing a target on a table. Hold the funnel above target and drop the marbles one-by-one through it, marking where each hits the table. The result: the marbles do not hit the target. The pattern made by their hits fits within a circle far larger than we had hoped (shown in figure 1.1).
>
> Again drop the marbles through the funnel, but this time try to reduce the diameter of the impact pattern by adjusting the location of the funnel based on the last result (or on a series of the last few marks). The result: much greater disappointment—the diameter grows by 41 percent!
>
> Finally, try again to improve results by using the target as a guide. For instance, if the last marble hit the table an inch to the left of the target, move the funnel so its opening is now an inch to the right of the target. The result: the pattern grows dramatically larger!

It is important to understand that the underlying cause—the reason the marbles miss their target—is not some sort of error, as is implied by the subsequent corrections. Instead, these deviations are inherent to the design of the experiment itself, caused by everything from the dimensions of the funnel, to the size of the marbles, to the funnel's height over the table. Simply reacting to its outcomes—in this case, adjusting the location of the funnel when marbles miss the target—without first understanding the contributions of these underlying causes constitutes nothing more than *tampering*. [10]

FIGURE 1.1   A Demonstration of Lag

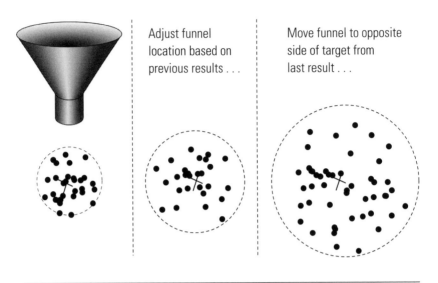

Adjust funnel
location based on
previous results . . .

Move funnel to opposite
side of target from
last result . . .

This same effect applies to businesses of all types; the potential exists for outputs to degrade whenever action is based on assumptions that are different than reality. And this is all too common; it is driven by the existence of disconnects much like those we see in everyday life. Consider an example described by Peter Senge, a professor at MIT, in his book, *The Fifth Discipline*:

> Adjusting the shower temperature . . . is far more difficult when there is a ten-second delay before the water temperature adjusts, then [*sic*] when the delay takes only a second or two. During that ten seconds after you turn up the heat, the water remains cold. You receive no response to your action, so you perceive that your act has had no effect. You respond by continuing to turn up the heat. When the hot water finally arrives, a 190-degree water gusher erupts from the faucet. You jump out and turn it back, and, after another delay, it's frigid again.[11]

The lesson is clear. The greater this gap between cause and effect—or *lag*—the greater the potential for a company's actions to further amplify its variability. We will see later that this lag can come in many forms, extending from information to actions, and even to innovation. Unfortunately, such lag is central—built by design into today's system of management.

Beyond the Span of Insight

More than two hundred years ago, Adam Smith described in *The Wealth of Nations* a breakthrough strategy for increasing the output of manufacturing operations. Using the example of a pin factory, he showed how a sequence of workers specializing on individual processes could produce hundreds of times as many pins as the same number of workers who performed all of these steps by themselves. Corporations ultimately learned to draw tremendous efficiencies by aligning work based on this *division of labor,* powering their system of management to become the envy of the world.

Smith attributed such efficiencies to three separate causes: "first, to the increase of dexterity in every particular workman; secondly, to the saving of the time which is commonly lost in passing from one species of work to another; and lastly, to the invention of a great number of machines which facilitate and abridge labor, and enable one man to do the work of many."[12] Combined with such innovations as the standardization of products and processes, development of specialized tooling, and ultimately the introduction of automation, companies found themselves able to extend these advantages by expanding their operations to a tremendous scale.

Yet, in doing so, they introduced a new set of problems. Factories were now filled with highly specialized workers who lacked the insight to understand how their activities related to the final product. At the same time, production flow became increasingly complex; the sequence of activities that turned raw materials into parts and then assemblies grew to enormous proportions as products and processes became more and more sophisticated. Maintaining stability, a task that seemed so straightforward for a simple pin factory, became inordinately complex.

The solution? Create a management infrastructure charged with keeping operations in lock-step, assuring their smooth flow despite the fragmented nature of how work was now performed. And this organization, too, was broken down into functional departments, permitting managers to specialize and to gain similar efficiencies as those seen in their workforce.

Just as was the case on the production floor, Smith's principle brought to management an array of new challenges. This functional division it created seriously constrained managers' span of insight, causing a serious lag in information flow. Managers found themselves forced to make plans and take actions in response to the outputs of other departments—often without any understanding of their cause.

This constant state of disconnect set the stage for repeated bouts of disruption and crisis. With each case, managers ultimately regained control, but only after accumulating new waste, hidden away as part of a general category known as *overhead*—a way of accounting for those costs not directly attributed to the products or services the company sells.

Over time, such overhead has become enormous, dwarfing even those activities it was originally put in place to oversee. In aerospace, for instance, "touch labor" now accounts for as little as six percent of the cost of the final product as compared to huge percentages of overhead—despite the labor intensiveness typically attributed to turning out these products.[13] The end result for many is a vast sea of waste, damaging and disruptive, yet hidden from view—a condition that is both an outcome *and* cause of lag.

The Concealing Nature of Workarounds

Many times I have been astonished at the reaction I receive as I challenge even enormous wastes—those activities, delays, or materials that consume resources but do not contribute value to the end result. Vast inventories, padded lead times, and workarounds acting as buffers against schedule delays impact value creation by distracting resources from everything important to the firm—from its day-to-day work to creating and introducing new innovations needed to capture the attention of the marketplace. As long as conditions remain stable, however, these go virtually unnoticed; it seems as if only an outsider would view them as loss.

Figure 1.2 compares this condition to a ship riding on a sea of buffers.[14] From its deck, operations seem to be effective, generally delivering results on time and within projected costs. Only those seemingly random hazards that breach the surface of the vast inventories and workarounds that protect operating schedules from deviations are seen and acted on. Corporations depend on these buffers during times of stability to keep operations steady despite the underlying churn that would otherwise cause a crisis. Yet, these outward signs of calm also mask the underlying unpredictability that acts to undermine innovation and send corporations into crisis when conditions shift.

With so much waste to conquer, it is no wonder that even modest efforts to reduce it can produce quick results. Corporations achieve great

FIGURE 1.2   Obscuring Variability with Inventories and Workarounds

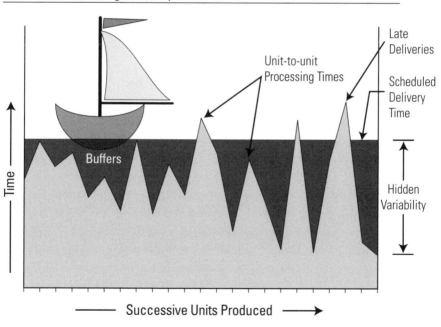

savings by slashing variability—driving down the need to hold these buffers. However, these gains can be temporary, requiring constant effort to protect them from backsliding. Furthermore, those successful in their initial attempts often run into problems when they try to broaden their application. One study suggests that companies are widely unsuccessful in transferring their own successes to other areas of their business.[15]

Worse yet, managers many times do not realize when their efforts have failed. I saw this firsthand during visits to manufacturing firms; I received management briefings extolling dramatic savings realized from one initiative or another—yet my subsequent findings frequently did not support these claims.

Such a disconnect often results from how people look at a problem. By attacking individual issues within the context of their own functional areas, their solutions can miss the underlying cause: the variation that causes these indications. Reacting to crisis only exacerbates this. With so many issues to be addressed it just makes sense to put as many to rest as quickly as possible so that new problems can be dealt with as they emerge. As a result, their initial benefits are not lasting; they may give the temporary illusion of success, but gains can quickly slip away, a point made by researchers Richard Foster and Sara Kaplan in their book, *Creative Destruction*:

> ... almost as soon as any company had been praised in the popular management literature as excellent or somehow super-durable, it began to deteriorate. Searching for excellent companies was like trying to catch lightbeams: They were so easy to imagine, but so hard to grasp.[16]

Visualize a mouse's journey as it maneuvers through a maze. By following those passageways that first present themselves, the mouse is often misdirected. As a result, it scurries aimlessly without making real progress toward its goal: reaching the cheese on the other side of the structure. Its missteps may lead it through doors that open into entirely new compartments, causing the maze to become dramatically more complex.

Such missteps can lead managers to broadly expand, even institutionalize, faulty strategies across their corporation. These can affect how businesses are structured, perhaps leading managers to arrange them-selves around products or services whose demand might vanish once conditions later shift. This is perhaps the worst form of loss—it sets in motion programs and new infrastructures with uncertain impact of their effect.

Seeing the Consequences

Today's growing awareness of operational waste has driven the prolif-eration of improvement initiatives. Too often, however, these run into problems. The reason is simple: The same disconnects that caused this waste often thwart its reduction.

A growing number of managers, for example, know that their em-ployees possess detailed knowledge of their operations that can help to uncover hidden waste. Some create programs to draw out these insights. Yet, in doing so, they can find that their system of management itself is stacked against them.

Consider, for example, GE's "Work-Out" program (the company's version of *kaizen*—or continuous improvement—a practice also used by Toyota that is gaining in popularity). In facilitated events, employees stepped away from their daily activities to identify ways in which their jobs could be streamlined; in other words, they looked for how they might remove unnecessary work steps from the activities of their shops (hence the name "work-outs"). Their most popular recommendation? Remove the management bureaucracy, as Robert Slater reports in *Jack Welch and the GE Way*:

> It became fashionable to launch assaults against bureaucracy. But the bureaucracy had been erected in many cases to help impose discipline that assured the quality of products and pro-cesses. All too often, the assault on bureaucracy had the effect of getting rid of some of that discipline.[17]

This illustrates a key problem. While workers can quickly hone in on *what* problems or wastes stand in their way, they often cannot know *how* to mitigate them. Simply eliminating their bureaucracy, as they suggest, can lead to chaos; governed by "division of labor," corporations' very way of doing business in fact requires such a management structure to maintain order. Yet, this understanding is usually beyond workers' span of insight.

Peter Senge referred to this as *the learning dilemma.* As he put it, "we learn best from experience but we never directly experience the consequences of many of our most important decisions."[18] For one reason, many of the most important problems cross departmental lines. This is the Achilles' heel—or crucial weakness—of many improvement activities; the division of responsibilities makes it difficult for workers and managers alike to see the consequences of everything that results from individual actions or management initiatives. Tremendous resources are applied to make changes that, on a broader perspective, simply create no value. Instead, they may simply accelerate a downward spiral of loss.

Overcoming the Cycle of Loss

If waste, crisis, inflexibility, and *loss*—poor efficiencies that drive up costs, misdirected strategies that impact sales, lost opportunities to innovate, and sharp drops in revenue that can impact profitability—are so prevalent today, why have so few corporations changed directions? In this chapter we have seen a large part of the reason. Their current system of management can make it difficult to see the problems it creates—how its methods and mindset can actually promote disruption and loss. Thus, the first step to lasting improvement, it seems, is to understand those causes we have begun to explore throughout this chapter:

- Today's growing unpredictability frequently translates to some form of *waste*—in materiel, facility and equipment utilization, time, man-hours, and dollars that must ultimately be passed to the customer.
- Waste is often widespread yet hidden within today's corporations. Each of these wastes can be linked to a common underlying condition: *variation.*

- The greater a firm's disconnects—or *lag*—the greater the potential for changes to amplify variation and increase its disruptive outcomes. This lag can come from a range of sources—from disconnects between measurement and outcome, to discontinuous flow of information, activities, or decisions. And it is built-in by design to this system of management—a by-product of its foundation in Smith's division of labor.
- The bottom line result is a *loss* in value—the adverse outcome of everything that can lead to lower bottom-line value, making a firm vulnerable to severe, long-term consequences.

We have seen how these elements work together to impact firms' ability to create value. Change drives up operational variation—amplified by the lag that is basic to how they do business. This creates disruption, workarounds, and even more lag. For many corporations the result is a downward spiral of loss with which they have simply learned to live—a condition that is widely accepted as the norm.

Firms like Toyota, Wal-Mart, and Southwest Airlines have found a better way. Rather than accepting the loss and buffering outcomes using extended schedules, long lead times, and mountains of inventories, these companies demonstrate a different set of principles and practices, or *lean dynamics*—a fundamentally different way of managing how value is created. With this, they have come to stand out above the rest, achieving a kind of lasting success that continues to gain in intensity during times in which this has traditionally been seen as impossible.

What exactly is lean dynamics? It is a system of management that creates and sustains strong, steady bottom-line value for corporations and their customers even as they encounter severe, dynamic conditions. Rather than avoiding change or suffering its devastating effects, lean dynamics harnesses the variation that comes with it to achieve astounding results, including:

- Greater output using a fraction of the resources (people, facilities, and equipment) and substantially less waste (such as lower inventories, shorter lead times, and fewer defects)
- Strong innovation and smooth introduction of new products and services, largely undeterred by industry downturns

- Operational agility that enables the pursuit of *dynamic* business strategies—turning today's uncertainty and constant change into a goldmine of opportunities; and
- Industry-leading returns as demonstrated by traditional measures: profitability, market capitalization, and growth.

The next chapters describe how businesses of all sorts can quickly begin to realize these powerful advantages. They will show an entirely new technique for mapping corporations' progress—an unconventional method for distinguishing sustainable excellence. With this we can focus on those firms that stand out, isolating their underlining characteristics—those common elements that make some firms consistently succeed. Finally, we will look at how small and mature companies are applying these same principles to advance their competitive edge.

But putting in place such a system of management requires stepping away from the belief that change is by nature temporary and uncertainty transient. Next we will see that this mindset, once central to the success of American business, has become its greatest obstacle—leading a growing number of once-mighty firms to struggle against sustained loss and ultimately failure.

Two

Shattering the
Illusion of Stability

If American business is going to prevail, and be competitive,
we're going to have to get accustomed to the idea that business
conditions change, and that survivors have to adapt to those
changing conditions.
—Sam Walton[1]

IN 1907, THE FORD MOTOR COMPANY was one among a pack of
hundreds of companies scrambling to capture a share of the emerging automotive market. Like so many others, Henry Ford struggled; for
years it was failure rather than success that marked his firm's efforts. It
was not until his twentieth design—the Model T—that he finally broke
away to dominate this business.[2]

Remarkably, it was not so much *what* he produced, but *how* he produced it that made the difference. Ford had found a new way to adapt
Adam Smith's division of labor to the production of his vehicles. To create the tremendous efficiencies that fueled his success, Ford broke from
custom-building large components or entire vehicles from beginning to
end—the standard practice of the day. Instead, he divided workers' jobs
into small, simplified, and repetitive tasks. By carefully sequencing and
managing these steps he was able to produce each unit in a fraction of the
time and at a much lower cost.[3]

This division of labor was critical in that it no longer left to the dis-
cretion of a particular artisan how a task should be completed, based on

nothing more than his own personal experience. With these individual tasks now broken apart, Ford could instead make them more repeatable and teachable.[4] Moreover, he could much better understand and manage the variation each time a step was performed, creating a high degree of consistency in everything from the time it took to complete to the dimensions it produced.

Still, Ford faced another, much greater challenge. His Model T line represented a substantial leap over previous applications of the division of labor. Whereas Adam Smith's example of an early pin factory dealt with only a few parts whose assembly was straightforward, Ford's operations involved a complex string of sequential tasks, each one dependent on preceding operations. This brought a new complication, notably the need to deal with *end-to-end variation*—those overarching perturbations that span beyond individual steps.

To understand what this means, think of what happens as a car moves down a production line. At each station workers cannot begin their tasks until those ahead of them have finished. They might need to retrieve materials, stop to replace worn-out drill bits, or wait for others who might be similarly delayed. If by doing so one station's output slows down, others cannot make up this lost time. Instead, their individual delays accumulate as the product moves down the line.

The end result? A wave of disruption that overshadows even the greatest of processing improvements. What good does it do, for instance, for a factory to cut the time it takes to perform individual production steps if delays from other work stations continually impact when they can begin? Their local gains get swallowed up—lost in the much greater uncertainty that dominates the factory's work flow. Such broader disruption similarly undermines other types of improvement; success in reducing defects or automating work steps, for instance, might make little difference where overall variation remains high.[5]

Ford's genius was in devising a way to overcome this broader variation—smoothing the flow and more precisely synchronizing the steps across his operations. In doing so, he made it possible to expand Smith's division of labor to an unprecedented scale, standardizing and tightly controlling long sequences of repetitive tasks to create great numbers of automobiles with unprecedented efficiency.

A Foundation in Control

Central to Ford's success in regulating the movement across his operations was the stability he gained from controlling everything. From raw materials to the vehicles that transported them, Ford sought to tightly manage all aspects of his supply chain, leaving nothing to chance. This way he could better protect his operations from the broad spectrum of factors that might otherwise cause them disruption.

To ensure that finished parts would match up properly without the need for trimming, he insisted that everyone involved in their processing—from fabrication to assembly—work to the same standardized gauges. He came up with new controls to keep subsequent steps from affecting their shape or dimensions, such as preventing them from warping during operations like heat treatment.[6]

Ford progressively increased his direct influence over anything that could disrupt the flow of his activities. In doing so he entrusted less and less of what he needed to his suppliers, bit by bit bringing their functions within his own operations. Eventually he owned all that it took to produce his vehicles—everything from the trees whose lumber made the floorboards for his cars to the trucks that carried them to his factories.

Ford seemed determined to smooth out the day-to-day demand variations coming from his customers' orders, giving his factories even greater efficiencies by letting them produce at a consistent rate. To do this, he pressed his network of automobile dealers to serve essentially as his factory's final customer. He required their full payment upon receipt of the vehicles (rather than once they were sold to final customers) and demanded that they hold inventories based on projections of sales.[7] With his dealers buffering peaks and valleys in actual demand with their own inventories, Ford's factories could produce for a predictable demand.

His capstone innovation was his introduction of the moving assembly line. With this he slashed the variability between assembly steps, virtually eliminating the potential for one work station to disrupt the pace of those behind it. This tight synchronization was what gave Ford *predictable operational flow,* making possible the quality and efficiencies that drove his success.

Ford was ultimately able to exert tremendous control over nearly every aspect of his environment, from his self-contained operations to his workforce (a key benefit of his unprecedented increase in pay to employees) and even to his marketplace. By reducing prices and permitting more people to afford his vehicles, Ford expanded the automotive market to unprecedented levels, gaining tremendous control. As Ford put it, "Every time I reduce the price of the [Model T] car by one dollar, I get one thousand new buyers."[8]

As a result, Ford found himself substantially less affected by the distractions of external perturbations, freeing him to almost single-mindedly focus on honing his internal activities, testing the limits of what his approach could achieve. He set his operations to produce essentially a single product at a predictable rate of customer demand—the optimal condition for his system of management. And his efficiencies permitted him to slash the price of his Model T by nearly two-thirds, expanding his output to an all-time record of over two million vehicles per year![9]

As explained by James Womack and Daniel Jones in *Lean Thinking,* Henry Ford's achievements, while truly remarkable, represent only the "special case" condition that proved impossible to sustain.[10] Despite this, his apparent mindset—that a largely predictable, growing demand should somehow be counted on—became the foundation for how this and other industries would manage for decades to come.

Leading the Marketplace

In 1921 General Motors mounted a fateful attack on Ford's automotive empire, adopting a finely sharpened customer focus. The firm drew from Ford's manufacturing techniques, recognizing the need to gain similar efficiencies if its vehicles were to be at all price competitive. But instead of challenging the Model T head on, the company took a different aim altogether. Through five separate product lines, its Executive Committee planned a coordinated range of offerings to serve "every purpose, every purse." The result: By 1927, after nearly a generation, Ford's reign was coming to an end.[11]

Leading the way was GM's newly appointed president, Alfred Sloan, who put into place the competitive strategy he himself had helped to formulate. By around 1925 he had succeeded in setting up a structure under which customers could purchase and trade up along an evolving continuum of models and options in a coordinated manner. In doing so he brought variety and choice within the reach of a growing number of customers, moving beyond the presumption of a largely static marketplace in favor of a strategy that constantly pressed the customer with new reasons to buy. And buy they did, launching GM to become the dominant company within what was to become the largest manufacturing industry in the world.

GM's strategy encouraged more people to drive better and better cars, a shift Sloan later characterized as one from a mass-market to a "mass-class market."[12] This trend became particularly important as the marketplace grew increasingly saturated with used automobiles (primarily those serving as "basic transportation"—further challenging Ford's ideal that he could endlessly expand the market for his Model T). The result: More people now wanted to move up, and they were prepared to pay more.

Ford previously had led the world by adopting an approach whose success had in large part stemmed from his ability to generate enormous efficiencies from producing great quantities of a single product, which he, in turn, used to stabilize his product's demand. By driving down manufacturing costs, he found he could offer the cheapest product on the market. This allowed him to hold his competition at bay, giving him no compelling reason to split his efforts between different vehicles or to make substantial product changes. Thus, he avoided the array of related disruption he must have known would have followed (something he later encountered when he shut down his largest factory for nearly a year to changeover to produce the Model A). Instead, he turned his sights to refining his operations for even greater economies of scale—and presumably greater inflexibility—enabling price reductions that fueled his continued control of the market.

With GM's challenge, things had become much more complicated. Ford could no longer endlessly generate sales simply by increasing efficiencies and offering lower and lower prices. With Ford's lock on the mass market now gone, so too was the stability on which his low costs were built. And as new competition created more and more variety, the gap between the new form of value his customers now demanded and his capability to produce it only widened. Ford's near-perfect relationship between his operational precision and his ability to drive the marketplace was gone forever.

Sloan's strategy meant striking a new balance between his factories' need for attaining great economies of scale while also producing the variety his customers demanded. His product variety meant he could not create efficiencies by producing mass quantities of one product, like Ford did with his Model T. Instead, he showed he could gain economies of scale by coordinating production of one car model with another, reaching across different price classes. He proved that creating variety no longer meant sacrificing efficiency—or driving prices out of reach.

GM's success, however, did not come without a price. Change had now become the norm, and with it came ever-increasing uncertainty, over time placing tremendous strain on a system of management built to deal with a constant, stable environment.

Managing by the Outcomes

The answer could not come from applying Ford's approach of total control—it stifled product variety, and variety was what was now needed in order to compete. Instead, Sloan succeeded in modifying Ford's methods, using something he described as *coordinated control of decentralized operations*.[13] Sloan used decentralization as the means to promote product diversity, giving his managers the degree of autonomy he felt they needed in order to succeed. Rather than track the details of each division's operations, he reviewed standardized monthly reports of their total operating results. He held those who ran them accountable for their outcomes, deciding who was doing well and who should be replaced.

To make this assessment possible, Sloan introduced an approach under which his managers reported their results based on their *average* production levels—something he termed, *standard volume*. He and his managers could now directly relate any increases in unit costs to their driving factors, from changes in wage rates to material and inventory costs. This allowed them to see beyond short-term fluctuations (including such accounting effects as the allocation of overhead)[14] to determine where corrective action was needed in order to keep costs from spiraling out of control.

But his company's use of standard volume had other far-reaching effects. With managers' attention set on the averages, success no longer meant carefully sequencing and synchronizing work as it flowed from station to station, a practice that Ford so ardently pursued.[15] Instead, managers set their sights on optimizing factories for their desired outcome: turning out huge batches of identical items at or near standard volumes.

The end result was that factories came to operate well at or near their intended rates, but their efficiency dropped off quickly if they had to shift too far from this production volume for which they were optimized. Anything short of ". . . absolutely level production—or the nearest to it that could be attained" would leave equipment idle and huge batches of materials, parts, and finished products unused and unsold.[16] This meant that surges or drops in demand could significantly drive down efficiencies. And its impact became even more pronounced with the introduction of super-sized, automated equipment, driving factories to make even larger lots of items at these predetermined volumes.

Yet, these expectations fit in well enough with the expanding conditions of the early automotive industry. Business thrived; nothing seemed to work better. Sloan's methods spread from industry to industry, completing the American system of mass-production Ford first set in motion.

In Search of Stability

By the 1970s, however, everything changed. Consider the pattern for automobile demand depicted in figure 2.1. During the late 1950s and throughout the 1960s, managers had become accustomed to growth; while demand had always been variable, fluctuations tended to be of relatively short duration with a clear upward trend. Suddenly the steady growth on which they came to depend fizzled; relative stability was replaced by unpredictable surges and slumps of increasing severity.

FIGURE 2.1   Growth of Demand Variation

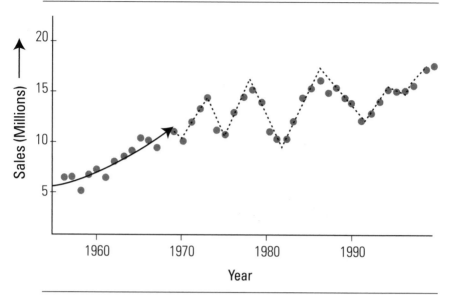

Data for 1965–2001 from: *Ward's Motor Vehicles Facts & Figures 2005*, Ward's Automotive Group, Southfield, MI USA. Data for 1956–1964 from *MVMA Motor Vehicle Facts & Figures 1986*, Motor Vehicle Manufacturer's Association of the United States, Inc.

At the same time, customers' buying behaviors were becoming less and less dependable. As this new system of management spread from industry to industry and around the world, it gave rise to an increasing number of companies who could now offer affordable alternatives. Customers now had choices, fragmenting what was once considered a "mass market" and making demand increasingly difficult to forecast. This placed enormous strains on operations intended to produce at a constant, predictable rate of flow.[17]

In order to stabilize factory operations, managers adopted practices that promoted the growth of enormous inventories and other wastes, creating long-term consequences in order to smooth workload across their factories. Buffering demand spikes or smoothing out downturns meant carrying enormous warehouses of inventory—a practice that managers unquestioningly accepted as how business is done. And the loss that accompanied this was viewed as acceptable, so long as it permitted their companies to achieve their objectives.

This same mindset seems to have gone beyond the factory floor; for instance, it seems to have impacted management's long-term arrangements with labor. During the industry's dominant years, automotive executives conceded to substantial retirement and healthcare benefits—costs that they tucked away as part of overhead. Its burden probably seemed to be manageable, so long as product demand remained stable and strong. Yet, the substantial per-vehicle costs these arrangements create today seem to support the conclusion that such agreements were based on "faulty assumptions of rising production."[18]

As hidden costs accumulated to enormous levels, maintaining optimal production volumes to offset them became more and more critical. Each new challenge sent businesses searching for new strategies with the aim of growing their market share—the only way, it seemed, that firms could secure the strong, stable product demand so critical to their operations. Corporations tried everything from acquisitions and mergers to price breaks in order to gain a greater share over the marketplace.[19] Despite this, achieving the sort of results they once found so straightforward became harder and harder to do.

Today, a few firms have visibly split from this mindset. Herb Kelleher, founder and former CEO of Southwest Airlines, remarked: "Market share has nothing to do with profitability." He further explained, "In order to get an additional 5 percent of the market, some companies increased their costs by 25 percent. That's really incongruous if profitability is your purpose."[20] The firm continues to show today (under CEO Gary Kelly and president Colleen Barrett) that sustaining excellence means taking on a very different mindset, one that makes turning out steady value possible no matter how conditions change—and driving out the tremendous loss that too often characterizes how businesses have come to operate.

To do this, businesses must come to better understand the interaction between what it is that their customers seek and their own ability to deliver it across a broad array of circumstances. Loss in value can no longer be looked at as something to be addressed only when it rises to a level that threatens a firm's stability and other near-term objectives. Instead, managers must form a more complete picture of its varying impacts on their business across their continuum of circumstances.

Loss as a Continuum

Many years ago the renowned Japanese statistician, Genichi Taguchi, forwarded the concept that loss does not suddenly appear when a preset limit, or threshold, is breached. For instance, quality does not suddenly diminish when a machinist exceeds a blueprint tolerance; instead, loss grows continuously as outcomes deviate farther and farther from their intended target. How much of an impact this has depends on the situation. Loss might rise abruptly if a product's performance requires parts to fit together precisely; it might have little effect if the design calls for a looser fit-up.

In the early 1980s the Ford Motor Company ran into what has since become a classic example of this phenomenon. After finding that a large number of its transmissions were wearing out prematurely, the company's analysis revealed a clear trend: Problems with its transmissions related to the factory in which they had been built. Ford found that most of its problem components came from its *own* factories; those manufactured by its other source—Mazda (a company in which Ford had taken a large financial stake)—had a much lower failure rate. Yet, Ford and Mazda had built their components to the same dimensions, checking and certifying them to the same blueprint drawings. Still, Mazda's transmissions outperformed Ford's.

What, then, could have caused such a major difference? When engineers examined the Ford-produced components, they found their dimensions generally hovered just within the company's tolerance limits. Conversely, the Mazda parts fell much closer to the nominal dimensions, or nearer to the optimal size and shape called out by the drawings. Thus, reducing their deviations in size, or *dimensional variation*—even inside of the acceptable tolerance range—caused parts to fit together more precisely, mitigating the abnormal wear that caused their failure.[21]

Quality inspectors have long applied pass-fail criteria just as Ford had done in this case, as if all points that fall within an "acceptable" range are of equal value but assessing those that fall outside as faulty. In reality this cannot be true; the results of the Mazda plant demonstrated that there is, in fact, significant value to be gained by further drawing down the variation of their dimensions.

Using what he termed the *loss function,* Taguchi graphically depicted this effect. With a curve like the one depicted in figure 2.2, he showed that loss is minimal at a system's optimal state (Deming argues that a certain amount of loss is normal); it incrementally increases as conditions move farther and farther from this point.[22] Thus, substantial loss can accumulate even *inside* of accepted tolerances, just as it had done in the case of the Ford transmissions. As we see in the figure, loss can grow substantially by the time variation reaches the upper or lower tolerances (causing parts to fit together either too loosely or too tightly).

This same concept applies to just about any system where variation is involved. From product dimensions (as was just described), to deviations in supplier shipments and airline's flight delays, we can depict the rate that loss increases for any given activity as its outcomes vary from their intended objectives. And how well an activity's execution is matched to its design is of critical importance—*systems in which normal variances create an elevated state of loss can have serious implications on their stability and overall outcomes.*

FIGURE 2.2   The Taguchi Loss Function

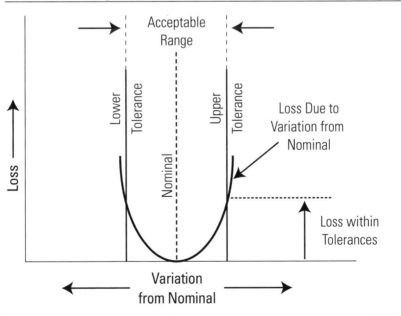

The Impact of Variation on Loss

During a visit to an aerospace producer it was not hard for me to see that its operations had been struggling against just such a condition. First-time production yields were low; countless cycles of testing, rework, and retesting to correct defects had become the norm. Delivery delays, expediting, and other workarounds routinely disrupted factory work plans. It almost seemed as if its mountains of inventories and the armies of expeditors were all that stood in the way of outright disaster.[23]

Driving this loss was a severe state of variation, creating uncertainty and disruption across the factory. Not only were its different work stations struggling to keep pace with their individual demands, but the effects of their unstable results impacted other activities up and down the line. At the end of the line these accumulated effects drove enormous *cycle time variation*—the time it took to assemble each successive unit spanned as much as thirty percent from the nominal (depicted in figure 2.3).

What was it that created such volatility? Precisely those things that today's management approach has emphasized: large-batch produc-

FIGURE 2.3   Variation in Factory Assembly[24]

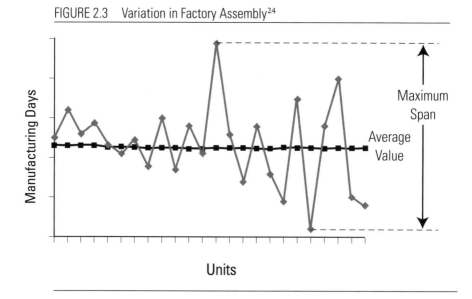

FIGURE 2.4   The Effect of Cycle Time Variation on Loss

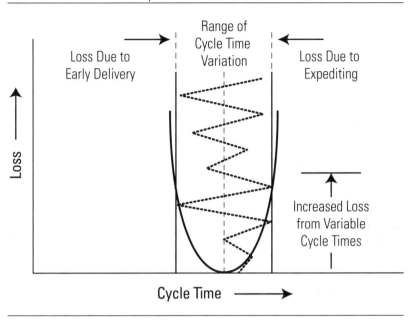

tion, super-sized equipment, and narrowly specialized operations—everything managers have come to embrace in order to maximize output when operating at or near a standard volume. The lag this creates results in steep, inflexible loss functions, probably looking a lot like that shown in figure 2.4. Superimposing a firm's variation on this curve is particularly revealing; in this case its intersection at such an elevated level of loss strongly suggests a mismatch between the firm's capabilities to accommodate the wide span of deviations it must face.

Such a steep curve means that each station must perform work very closely to when it is planned. Delaying even slightly can lead to substantial loss, causing factories to temporarily idle expensive equipment and their operators. Pressing to finish early to expedite orders could create other kinds of loss, perhaps undermining quality, disrupting schedules, and thus impacting other workstations. Either might create a domino effect, causing shortages or expediting of other activities, thus driving up similar loss for workstations across the factory.

The Dynamic Effects of Change

Many years ago as a newly graduated engineer embarking on a career in aerospace, I stood in awe of American innovation. Working alongside spirited test pilots, respected program managers, and the world's most capable design engineers, my appreciation continued to grow. Over time, I came to believe in this nation's ability to overcome nearly any hurdle, to reach almost any goal.

More than a quarter-century later I now see that even such tremendous spirit and ingenuity cannot stand on its own. The best technology in the world offers little advantage if its introduction lags the competition; it does no good at all if it fails to reach the marketplace. Continued leadership demands change—rapid and frequent change that displaces the competition before it can gain a foothold. With change, however, only one thing is certain: There will be variation, and with it will come disruption.

Since disruption compromises stability, it causes managers to approach change of all types with caution and concern. Consider the shift reported in a major aerospace firm's thinking on how to improve the value it provides to its customer. In order to control costs, managers decided that new technology must now "buy its way onto the plane."[25] In my own travels I have heard such statements as well; my own reaction was one of concern. In an industry where a company's leadership depends on building products that have the latest technology, where is the value in avoiding its use?

What makes such change particularly damaging is not so much its direct result—the elevated loss it creates for individual workstations. Instead, the real problem is its *dynamic effect*—the overreactions from the uncertainty that these deviations create. We can see this if we look back to the earlier analogy of driving a car in heavy rush hour traffic:

> Imagine yourself driving home from work. At first, traffic appears to be moving forward steadily, allowing you to travel at the speed limit. Suddenly, you see red taillights on the cars in front of you. The traffic slows to a crawl. You look around for an accident, but see nothing. There is no road construction; there are no entrance ramps. Nothing can be found that could have

caused this delay.... It takes 15 to 20 minutes traveling at this slow pace until the traffic abruptly speeds up again.[26]

What causes this to happen? The answer can be as simple as one car making a sudden change in its movement, startling those behind it. Perhaps the driver hit his or her brakes or suddenly changed lanes. With little to go on other than the sudden appearance of brake lights in front of them, the drivers who follow will in turn overreact, slowing down sharply themselves. The end result is a chain-reaction that progressively clogs the flow of traffic until it comes to a halt.

Just as the movement of individual cars makes up the overall pace of traffic, a firm's work steps act together to form the flow of its operations. Each of these steps moves independently, speeding up or slowing down to some degree, their variations adding together to form one overall result. When one of these cars—or steps—suddenly changes pace, it sends a shock wave triggering extreme variation and disruption up and down the line.

How much loss does this create? Its impact can be dramatic and far-reaching, as can be seen in corporations' enormous savings when such variation is later controlled (an effect that is notionally depicted in figure 2.5).

In one case, even moderate reduction in cycle time variation correlated to huge inventory and lead time improvements (as much as eighty percent and sixty-eight percent, respectively).[27] In others, narrowing variation using Six Sigma has purportedly created savings into the billions of dollars.[28] This substantial impact of changes in variation on loss—indicative of steep loss functions—suggests the systems under which these firms operate are poorly suited to change.

Facing such tremendous potential for loss, why would companies pursue activities that would introduce such change—any change— unless they absolutely must? For that matter, why introduce new designs or product upgrades—activities that would surely drive up variation and loss—unless these have become absolutely necessary? Why not instead stay with existing products or service offerings for as long as possible?

Such a mindset of resisting change and regulating innovation can no longer be accepted. It may lend a sense of security for the short

FIGURE 2.5 The Impact of Change on Loss

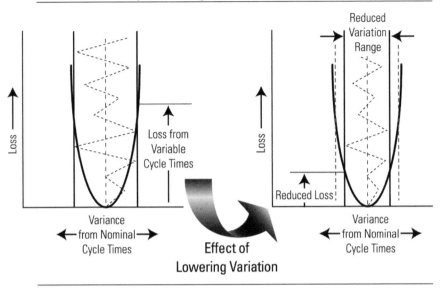

term, but in the long term it will lead to repeated crisis and declining competitiveness.

Adopting a Focus on Value

We have seen that management techniques based on a presumption of stability have led corporations to create narrowly optimized capabilities that respond poorly to change. Any shift, causing even moderate increases to variances, can lead to widespread disruption and tremendous loss. Their response is natural: Cling to their current offerings as long as possible to avoid the disorder they know will be so hard to stabilize. But this solution is really no solution at all. It only succeeds in putting off the inevitable, while delaying the fresh new offerings companies increasingly need to compete.

Ford's dramatic downfall early last century should have served as an early warning of this unfortunate dilemma. Simply preserving the firm's hard-earned efficiencies in bringing its existing product—the Model T—to the customer was not enough. Corporations today face much the same issue; they must see that continuing to thrive takes more than "damage containment."[29] They must look beyond simply trimming costs or optimizing operational effectiveness. Success now requires striking out with new innovations at a pace faster than before, making them more cost-effective and thus ensuring more and more of them find their way into the marketplace. This means rethinking their existing operating structure, beginning at a very basic level, as is pointed out by Clayton Christensen in his book, *The Innovator's Dilemma:*

> . . . managers who face the need to change or innovate, therefore, need to do more than assign the right resources to the problem. They need to be sure that the organization in which those resources will be working is itself capable of succeeding . . . [30]

A growing number of firms are doing just this, demonstrating a way of doing business that is better-suited to their environment of change. Together their lessons form the tenets of lean dynamics, enabling them to introduce exciting new innovations and then turning them out faster and more reliably at a lower cost—despite facing some of the business world's most dynamic circumstances.

Which firms are able to do this? To find the answer, we need a means for isolating excellence from anecdotes; we need a structured way for mapping and tracking their overarching components of value. After years of research and poring through data I found such a tool, a roadmap of sorts that draws on existing business theory, but in a much different way. The next chapter shows that, much like this business approach itself, the real difference comes from the way it is applied. Laying out this roadmap requires taking an unconventional perspective and drawing from a very different model.

Three

Creating a Roadmap for Change

> Today's planning must assume that the future
> can't be predicted—only prepared for.
> —Michael Hammer [1]

THE ADVENT OF THE JET ENGINE brought performance as well as
peril. With it aircraft could fly faster and higher than was ever before
imaginable. Despite their planes' high-end performance, pilots quickly
realized this new innovation caused new problems at low velocities. In
order to maintain thrust, pilots now had to land at very high speeds,
sometimes at hundreds of miles per hour—at the limits of their brak-
ing ability. Any mistake could prove fatal; power "spooled up" so slowly
that their aircraft might not be able to climb out of harm's way in an
aborted landing attempt. [2]

This new limitation was a real concern. Propeller aircraft using certain maneuvers could slow to very low speeds and altitudes and then
quickly accelerate. Because jets could not do this, a pilot had to remain
vigilant so as not to fall to a point where it would be impossible to recover if conditions suddenly changed. In other words, he had to keep the
aircraft from getting, as the expression goes, "behind the power curve"—
slowing to an airspeed where a plane cannot maintain its altitude and is
at risk of crashing.

The *power curve* itself is nothing more than a graphical depiction of
the two competing forces that together dictate how well an airplane will
perform at any point in its flight. [3] One is the thrust that can be generated

from its engines—their *power available* to make flight possible (drawn as a straight line for a jet aircraft). The other is the thrust the plane needs— the *power required* to overcome all the negative forces (or drag) acting on it through the course of its flight. Like loss, a plane's *power required* varies throughout its flight; it is lowest at its point of least drag (dictated by the design of the system) and increases as it speeds up or slows down from this point. And it is displayed as a curve that looks remarkably like the loss function.

The interaction between these two components serves as a pilot's roadmap to a plane's performance at any point in its flight. Where they meet dictates the upper and lower limits of the plane's flight. From figure 3.1 we can see that their right-hand intersection occurs at the point where rising loss can no longer be overcome by its engines, and thus the plane can go no faster. The left-hand point identifies its lowest speed for stable flight.

For a fighter pilot, ensuring the plane has the excess power to quickly accelerate or climb with the sudden appearance of an adversary is of critical importance. Doing this means tracking the vehicle's *power margin*— or the distance between its power required and power available at any

FIGURE 3.1   The Power Curve

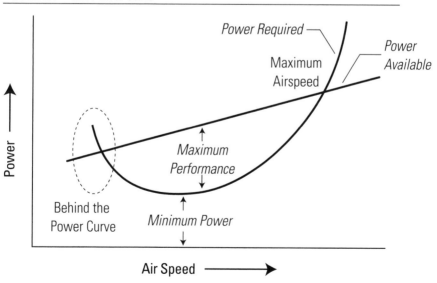

point in flight. Maintaining a large power margin at all times is essential to preserving this ability to maneuver.

How does this relate to business? Corporations everywhere operate under a power curve of sorts. Just as an aircraft does not perform at one speed throughout its flight, neither does a business operate at a constant pace of activity flow. And just as the fighter pilot must do, a manager must match the firm's capabilities to the dynamics of its environment to ensure it will not fall into harm's way when conditions ultimately shift.

Minding the Value Curve

Much like the power curve, we can graphically portray how a company performs at each point across the range that its activities will flow, using something we might term its *value curve*. Much like we saw for an airplane, this value curve consists of two parts: *value required,* which is the sum total of loss from each of its individual activities that it must overcome; and *value available,* or what the customer pays for the output these activities produce (a direct means for gauging value as perceived by the customer). Together, these set the limits of the firm's performance; their relationship defines the *value margin* so critical to driving its competitive strength.

The best way to map out a value curve is not by aggregating all of the individual loss functions that help shape its value required; this would be difficult because of the complex effect of their individual interactions (described in Chapter 2). For an airplane, engineers instead measure its overall outputs while simulating different rates of speed in a wind tunnel—or better yet, during actual flight tests. In much the same way we can calculate a firm's value curve by taking measurements of a firm's response as it changes its rate of flow. And just as with a flight test, this means pressing the system to its limits—subjecting it to the very worst conditions it might see during its operation.

For a glimpse of the value curve for a classic American corporation, we need look no further than to its first complete example: Alfred Sloan's General Motors. Remarkably, it was only a handful of years after Sloan first prototyped his system that he had the chance to fully test its limits.

Figure 3.2 depicts GM's value curve between 1926 and 1936—a string of years marked by greatly shifting flow in automotive production, as world markets swung from prosperity to the Great Depression, and then to recovery.[4] *Value required* is calculated as the total cost it takes to produce each unit. *Value available* is the income the company gains from the sale of each vehicle. (Scaling these to a constant value required as described in the Appendix makes trends clearer by highlighting their proportional relationships).

As we see from the intersection of these curves, Sloan's operations were ill-prepared for such a wide span of activity. Designed for a preset rate of flow (volume serves as a proxy for flow, which was apparently somewhere around one-and-a-half million cars per year), GM's value margin suffered greatly as it moved from this ideal. When faltering markets drove down production, the firm's value required rose beyond what could be supported by its value available. For a time, the firm's *value margin* became negligible as the company nearly fell behind its value curve.

FIGURE 3.2   The Value Curve

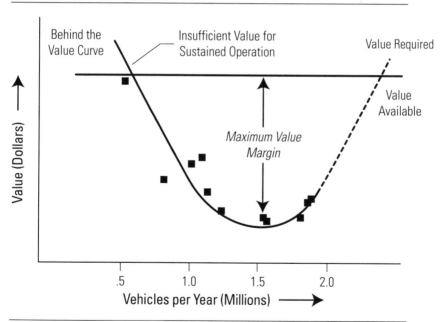

Managers could do little to improve their situation; they were left to focus on damage containment until the level of demand for which they had prepared once again returned.[5]

The value curve provides us with a powerful tool in our study of lean dynamics. It maps out firms' capabilities based on their *creation of value*—a key focus of lean business practices. But the value curve goes a step further by offering insights into *dynamic flow*—showing not just what happens at a given state of flow, but how well corporations sustain positive results even in response to dynamic conditions. This lets us begin to gauge to what degree internal activities will be interrupted when firms are pressed to operate outside of the normal range of conditions for which they built their business.

Most of all, the value curve gives us the means to see where individual companies stand across a competitive field, making clear those that have gained only temporary advantage while distinguishing others that consistently create strong value over time. Later in this chapter we will see that we can compare different firms' results in this way, giving us a clear picture of which have sustained excellence using the fundamentally different principles and practices of lean dynamics.

Tracing the Progression of Value

Nearly a century later, most corporations continue to operate under a value curve that looks remarkably similar to that of Sloan's GM. As we saw in Chapter 2, businesses seem to insist on optimizing their activities from beginning to end based on the presumption of a static environment.[6] When change does occur it creates disruption and loss, impacting everything they do. Not only can this cause loss to skyrocket (shown by their steep U-shape), it creates barriers to generating the revenue they need for sustained innovation. Clayton Christensen describes this struggle with change in *The Innovator's Dilemma:*

> One of the dilemmas of management is that, by their very nature, processes are established so that employees perform recurrent tasks in a consistent way, time after time. To ensure consistency, they are meant not to change—or if they must change, to

change through tightly controlled procedures. This means that the very mechanisms through which organizations create value are intrinsically inimical to change.[7]

Overcoming this means understanding the effect of constantly changing or dynamic conditions on the mechanisms through which value is created as a whole—the components that together make up how it progresses from beginning to end. This helps us see how the variation that these conditions cause impacts the way value flows, and how it produces the outcomes we see in the value curve.[8]

This effect is most visible in the progression of a firm's tangible activities—the component of flow we will refer to as *operational flow*. Operational flow interacts in a complex manner with three parallel elements that together make up the end-to-end flow of value: *organizational, information,* and *innovation*—each of which are more difficult to see.[9] Ultimately, it is not disruption to these individually but rather their combined effect that causes loss to skyrocket when firms operate at the outskirts of their value curve.

To better understand this phenomenon, we will now look at each of these elements and the role of each in enabling the flow of value:

Operational Flow

Operational flow is essentially the progression of those activities involved in transforming products or services from their basic elements to their finished state, delivered into the hands of the customer. This might include a network of suppliers, each involved in some aspect of creating these final products. It is this physical flow that we most often think of when we picture the buildup of value—and it is this that is the most visible casualty when operating conditions shift.

Henry Ford's Model T line was a classic case of smooth operational flow. By making constant refinements and tightly controlling the variation across his activities, he was able to closely synchronize their buildup, driving out buffers of inventories and lead times from each activity along the way. He succeeded in driving out so much waste that he could assemble his vehicles all the way from their most basic materials in only three days. But he did this without facing substantial change—something few firms can count on today.

What happens to most firms' operational flow when change suddenly strikes? As we saw in Chapter 2, frantic activity takes over as narrowly optimized workstations struggle to stay in control. Ad hoc activities replace preset work plans, overpowering standardization and driving up their variability. The result is a breakdown of synchronization, with disruption rippling up and down their stream of work—just like the reaction of a pebble tossed into a river.

Now, think of what happens when this same breakdown originates at many different sites at the same time, as would typically be the case. Disruption is spread in a complex pattern from suppliers to customers and everywhere in between. Instead of just one pebble, the result is like that of a handful tossed into the stream; together they create a reaction that is complex and widespread. The end result of all of this is the *dynamic effect* discussed earlier—amplifying disruption and crisis through a complex pattern of interaction, until finally stabilizing at a total state of loss that can be many times greater than before.

Firms today face an environment in which their ability to sustain smooth operational flow is constantly under assault. And each time it leads to this same chain reaction, causing workarounds and loss and driving this broader dynamic effect. Further amplifying this effect is operational flow's interaction with two other forms of flow: *organizational* and *information flow.*

Organizational Flow

As corporations grew to enormous proportions over the last century, they lost the organizational simplicity that marked Adam Smith's example of an early pin factory. Gone was their logical, almost intuitive authority for managing work. And with this went the adaptability that once marked their decision making—a key to sustaining smooth flow.

Why did this occur? Chapter 1 describes how today's management ranks grew to make possible Smith's division of labor and its way of aligning work. Just as was done on the shop floor, manager's responsibilities were broken down as well, narrowing their focus to specialized areas, from design to production, order fulfillment, and customer support. Large, rigid hierarchies came to define management authority, dictating how organizational decisions are supposed to flow. The net effect was to limit managers' span of insight, creating the potential for lag that can amplify disruption when operational flow is disturbed (as described in Chapter 1).

Moreover, such a structure for making decisions is designed to work best for a firm's *normal* conditions—those near or at its forecasted flow. Those decisions that are routine in nature are made at local levels; broader, less time-sensitive decisions are reserved for those nearer to the top. This promotes rapid resolution of urgent issues while elevating those of broader impact to the firm's more senior managers.

When crisis strikes, however, all of this quickly changes.

Think of what happens when disruption ripples up and down a production line. Anything that interferes with regaining smooth operational flow, from materiel shortages to missed deliveries, becomes worthy of high-level attention. This drives a complete turnaround in decision making. Managers in senior positions take on a new level of interest in day-to-day activities, determined to keep chaos from derailing their strategy and plans. Executives insist on staying informed—sometimes taking over decision making completely. Those closer to the action quickly lose authority, their positions now relegated to gathering data and reporting them up the line.

Although this higher-level attention brings with it the span of authority to overcome intradepartmental disconnects, it introduces another form of lag. What were once quick decisions now take time; corrective measures that previously began almost instantly might now be delayed for days. And, by the time action is finally decided on, conditions might look very different than they did when the problem arose—a delay that might cause these actions to now miss their mark.

Worse still, the higher such decisions move, the bigger they tend to grow. Something that might once have needed only a small tap to set straight might now be fixed with a sledgehammer—overcorrections that might draw greater resources and create additional unanticipated results.

Sadly, workers and managers have become particularly adept in their abilities to react amid the onslaught of crisis. This has become a critical skill as corporations face an ever-increasing pace of change with a system that was never designed for managing within such conditions.

Think of what all of this does to a corporation's ability to think ahead. With everyone tied up in the day-to-day struggle for stability, who is left to navigate? Executives' attention must be turned to matters inside of the business, rather than focusing on customers and markets. Companies can easily lose sight of less pressing but critical needs; for one, they can lose sight of the need for reaching out to capture new opportunities—something that clearly is essential to their ability for creating and sustaining value.

Information Flow

Managers know that receiving accurate, timely information is key to making sound decisions. It affects how they see the outside world and how they relate it to their own operations; it is thus critical for preparing them for changes coming their way. Any disruption to the flow of information means they will face the full force of any changes with little notice—driving up variation and loss.

Think back to our earlier scenario of a car in traffic. We saw that a traffic jam can be caused by something as simple as one car making a sudden change in its movement, startling those behind it. Others must act instantly, on information that is insufficient to understand what they are up against—making adjustments based solely on the appearance of brake lights. Their instinct is to overreact, causing a chain reaction that progressively grows to overwhelm the flow of traffic.

This same basic principle applies to just about any progression of interdependent steps. We saw how sudden change can impact a firm's operational flow, quickly spreading crisis and workarounds from suppliers to customers. Without knowing to any real degree how big the danger is, those affected by this must overcompensate to ensure they keep out of harm's way. Such overreaction might translate to buffers and workarounds to prevent shortages, or reroutings to steer clear of problems while they are being solved. All of this contributes to the dynamic effect, amplifying disruption with each sudden change to operational and organizational flow.

Information systems such as ERP (Enterprise Resource Planning) can help to mitigate some of this in much the same way that traffic reports can help avoid a commuter's delay. Advance notice of a traffic jam gives drivers the information they need to decide whether to change routes. Informing workstations of activities or issues down the line can do much the same thing, enabling them to adjust their activities while it is still efficient to do so. In theory, such a constant flow of information can dampen much of the dynamic effect, helping avoid overreaction and workarounds that disrupt operations.

Still, even the best information can do only so much. A car can do nothing to change its route if there are no exits from the highway. Similarly, a company whose activities are optimized for a narrow range of conditions can do little to prevent loss even with advance notice of major changes. And the way information systems are applied can even *add* to such operational limitations (as is described in Chapter 8).

Further complicating matters is that, in order to be useful, this information must be accurate as well as timely. This is particularly problematic during times of crisis, when much of an organization's attention goes to its workarounds. Think of how a crew deals with routine chores aboard a ship—keeping the decks clean is not something they concern themselves with when sailing into a storm. For a corporation, data integrity quickly suffers when people sidestep normal procedures in their struggle to keep their "ship" upright. This can be quite damaging, since sustaining an accurate, relevant flow of information is critical to everything from managing basic activities to picking the best course for steering clear of danger.

The Flow of Innovation

Firms' efforts to flow new innovations to their customers create a tremendous potential for amplifying disruption and loss. Introducing fresh new products and services that use the latest technology can force significant changes—from changeover of procedures, tooling, and materials—each creating variation that can seriously disrupt operational flow. Organizational and information flow can be interrupted by streams of last-minute design or tooling changes as engineers struggle to correct start-up problems. The result is higher variation, crisis, and loss until stability is once again attained.

All of this can have the same impact as a sudden economic slump. Factories turning out new products might find that they must sustain substantial loss for an extended period of time as operations restabilize. Thus, each new innovation can undermine the very value margin it is intended to create.

But there exists a greater hazard still. Since this "economic slump" affects no one else, it can be exploited to a competitor's advantage—much like Henry Ford found when he finally replaced his Model T. Shutting down his River Rouge factory for nearly a year to retool meant opening the doors for others to gain a foothold (in particular Walter Chrysler used this as the chance to advance his Plymouth model, launching his company to become the strong competitor it remains to this day).[10]

It should be no surprise, then, that firms tend to keep their changes smaller and less disruptive, thus making their rapid recovery much more possible. Alfred Sloan's approach set the pace for this; despite maintaining largely stable offerings, he gave his customers the *perception of change*. By laying out a well-structured array of products, he created a path for his customers to seamlessly climb through his relatively static lines of offerings, customizing vehicles with add-ons or stepping customers up to more expensive models. In this way he could minimize product redesigns and the need to interrupt his production lines, instead rolling in needed changes when seasonal demands were at their lowest—and then billing them as new model year designs.

Others followed; regulating innovation became a centerpiece of the American system. Companies extended their existing products and services as long as possible, replacing them only when a fresh new design was clearly needed to maintain sales. Doing this, corporations have been able to successfully work around the constraints marked by the "U" shape we see in their value curves.

Most firms today are governed by this same narrow and regulated flow of value. Their inflexibility to change creates a reluctance to press forward with new products or services—even where there exists a clear demand. Worse yet, most seem to view this condition as acceptable, the inevitable outcome of their American system of management that has served their needs since their early days of industrial dominance.

But a few no longer subscribe to this belief.

A new breed of companies has emerged that has risen above these constraints. Their way of flowing value is very different, and so too are their results—from their smooth, streamlined operations to the flexible way they introduce new products and services. What stands out about them most, however, is how they seem to meet extreme conditions head on, attaining and sustaining excellence by embracing or even creating the change that others seek to avoid.

Managing for Change

In the spring of 2004, US Airways found itself in its second fight for its life in as many years. Struggling to drive down costs as it tried to regain its footing after emerging from bankruptcy, it suddenly faced a new threat. Southwest Airlines was coming to Philadelphia—one of US Airways' most critical hubs.[11]

It is not hard to see why so many view Southwest as an increasing threat. From its humble beginnings flying a few simple routes from a small Texas airfield, it learned to thrive amid its industry's extreme cycles of boom and bust while waging battle after battle against large competitors. Wherever Southwest goes, regardless of how strong or weak the conditions, it manages to create new value where others find none. [12]

This company particularly stood out during the weeks and months after the tragic events of September 11th and throughout the downturn that extended for years beyond. While others stumbled and failed, Southwest moved forward, growing its fleet and adding new routes almost as if it had prepared for such a crisis.

And in a way, it did.

To understand how, let us look at its value curve—our graphical depiction of how it performs at each point across its range of conditions. Figure 3.3 shows that Southwest Airlines' value curve is not a curve at all (depicted on the left side of the chart). When we map out how its value varies as a function of passenger flow (with value available depicted as a constant for graphical clarity, as described in the Appendix), we see strong, steady flow of value across a wide span of volumes—a straight line rather than the classic U-shaped curve!

This really stands out when we compare Southwest's value curve to others over a period from the mid-1990s through the beginning of this decade—a particularly difficult time frame for Southwest's rivals. Figure 3.3 depicts one case for comparison (United Airlines' curve is depicted,

FIGURE 3.3   Southwest versus the Airline Industry [13]

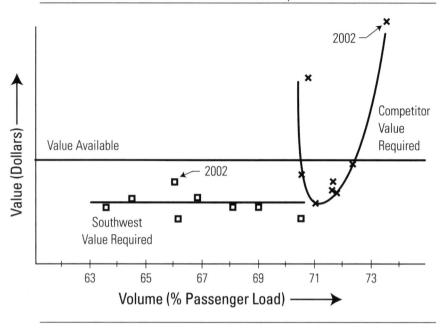

but others illustrate this characteristic "U" shape as well). Southwest Airlines kept its loss in check, maintaining a flat value curve as its competitors' followed the classic "U" shape. This let it continue to profit despite swings in passenger volumes that threw most others out of their "optimal zones" (the depicted firm struggled against crisis, and ultimately fell into bankruptcy).

Southwest did not face the frantic activity or broken flow that beset its peers; even after September 11th its operations, decisions, and information moved along much as they had done before. While others were grounding aircraft and slashing fares—artificially boosting the passenger flow for their much fewer remaining flights, as conventional wisdom would dictate—Southwest continued to reach for new value. And not only did it keep its fleet in the air, it added new planes and new routes, filling gates dropped by others left reeling from this harsher environment. The result has been phenomenal; for instance, the company reports that it has increased its capacity (as measured by available seat miles) by more than sixty percent since 2000.[14]

Others have tried to emulate it; from United's Shuttle, to Continental Lite and US Airways' own MetroJet, each of these airlines has tried to implement different aspects of Southwest's way of doing business.[15] But none of these experiments matched Southwest's success—perhaps because these firms, like so many others, failed to understand the real reasons for Southwest's success.

One persistent belief is that Southwest Airlines somehow treats its employees differently than do others. Cheaper labor that could be hired and fired at will would certainly help to explain its ability to control costs—particularly during times of crisis. Statements such as, "Southwest is not shackled by traditional unions" probably add fuel to this perception.[16] Such a view is clearly attractive in that it fits neatly into today's concept of business. However, it is far from true.

Southwest is, in fact, unionized—"one of the most highly-unionized airlines in the U.S. airline industry, with employees who are represented by some of the most traditional unions in the United States."[17] And while the firm does treat its employees differently than do others, it is not in a way that one would normally equate to cost reduction. This was particularly evident in the weeks and months following September 11th. Rather than lay off huge numbers of people as did nearly all of its peers, it managed to keep to its no-layoff approach, retaining virtually all of its workers.[18] Many hold other beliefs that are similarly flawed; these can lead those who try to follow down a difficult path.

What is hard for so many to see is that Southwest's success comes from something very different. It comes from more than honing the standard methods, applying quick fixes to squeeze more out of the same methods that govern others across this industry. What Southwest has done instead runs much deeper. As we will see, the company has demonstrated the principles of lean dynamics, transforming its progression of operational, organizational, information, and innovation flow to achieve a seemingly impossible result.

We see this very same phenomenon with Wal-Mart. It, too, grew from humble beginnings through a series of challenges that shaped the way it now does business. And just like Southwest, this firm now stands above the rest, advancing in all directions and leading the way in both good times as well as bad.

Wal-Mart's story can almost be compared to that of David taking on Goliath. In the mid-1970s this modest chain of discount stores was widely seen as no match for the likes of Kmart. Wal-Mart, observers thought, had found its niche in small, out-of-the way places where Kmart was not interested. As one analyst wrote, "It is clearly easier to operate in this kind of a situation than a competitive one: pricing need not be so sharp, and the 'right' merchandise is less critical, simply because customers have no alternative . . ." [19] Many seemed convinced that at the first sign of threat Kmart would unleash its fury, and Wal-Mart would surely succumb.

But this was not to be. Not only was Wal-Mart able to hang onto these sites despite Kmart's onslaught, but it would soon expand to challenge Kmart's stores on their own turf. And in the early 1980s, when the surging demand that had fueled the growth of the discount retail industry began to deteriorate, Wal-Mart continued its strength while firms like Kmart found it more and more difficult to profit.

Today, any questions about Wal-Mart's might within the discount-merchandise business have long since disappeared. After years of struggle, the once-dominant Kmart fell to bankruptcy. Wal-Mart, however, thrived; just as its long-time competitor suffered defeat, it topped the *Fortune* 500 list, becoming America's largest corporation. [20]

How was this possible? The answer is clear when we look at the shape of its value curve. Figure 3.4 shows that, over a period spanning a decade, Wal-Mart held its value margin (the value it retains — the difference between the value it brings in through sales and its value required) virtually constant (its construction is shown in the Appendix). This stands in stark contrast to Kmart's steep slope and often negative value margin during the same time frame (note that the time frame depicted is prior to Kmart's bankruptcy and subsequent restructuring). Even as its industry stagnated, Wal-Mart increased sales by as much as forty-nine percent, expanding its reach by opening new stores. [21]

Fueled by its strong, sustained value margin, Wal-Mart's challenges continue to succeed against even entrenched rivals across a range of retail businesses. The company's foray into groceries has been wildly successful; it has built a commanding presence in consumer electronics; and its movement into children's toys has landed leading competitors

FIGURE 3.4   Wal-Mart versus Kmart[22]

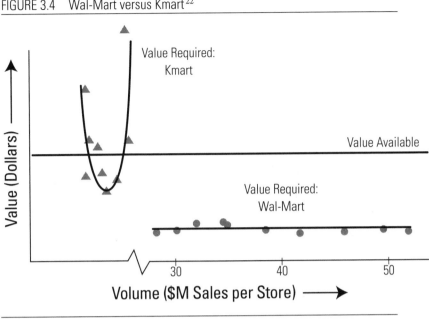

on the ropes. For Wal-Mart, its operational efficiency combined with its seemingly unstoppable ability to expand to new offerings (now including prescription drugs and even banking) seems to be the perfect formula for success.

The same can be said for the Toyota Motor Company. This corporation has been widely credited with starting the worldwide revolution in *lean manufacturing*—a revolutionary system that turns out greater quality at higher speeds using less of everything, from factory space to labor hours and inventories. Figure 3.5 shows another measure of the company's success. From 1995 to 2002—years fraught with particularly severe conditions—Toyota's value margin remains stable, even growing in magnitude (its subsequent leap in performance is described in Chapter 8). While its competitors closed factories and offered huge incentives, apparently to stabilize demand (Ford's value curve is depicted in the figure; its shape is shown in Chapter 8 to later become much more pronounced), Toyota's value skyrocketed by all conventional measures. Its profitability is now greater than Ford, Chrysler, and GM combined; the

FIGURE 3.5   Toyota versus Ford[23]

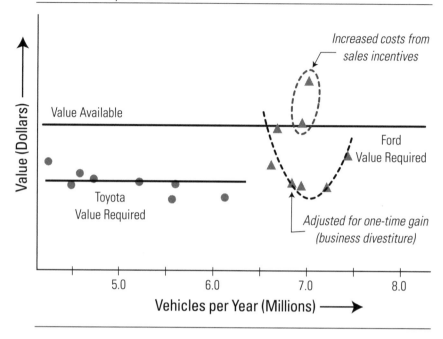

company is now challenging GM's title as the world's largest automobile producer.[24]

What seems difficult for many to grasp is that, for these firms, traditional rules of business no longer apply. Attacking waste does not seem to be the key (Chapter 10 shows that, despite enormous purported savings, Ford's "6-Sigma" program did little to change its value curve); neither is hiring and firing employees to offset complications of their environments. Firms like Toyota, Wal-Mart, and Southwest Airlines seem to see such actions as counterproductive. They do not seem to trust in such age-old "truths" as the stability of mass markets, the need to optimize for large scale. Instead, they have come to operate under a different set of rules—rules that require looking at their business in an entirely different way.

In the next chapter we will see that the value curve is a particularly powerful tool for examining the reasons for these successes. It gives us a window through which we can better understand what makes these firms different, isolating the set of common characteristics that make them stand out. We can see from this that their results come not from discrete tools or practices, or from applying new targets for quality or variation that can be added to whatever approach a firm already uses. Instead, their ability to create value when others face crisis comes from something much deeper—a new way of managing that seems to thrive on the dynamic conditions they face today.

A New System
of Management

The assumptions on which the organization has been built
and is being run no longer fit reality.
—Peter F. Drucker[1]

CONSIDER FOR A MOMENT Sir Isaac Newton's explanation of the notion of gravity. For centuries his mathematical description of this and other physical phenomena served as the underpinnings for modern science. Yet, hundreds of years later, Albert Einstein's new explanation of these same physical realities changed everything.

Neither was wrong; both were right. However, Einstein's discovery showed that Newton's underlying principles of physics relied on approximations that could no longer be made within the context of much more extreme conditions. And this new understanding of how to deal with these ultimately opened the doors for mankind's advancement to the nuclear age and beyond.

Much in the same way that Newton's theories set the course for the scientific community, Adam Smith's concept of the division of labor forms the basis for the prevailing mindset of today's business world. And much as was the case with Newton, Smith's philosophy draws on assumptions that no longer hold true.

The complications of Smith's principle, once dealt with almost transparently in a pin factory, have become overwhelming in a time marked by complexity, instability, and rapid change. Shifts in business cycles, customer tastes, and world events induce changes that generate crippling disruption to producers and their suppliers. Fragmented work and compartmentalized oversight, the driving force behind Smith's approach, now fuel this cycle of loss.

Lean dynamics offers the answer to advancing within these extreme conditions that corporations face today, overcoming the disruption and uncertainty they have learned to accept. At its core is something quite different from the fragmented work and management tasks laid out by Smith's division of labor. It does not target economies of scale, seeking efficiencies that break down outside of the special case of predictable, stable conditions. Instead, lean dynamics focuses on creating stable yet ever-advancing value—for benefits that are clearly visible in Toyota, Wal-Mart, and Southwest Airlines' value curves.

This shift—from managing discrete tasks to flowing value—is key to turning dynamic conditions into the tremendous advantage that continues to widen over time.

Five Characteristics of Lean Dynamics

In many ways, those who employ lean dynamics appear to be no different than their peers. They offer similar products or services, and even implement similar initiatives. Upon further study, however, we see that others only *seem* to have followed the same path; in reality they often have missed the mark.

What is it, then, that distinguishes those that apply lean dynamics from all the rest? A closer look at the examples of Toyota, Wal-Mart, and Southwest Airlines shows that, despite their very different businesses and underlying constraints, they exhibit an array of commonalities: lean dynamics capabilities they seemed to create entirely independently of one another. These all relate to five overarching characteristics that make their value curves look much alike—characteristics that are central to making these firms the juggernauts of excellence we see today. We will now review each of these one by one.

Planning for Chaos as the Norm

The most basic of these firms' common characteristics is their almost uncanny *preparedness for crisis*. While others seem to plan for stability and then react frantically to change, these firms instead seem determined to meet external variation head on. This was clear from Southwest's response to September 11th, Wal-Mart's strength during severe market conditions that overcame Kmart (and later in its reaction to hurricane Katrina), and Toyota's ability to thrive despite today's skyrocketing gasoline prices. It is their active way of dealing with change that seems to inoculate them against the ill effects that disrupt all the rest.

Dr. W. Edwards Deming, the statistician whose writings prompted a major quality movement in the 1980s, observed that two distinct types of variation exist: those he categorized as *common causes,* which are normal occurrences that should be expected and planned for as part of doing business, and those he termed *special causes.* Special causes are the result of some extraordinary outside influence and cause results to fall outside of the system's statistical control limits.[2] Since these cannot be reliably predicted, they cannot be readily planned for, and therefore they can lead to disruption and crisis.

Most corporations react to sudden swings in environment as extraordinary conditions—special causes that drive up loss and shrink value margins. In the airline industry, these include anything from spikes in fuel prices to major storms, and even war. And although such events are becoming more and more typical (it seems that not a year goes by without some sort of major crisis), they continue to take most firms by surprise.

Just one look at Southwest's value curve (figure 4.1) makes clear that this firm is different. It did not react to the severe downturn and other events following September 11th as its competitors had done. In the midst of this series of circumstances that shook this industry's very foundation, its value curve remained stable *and within statistical control limits.* Rather than suffering skyrocketing loss as others faced, Southwest seemed to manage these circumstances as if they were just a normal part of doing business.

Toyota and Wal-Mart display this same ability to sustain predictable results, holding their strikingly constant value margins within predict-

FIGURE 4.1   Southwest and "Special Causes"

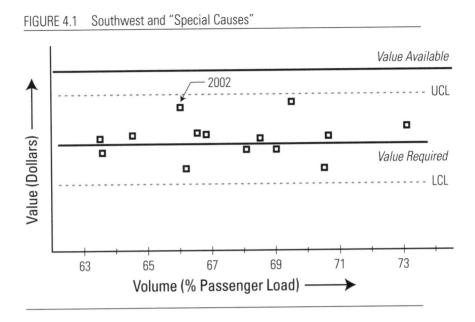

able limits even in the face of what others see to be extraordinary circumstances. In fact, we will see in Chapter 9 that Toyota used the most recent industry downturn as an opportunity for *expanding* its value margin—advancing as its competitors struggled with huge losses.

What does this ability to excel across such a wide range of conditions mean to these firms' ability to compete? At the same time that others must abandon normal day-to-day practices as they react to event after event, these firms can continue to operate largely as they had done before. And rather than striving to sustain their progress only when conditions are at their peak, these firms manage to advance new or improved offerings through the troughs as well—just what succeeding in today's competitive marketplace demands.

Managing for "A Rising Tide"

As was noted earlier, Toyota, Wal-Mart, and Southwest Airlines did not attain their results by charging straight ahead with those initiatives that are most visible on the surface. Instead, they began by building the broader, underlying foundation of smooth flow on which these activities depend. These act like a rising tide on a procession of ships, lifting them smoothly above obstacles without the frantic maneuvering that might otherwise separate them or disrupt their journey.

While it is true, for instance, that Toyota's *kanban* (a technique for regulating parts production) is important to making its activities progress smoothly, this alone is not enough. Taiichi Ohno, a founder of the Toyota Production System, made it clear that this makes up just one part of a broader system of management that remains largely unseen.[3] A range of other principles and practices (described in subsequent chapters) together create the structure of flexibility and smooth flow that enables their kanbans to work.

Similarly, it is overly simplistic to say that Southwest Airlines' success comes simply from cutting its planes' time at the gate, as many have come to believe. While it is true that speeding gate time means that airplanes spend more time in the air flying passengers, this, by itself, is not the answer. Others have shown that targeting this outcome without first putting in place the needed enablers only disrupts flow, leading to *increased* delays and loss.[4]

We will see later why these outcomes depicted by their value curves are not the result of some quick fix, some new fad or business initiative for adapting an old management system to new constraints. It is not simply lower wages, cheaper equipment, or greater scale that makes these businesses outperform the others. Sustained leadership does not come from any one "silver bullet," as so many continue to seek. Rather, it comes from something much deeper: a broader, much more basic system of management that helps firms thrive no matter what the circumstances — one that must be put in place long before a crisis ever starts to unfold.

Creating Dynamic Stability

Perhaps the most powerful characteristic these firms share is their ability to create stability where others find none. Not by trying to buffer against its fluctuations — something that is becoming increasingly difficult — but by putting in place a mechanism that lets their activities adapt to them, *dampening out internal variation even when major external disruptions are thrown their way.*

To see why this is important, let us look back to our earlier example of what happens to the supermarket during a snowstorm. Sudden change creates variation that quickly expands to overwhelm its management system, driving widespread shortages. Why does this happen? For most companies, lag that is basic to their way of doing business (as described in Chapter 2) causes the flow of operations, information, and decisions to become less and less certain. Such a disconnect leads to rapid escalation of loss—a condition that is *dynamically unstable.*

A simple model illustrates what this means. Turn a bowl upside down and place a marble on top. As depicted in figure 4.2, with even the smallest perturbation from its center point, the marble tends to roll outward, diverging from the center. A system that does this is unstable—its outcomes naturally tend to move away from its desired or nominal state. Only through constant external intervention will the marble remain at this desired location.

This is analogous to what happens when traditional firms are pressed to perform outside of their intended range of conditions, operating on the steep slope of their value curve. Just like pushing a boulder up a hill, it takes constant focus and energy just to maintain basic control. Only when "normal" conditions return can they again turn their attention to critical

FIGURE 4.2   An Illustration of Dynamic Instability

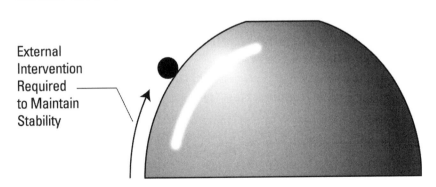

External
Intervention
Required
to Maintain
Stability

but less pressing matters, such as planning and implementing strategies for advancing the underlying competitiveness of their corporations.

Toyota, Wal-Mart, and Southwest Airlines are different in that they do not simply create better ways of pushing the boulder uphill. Instead, they tend to sidestep such hazards, putting in place measures that *flatten the hill*, so to speak, so that there is no need to push the boulder at all.

Toyota, for instance, takes the unlikely approach of *building variation right into its work flow*. As we will see in Chapter 7, the company constantly shuffles what it makes, deliberately varying the types and quantities of different items it manufactures on a given production line. This keeps production lots small—very close to what is needed at each step along the way. Doing so virtually eliminates the expansion of variation seen by others who build enormous batches based on forecasts that depend on demand stability—and then react to crises when conditions do not turn out as planned. By avoiding the lag this creates, Toyota's approach essentially builds in a self-dampening tendency that maintains stability even when conditions inevitably change.

Southwest Airlines achieves this same variation-dampening effect through a combination of activities—its quick turnarounds, short direct routes, less congested airports for many of its flights, and single type of aircraft—all working together to smooth out variation before it has the chance to build. The company's organization and well-known work culture make up key parts of this puzzle, creating a system that does not diverge when pushed beyond normal limits, but instead rights itself when thrown off course.

Wal-Mart follows this model as well, creating smooth flow through a complex array of interrelated techniques. It integrates its information systems with work flow and its people's broad span of authority in a way that responds well to change.

Each of their systems respond much as the marble does when it is set *inside* of the rounded bowl (now turned upright, as depicted in figure 4.3). When placed at a point that is away from its intended target, the marble now moves in a path that is *dynamically stable*—rolling back and forth, each time drawing closer and closer until it finally comes to rest at the center.

This deep-rooted difference is what helps these firms maintain order no matter what conditions they face. By dampening variation

FIGURE 4.3   An Illustration of Dynamic Stability

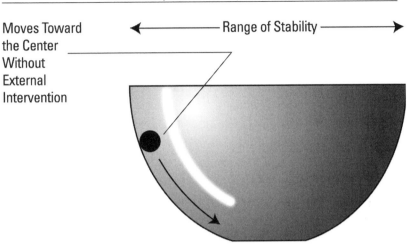

Moves Toward the Center Without External Intervention

← ———————— Range of Stability ————————→

before it has a chance to build, workers and managers maintain their focus despite facing even enormous shifts—keeping them from circling aimlessly as they otherwise might, blown off course by storm after storm.

For those seeking similar results, simply trimming their sails— adjusting what they are already doing—will not suffice. Instead, sustaining excellence requires rethinking everything, from the design of their products, to the layout of their factories—even the relationship and expectations they strike with their employees. It means intertwining their operational ability with their business strategy, becoming forward thinking rather than reactionary. But most of all, doing this means overcoming a culture that has been ingrained for nearly a century.

Overcoming the "Culture of Workarounds"

The next of these common characteristics is a corporate mindset that overcomes today's "culture of workarounds." This is central to their system's success; without it their system of management could not work as intended.

The need to maintain operational rigor was documented as early as the year 1911, when Frederick Taylor, an American engineer who sought to improve industrial efficiency, wrote of a new approach to business that could make firms substantially more profitable than all the rest. He showed that his now famous "scientific" approach to management—the careful identification and control of the individual tasks that make up each job—could generate unprecedented improvement in productivity and workforce morale. As Taylor noted, it is only when individual tasks are well-defined that precise planning can occur. Because workarounds by nature violate this standardization of work, they violate the core tenet of this philosophy on which firms today are based.[5]

Perhaps this is why my study of aerospace manufacturing showed that those most successful in their efforts began with measures that pre-empted the need for many of their workarounds. Rather than jumping first to cutting-edge initiatives, these plants worked at stabilizing key elements that permitted their operations to flow more smoothly and predictably. They progressively advanced up a framework (depicted in figure 4.4)—first implementing more basic elements like closely managing inventories and putting in place rigorous steps for managing production operations (the bottom two blocks) before proceeding to the next-level elements (implementing statistical quality control, tightening supplier relationships, and putting in place manufacturing cells). Those that did so exhibited a distinct characteristic: Their operations were marked by reduced cycle time variation—far greater reduction than that seen by their peers. This turned out to have a direct link to cost reduction—much more than reducing inventories or speeding operations alone. Unlike the others, structuring their efforts in this way gave them strong, measurable savings.[6]

To understand why this happens, think back to our earlier traffic analogy, in which one car's sudden shift causes a disruption that is amplified by others. Higher-order techniques for smoothing flow—like dispatching police cars whose presence makes drivers more cautious—can reduce drivers' disruptive behaviors, mitigating the chain reaction they caused and maximizing the highway's overall efficiency. Yet, the existence of a more basic condition—like road construction that narrows the highway—will undermine the effectiveness of this improvement; police cruisers will simply get stuck in the broader traffic jam this creates, preventing them from having a positive impact stabilizing flow. Without first stabilizing road conditions, higher-order improvements make little impact.[7]

This is much the same as in a factory. Automation, for instance, was shown to produce little effect when preceding activities (those more basic "road conditions") could not be made to deliver consistently and on time. Quick equipment changeovers did little to support speedier flow where inventory accuracy was poor, or where Bills-of-Materials were incorrect. Even statistical quality control methods did not seem to help much until more basic flow disruptions were overcome.

This need to avoid workarounds seems particularly important to companies that have built in the dynamic stability just described. To understand why, let us look at the effect of workarounds on a more visible sort of system: an airplane. For safety reasons, many aircraft are designed for dynamic stability—they automatically return to level flight even after stalling into a spinning dive. But regaining stability is

FIGURE 4.4   A Framework for Overcoming Workarounds[8]

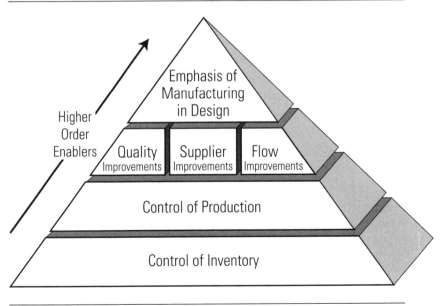

only possible if the pilot does not interfere—he or she must let go of the controls, or his or her input might actually prevent the plane from recovering.

Just as with an airplane, workarounds in a factory can cause even a stable system to become unstable. Instead of creating value, they might throw the system into a constant state of disarray. And as we saw in the previous chapter, these disruptions can domino to other forms of flow, greatly amplifying disruption and loss.

Firms' frequent reliance on workarounds can cause another, perhaps more disturbing outcome: It can cause workers and managers alike to no longer see it as just part of the job—it now *is* the job. In many corporations, conquering an issue that threatens the very goals of the company has become a badge of honor, and the rewards tend to follow. Those who are promoted tend to display tremendous skill in "firefighting," rewarded for producing results that are immediate and visible. This relates to Peter Drucker's observation:

> For many years I have been asking new clients to tell me who their best-performing people are. And then I ask: "What are they assigned to?" Almost without exception, the performers are assigned to problems—to the old business that is sinking faster than had been forecast; to the old product that is being outflanked by a competitor's new offering; to the old technology. . . . Then I ask: "And who takes care of the opportunities?" Almost invariably, the opportunities are left to fend for themselves.[9]

Firms like Toyota, Wal-Mart, and Southwest Airlines show that success is not tied to frantic activity; in fact, it is just the opposite. Without the need to constantly deal with workarounds, managers can shift more of their attention to actions that bring real value to the firm: taking charge of this newfound capability. Theirs is no longer the role of heroics, of last-minute saves. Instead, it becomes one of leadership—forging the way to the next breakthrough strategies and innovations, driving profitability, growth, and competitiveness.

Mitigating the Perception of Risk

The fifth common characteristic shared by these firms is their very different sense of risk. For them, change is not automatically seen as risk; instead it is something for which they prepare, using specific measures based on the realities of their circumstances. They seem to realize that the greatest risk lies not in pursuing change, but in the inability to do so.

Let us look again at a traditional U-shaped value curve (figure 3.2). What risks face such a company? The most obvious is that conditions might shift outside of the narrow range in which their operations are designed to thrive, leading to consequences that we have already seen can be severe. For many firms, such change will be frequent, if not constant. What were once occasional hazards that many firms presumed they could avoid, they must now expect to routinely face. Thus, the greatest risk comes not from the unknown; it now lies in what inevitably faces them.

But if risk has turned to reality, why are so many content to continue in this mode? Consider what happens in a classic business analogy. Suppose you place a frog into a pot of boiling water. The frog immediately senses danger and jumps right back out of the pot. But what if you instead put the frog in a pot of cool water, and then gradually turn up the heat. The frog (a cold-blooded creature) will continually adapt to the changing temperature, until the pot ultimately reaches a boil. By adapting to its gradually changing conditions, the frog stays in place, remaining comfortable within an environment that will ultimately lead to its demise.[10]

For many firms, the conditions they now face are very much different than those that were in place when their management system was first created. This shift was not sudden; bit by bit corporations adapted to meet its gradual change. And today they are rapidly approaching the boiling point, though most seem generally unaware of the hazards they face.

For Wal-Mart, Toyota, and Southwest Airlines, the difference is striking. Avoiding risk instead seems to mean always preparing for new challenges, constraints, and opportunity. They do not simply fix disruptions on the highway as they occur (from our earlier analogy); instead, they seem to constantly look well beyond the horizon—not just to those problems that lie over the next hill, but to the broader range of circumstances they might ultimately face. And when they do change, they appear to do so in an integrated fashion, leveraging the capabilities they have put in place to prevent hidden lag from obscuring their view and placing them at greater risk.

Regaining the Competitive Edge

The American system of management has changed twice already. Not as the result of gradual evolution, but as a series of abrupt shifts as corporations found themselves forced to adapt to new constraints. And after each change it looked starkly different from how it did before.

Henry Ford's innovations brought forth the first major shift. His Model T production taught us how to expand Adam Smith's principles well beyond what had been done before. By opening the door to bringing complex products to the masses, his approach transformed the world. Not only did the products themselves change the way we live, but so too did our newfound ability to create and respond to mass markets on a scale never before imagined.

Next came Sloan's transformation of American management to the form we generally recognize today. By breaking products into product lines, producers went beyond bringing their innovations within reach; now they broke them into ranges that more closely met individuals' needs. Customers were no longer forced to buy identical items; instead, these could be adapted to some degree to meet more refined needs. Variety became the norm, spurring innovation, growth, and the type of consumer market we see today. It also required a new way of managing the business—optimizing for average outcomes of a stable, common, and growing marketplace. The result? Another quantum leap forward for customer and corporate value.

Today we see that this is no longer enough. The success of this American system has driven competition to a fever pitch. Customers have come to expect more than basic choices; they want individuality. Globalized markets and advances in technology have given them greater information and access to incredible variety. They can now choose from niches around the world offering products and services that are better, faster, and cheaper. Within this environment, a system of management that can generate low costs and high quality only under stable, massive demands will no longer suffice.

American business once again faces the need to change. It can either embrace this change or suffer the consequences.

Staying competitive means looking at the world with a completely new perspective. It means moving beyond a system that was built for an ideal of consistent, limitless markets that no longer exists. This critical disconnect has driven a wedge between the two key components that must work together to create corporate value: the continuous change and innovation that customers have come to demand, and the operational efficiency that is so essential to giving them the quality, speed, and low pricing they expect. Today, this can no longer be accepted.

Bridging this gap means making fundamental structural changes. Just as shifting an airplane's power curve takes much more than adding on a few simple features, American business, too, must redesign itself from the wheels up. While it is true that some change is possible through modifications—adding fairings or even replacing the engines—these can create new problems and bring only modest improvement. At some point, "Band-Aids" will no longer suffice; it is only by making much deeper changes—a total redesign—that the true shift needed to stay ahead of the competition will result.

Part II

The
Foundational
Elements

L EAN DYNAMICS DRAWS ON *internal* measures to mitigate the effects of a corporation's *external* environmental dynamics. Based on *lean manufacturing* (derived from the Toyota Production System), the four chapters in this part describe how Toyota, Wal-Mart, and Southwest Airlines and others draw on its underlying principles and practices to create strong, steady, tangible value for corporations and their customers. [1]

Chapter 5 begins by examining the very different way in which these firms identify and measure *value*—a critical foundation for achieving sustained excellence. Chapter 6 shows how they define their *value streams* (their buildup of value from its basic elements to final products or services delivered to the customer) to avoid the traditional disconnects between work steps that amplify the effects of variation and create loss. Chapter 7 describes the underlying techniques that make this possible—dampening internal variation to maintain steady and predictable *flow*—the movement of work, decision making, information, and innovation across the value stream, even when external conditions suddenly change.

Chapter 8 concludes this part by examining a controversial issue: whether to *push*—scheduling activities based on internal plans and schedules—or *pull* operations at a pace driven by customer demand. It reveals the underlying philosophy that has enabled Toyota, Wal-Mart, and Southwest Airlines to rationalize these seemingly conflicting approaches as a way for achieving consistently strong results. Finally, we see how this enables firms to make substantial leaps in their journey in pursuit of perfection.

Five

Leading Through Measurement

> Whenever one analyzes the way a truly effective, a truly right,
> decision has been reached, one finds that a great deal of work
> and thought went into finding the appropriate measurement.
> —Peter F. Drucker[1]

THE AFTERMATH OF WORLD WAR II created the perfect context for the American system of management to thrive; and thrive it did. With pent-up demand suddenly unleashed, America's factories worked at a tremendous pace, turning out everything from automobiles to appliances at steadily increasing volumes.

By this time, the Ford Motor Company had fully embraced Sloan's strategy of breaking vehicles into product lines, and in the process it regained much of its earlier stature. Using the same approach GM demonstrated decades before, Ford created tiered but overlapping product lines to give its customers the choices they now demanded and to create the volumes so essential for its factories to run efficiently. This approach worked well; over a ten-year period, the company emerged from near-bankruptcy to become a major contender in both the American and European markets.

As part of its carefully orchestrated comeback, Ford was determined to turn out products filling each of the industry's four market segments. Through its basic line (simply known as "Ford") to the higher-cost Mercury and the even-pricier Continental, the firm had built a strong position in each of the first three. To gain a foothold in the final "upper-middle" segment, its designers amassed the "best information from market research, the best information about customer preferences in appearance and styling, and the highest standards in quality control."[2] By measuring everything that mattered, they sought to design a car to meet their customer's desires, and produce it in a way to ensure success.

This new vehicle was called the Edsel, and it became an immediate failure.

As it turns out, Ford's intricate measurements had been flawed from the start. They were based on a presumption of customer value that no longer held true: They assumed the existence of a thriving upper-middle market segment as others had since Alfred Sloan's original concept was put in place. In reality, this segment had all but vanished, leaving no real customer demand.

Management is based on theory. As Deming noted, "Rational prediction requires theory and builds knowledge through systematic revision . . . based on comparison of prediction with observation."[3] For Ford, even the most precise measurement did no good when the model on which it was based was fundamentally flawed. Only after the company acknowledged its error did it turn things around, designing a car the marketplace really wanted: the Thunderbird—one of this industry's greatest successes.[4]

Corporations today must heed this powerful lesson and recognize the need to ensure a sound foundation for what they measure. They can no longer blindly follow theories that are based on the presumptions of the past. Instead, they must take into account the great degree of change facing today's business world. Anything less might result in a similar fate as the Edsel, causing their strongest, most rigorous efforts to lead them down the path to irrelevance.

A Legacy of Lag

As H. Thomas Johnson and Robert Kaplan describe in their book *Relevance Lost,* today's basic approach to measuring progress was founded in the days when corporations were far less complex. "These organizations really had to do only one activity well: convert raw materials into a single final product such as cloth or steel, move passengers or freight, or resell purchased goods."[5] If a mill or a railroad's internal processes progressed smoothly and efficiently, its managers generally could count on a positive result. Because of this, managers concentrated on optimizing their firms' internal steps, with the expectation that this would lead to the outcomes they desired.

This is no longer a fair assumption. The age of straightforward, narrowly focused operations as the norm no longer exists. Products can be enormously complex, sometimes containing thousands of parts, often produced by geographically and functionally disparate suppliers. Firms' processes might consist of hundreds or even thousands of complex, interdependent steps. Because of this, the linkage between processes and their outputs is no longer simple and direct. Complexity has given way to lag, bringing with it a great disconnect between actions and the results they produce.

Sloan's way of measuring progress no doubt contributed to this disconnect. With his standard-volume approach, factories came to function best when turning out huge batches of identical items at or near optimal volumes (the narrow range for which they were designed to operate). Orders came to be filled directly from the mountains of inventories these batches produced. Thus, outcomes had less and less to do with the precision or speed of operations and more to do with the availability of inventory that might have been built months ago.

The consequences of such lag between actions and their outcomes became evident during the 1970s and 1980s as mass markets and predictable buying patterns began to break down (as was illustrated earlier in figure 2.1). Companies of all sorts likely were regularly forced to operate outside of their optimal zones. Bit by bit, factories became accustomed to reacting to demands that suddenly slowed and then surged ahead without warning. Forecasts that formed the basis for which factories built the inventories they operated on became less reliable; workarounds increasingly displaced normal procedures. Companies created teams of expeditors and a variety of buffers to protect their schedules; maintaining excess lead times and inventories became the standard approach for protecting against the next crisis.[6] And each time these brought greater lag, further expanding the gap between companies' internal measures and their bottom-line results.

Chapter 1 describes a key consequence of operating with no accurate means of relating process activities to outcomes: It can obscure reality, causing corporations to take suboptimal or even harmful actions. The result is all too familiar: Managers are perplexed as they spend ever-increasing time and resources dealing with crisis after crisis that never seems to completely go away.

Targeting Quality

This regular and widespread violation of work standards clearly contributed to the crisis that led to the great quality movement of the 1980s. With demand volatility spiking, disruption and workarounds were at full force, undermining operational controls and process repeatability. It is no wonder that American quality was under the gun.

The impact of volatile workloads on quality is much the same for service industries. In *The Fifth Discipline,* Peter Senge describes its effect on the business of assessing insurance claims.[7] He explains how, in order to keep up with growing case loads, a firm's overwhelmed adjustors were pressed to expedite their work functions. This gave them less time to perform key activities that created customer and corporate value, such as analyzing and explaining settlement sizes. They produced lower service quality and suffered a serious decline in bottom-line results—the company ultimately paid out more money while creating lower customer satisfaction.

Despite all their measurements, corporations often seem to lose track of how far they have drifted. Senge describes as the *trance of mediocrity* the downward slide in performance that, over time, simply becomes the way things are done. Corporations tend to lose sight of the loss they accumulate during crises; as a result, it becomes permanently imbedded, ultimately reaching across entire industries. Only after outside competitors emerge who are not affected by this "trance" do managers finally realize how bad things had become.[8]

Such a realization seems to have finally struck the American automotive industry in the 1980s when they saw that Japanese firms like Toyota presented a real threat to their market share. Forced to look at themselves with a fresh new perspective, they found that waste was everywhere. High inventories, rampant workarounds, and high defect rates brought poor flexibility and high costs, creating what seemed to be a constant state of crisis. Moreover, this disruption contributed to an increasing customer perception of poor product quality, impacting the demand so critical for regaining operational stability.

Desperate to get quality back on track, American corporations embarked on initiative after initiative—from Zero Defects (a methodology targeting perfect quality), to Quality Circles (teaming between workers to identify solutions) and Total Quality Management (a methodology based on the teachings of W. Edwards Deming, the well-known statistical-quality guru). However, rather than correcting the underlying cause for their waste—the inherent inflexibility in how they operate— each set their sights on chasing individual problems (the same approach we saw with the funnel experiment described in Chapter 1). And one by one, each of these efforts failed to overcome what their system of management had created.

Today, many see Six Sigma as the answer. Guided by their understanding that process outcomes can be made more reliable by tightly controlling their variation, firms of all types have begun setting aggressive goals for defect reduction. Yet many have come to apply this and other improvement methods as a tactical fix, attacking discrete problems without fully understanding their connection to the corporation's creation of value—a disconnect that undermines their ability to improve competitiveness.

Consider, for instance, what happens when a procurement organization sets its sights on "cutting the fat" in its contracting process. It is entirely possible for it to achieve this objective *without creating meaningful benefit to the bottom line.* How is this possible? While it is clear that speeding contract awards and increasing the number of long-term arrangements will slash *procurement's* workload, this benefit can be more than offset if awarded contracts offer no real increase to suppliers' production flexibility. Locking in existing methods—along with long lead times and other sources of lag—might instead *increase steepness of the firm's value curve,* creating a drag on suppliers' flexibility and their need for buffers (along with a high cost structure) that these long-term agreements will maintain for years to come.

Perhaps this is why so many improvement initiatives ultimately fail. Short-sighted benefits come at the price of lag and loss; initial gains might slip away as the variation companies seek to control simply reemerges when conditions once again change.

As we will see in later chapters, lean dynamics goes beyond applying targeted initiatives aimed at improving discrete outcomes. Creating lasting improvement means managers and workers must embrace a very different mindset; they must accept the need to make deeper shifts—fundamental, structural changes that address the many sources of lag imbedded within their traditional way of doing business.

Measuring for Internal Results

We have seen that, while the need to drive out loss is clear, corporations must resist becoming too targeted in this pursuit. They must be cautious in accepting any internal efficiency-oriented metric as their sole guide for making decisions despite the great promise it may seem to hold.

Consider one of today's widely accepted measures for improving efficiency: speeding inventory turns. *Inventory turns* gauge the overall rate that a firm transforms what it produces into value (often it is quite literally how fast companies turn warehoused inventories into customer sales). Low turns imply large inventories—a condition synonymous with waste (as well as sluggishness to responding to changing conditions). It stands to reason, then, that speeding turns is critical to improving a firm's chances for success.

But is this always the case? To answer this, let us look to the example of Toyota, a firm well-known for its almost obsessive attention to driving out excess inventories and other forms of waste. Historically, as one might expect, Toyota's inventory turns have been fast and ever increasing. But lately this trend has begun to shift; one study showed that

Toyota surprisingly fell among those firms whose turnovers have "plateaued" or worsened—an indication of growing waste.[9]

Does this mean that Toyota is losing its edge?

To answer this we must broaden our perspective and look at this measure in the context of its operating environment. During the 1970s and 1980s, the company faced conditions that were very different from those of American automotive manufacturers. In a distinct shift from its postwar years, Toyota's marketplace in Japan had become remarkably stable; substantially more so than that seen by U. S. producers selling in America. With the need for stability so fundamental to American business, this must have seemed for many competitors to be the underlying cause for Toyota's success.

What would happen, some came to ask, if Toyota's marketplace became less stable, if it was no longer protected from the severe demand cycles that plagued American businesses? Would Toyota become just like all the rest? An executive at GM at the time reached what seemed to be the clear conclusion:

> When the Japanese [meaning lean] producers encounter these gigantic market waves, they will quickly become as mediocre as we are. They will have to start hiring and firing workers along with suppliers and will end up as mass-producers in short order.[10]

Today, we can see the answer. Toyota has broadly expanded its reach far outside of Japan; its tremendous presence in America (now greater than that of Ford) subjects the company to the same "market waves" as GM, Ford, and Chrysler. At the same time, Toyota's sales base at home in Japan has grown less stable. Thus, it seems fairly clear why Toyota's measure of inventory turns might be tapering off: because of its need to combat the increasing uncertainty within this more chaotic operating environment. What, then, has been the impact? Toyota's bottom-line results have remained on track—*its value margin remains strong and is even improving* (a phenomenon that is described in Chapter 9).

We can see from this example that targeting even the best measures of internal efficiency can mislead corporations' actions. Inventory turns are a powerful indicator of internal performance, and can be useful for pointing to problems. This, however, is less reliable as a measure of bottom-line value. Companies must take care not to rely on internal measures for this purpose, even those that seem particularly compelling. Instead, managers must apply them within the broader context of achieving their real target: *creating strong and steady value for the customer and the corporation,* even as the nature of this value continues to change.

A New Model for Customer Value

When most firms think about value, they tend to do so within the context of their own goals or expectations. If only they could fully load their planes, sell more of their products and services, or turn over their inventory faster, surely this would create greater value.

It is this way of thinking that creates many of their problems.

Value begins with the customer. Those who put their own priorities first seem to assume that the customer will value their products and services simply because they exist. They fail to look beyond their own capabilities to recognize that the source of true value is providing just what the customer wants. This means looking outside of the business and anticipating customers' needs rather than assuming them or reacting to them once a problem emerges. [11]

Doing other than this can lead to serious lag.

Henry Ford clearly understood this; his Model T was successful not only in that his operations made it widely affordable to the masses, but because it fulfilled the broad range of what the customer valued at the time. Its durable structure suited the rugged roads on which it would operate (mostly horse trails). Its limited number of easily installed interchangeable parts meant that replacements could be made available and installed by the average user. This was critical since, with no service stations, the driver himself needed to be able to manage his own car's upkeep. [12]

Thus, Ford's success did not come solely from offering a cheaper product; instead, he beat out his hundreds of competitors by creating a *better customer solution*—displacing the horse and buggy with an alternative that met their full spectrum of needs. Moreover, he created a powerful interrelationship between internal and external value; he found that, as he improved his internal flow, he could reduce prices and thus meet the needs of a wider group of customers.

What Ford missed, however, was that value is not static in nature. Although he succeeded in controlling the market share for what he had created, he was not prepared when the market moved on. He ultimately succumbed to others better suited to meeting the rapidly evolving customer demand spurred by his own innovation.

Many firms today behave in much the same way. They focus to an extraordinary degree on increasing their share of those markets they know to now exist as they struggle for the large volumes needed to stabilize their operations. Such a focus is often at the expense of what should really be important to them; moreover, it assumes a greater degree of customer stability than what most really face. And, as in the case of the Edsel, the consequences can be severe.

A Focus on Flow

In the days following U.S. airline deregulation in 1978, most of the industry aligned itself to operate in a way that seemed to maximize its efficiency. Rather than flying passengers directly to their destinations, firms created routes using smaller aircraft to shuttle passengers to enormous airports where the core of their operations are gathered. Using a series of smaller flights, airlines bring together large volumes of passengers to fill up their much larger aircraft, generating the scale they need to produce much of their profits.

This approach parallels the "economies of scale" mindset that has driven most of American business since early last century. Just as managers seek to operate factory equipment at full capacity, a full airplane is considered to be the most efficient use of this central asset; how full an airline's planes are when they fly, or the *load factor*, has become one of the most-watched metrics in this industry. The philosophy is simple: The more seats an airline fills, the greater the revenue that can offset costs from fuel consumption and maintenance from the plane's time in flight.

FIGURE 5.1   Value Curve of Southwest versus Competitors

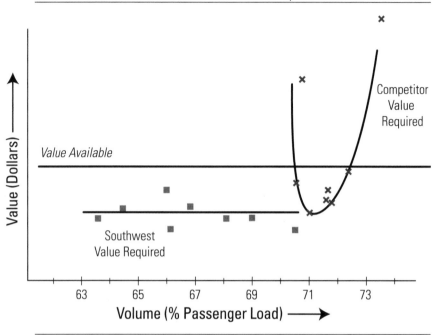

But is this really true? Do greater economies of scale really drive superior results? While it can be said that the hub and spoke system is an efficient way to *fill an airplane* (at least those long-haul flights to and from the hubs), is it really the best way for *maximizing the creation of value*?[13]

Figure 5.1 casts doubt on this traditional mindset. While the large infrastructure at competitors' centralized hubs works well for a given passenger volume (the bottom of the steep curve depicted on the right in figure 5.1), its efficiency quickly deteriorates if demand for airplane seats deviates. And this is precisely what happens too often today; volume has become anything but stable or predictable, and traditional pricing is becoming more and more difficult to sustain (it is no longer under an airline's control—owed in large part to Southwest's competitive presence).

Southwest Airline's emphasis stands in stark contrast. Rather than focusing on how full its planes are, Southwest derives its value from maximizing the time its planes spend transporting customers. This ability to generate greater value—even at lower volumes—makes it profitable for Southwest to serve even out-of-the-way airports, enabling it to expand into new areas that for other airlines would not have been possible. Perhaps more significantly, it permits the company to thrive despite major changes affecting flying patterns across its industry. The difference was clear in 2004 when its leading competitors struggled despite sustaining load factors of around eighty percent—while Southwest realized much greater value margins at a load factor that was more than fifteen percent lower.[14]

Toyota and Wal-Mart demonstrate this same effect. Their very different approach permits them to maintain operational stability and stave off loss even as industry volumes sharply fade while variation grows. Their ability to continue to profit during such conditions should serve as a lesson to others, smashing the myth that has driven American business for nearly a century: that there somehow exists an indissoluble connection between sustaining large, stable volumes and a firm's ability to succeed.

Lean dynamics means that *corporations must begin by redefining what value means.* Creating value for the customer and the corporation means going beyond some assumed relationship between activity and outcome that might no longer hold true; firms' measurements need to be revalidated to be sure they truly support their underlying objectives. Moreover, they need to validate that what they do consistently points to their end goals of value at each step of the way—and they must maintain sufficient transparency at each step to do so. With the value curve as their guiding light, they can gauge their real results, matching their activities against their own value-creating outcomes across a broad range of conditions that extend well beyond those they face today.

Measuring Beyond the Horizon

Those who succeed at lean dynamics seem always to be looking across the horizon, constantly preparing for whatever might strike next. This is certainly true for Southwest Airlines; as the firm's founder, Herb Kelleher, once put it, "Our pilots have accused me of predicting eleven of the last three recessions."[15] And this vigilance seems to pay off; the company consistently created powerful results even during the greatest downturns.

Even today, while others slash flights and abandon airport terminals, Southwest expands each, seamlessly extending its routes far beyond their traditional scope to offer cross-country flights: "As many of our competitors shrink due to massive operating losses, new opportunities arise. Fortunately, we are in a good position because we have more opportunity than people or aircraft."[16] And the firm's flexibility in reaching out seems to have been an important factor, helping to redistribute its planes at times when passenger loads thinned out. This keeps its fleet in the air gaining revenue and sustaining its strong, steady value margin.

For Southwest Airlines, creating value means looking beyond current markets or existing market share. "We will continue to assess needs and available gates in future cities," the company explains.[17] And there is no shortage of demand. The goal, however, is not growth for the sake of growth; the company steps forward only after carefully considering its many options, ensuring that each new move is consistent with its clear vision for value and is aligned with its lean system for smoothly and efficiently delivering value over time:

> Dozens of cities pitch for Southwest's attention each year. When selecting a city, we look for a market that is overpriced and under-served. Economic strength of the local community must be present. Overall, we look for opportunities to begin service where we will have the best probability of success and profit.[18]

When Southwest advances to a new airport or begins serving a different region, it does not seek to simply gain a share of existing passenger volumes. Instead, it completely transforms the marketplace with the low fares and increased passenger volume it brings to wherever it serves. (The U.S. Department of Transportation has coined a phrase describing this phenomenon, referring to it as "the Southwest effect.")[19]

Toyota and Wal-Mart show the importance of looking past today's circumstances to the next challenge. Toyota did not get caught up in the hugely profitable SUV market the same way others did. Instead, it seems to have balanced its output between passenger automobiles while pressing forward with new hybrid technology. The result? Toyota sold more hybrids in 2006 than Cadillac sold cars—a mix that left Toyota thriving even when skyrocketing gasoline prices undermined much of the industry.[20] And Wal-Mart has stretched to entirely different markets, from food to gasoline—far beyond its long-time core base of items— leveraging its powerful management system to overcome the ill-effects of uncertainty that periodically undermined the efforts of others across its industry (a variation leveling effect that is described in Chapter 7).

Firms that sustain value over time seem to consistently look beyond the traditional static measures of what customers buy today. By acknowledging the dynamics of their environment and applying a system of management that accommodates it, they instead create plans and actions that continue to thrive despite even substantial shifts beyond what they currently see. And in some respects, they go further still, raising the bar to actually *transform the customers' perception of value*—moderating customers' behavior to fit more squarely within their capability to deliver.

Mitigating Customer Variation

It is not hard for seasoned travelers to see that they must themselves take on a greater burden as a result of their airline's variability. Ensuring that they arrive on time for an important meeting, for instance, probably means departing well beforehand to offset the risk of running into flight delays. Protecting against lost luggage means bringing only what they absolutely must, fitting everything into bags that they can carry on to the plane. And then, there are all the irritations that travelers are asked to suffer along the way. During a three-hour connection at one of the world's largest airports, I was forced to drag my luggage three times from one terminal to the next to keep up with new departure gates as flight after flight was shifted.

To me the lesson is clear: *Customers like low variation.* Regardless of who they are—a business or an individual consumer—elevated variation causes customers to suffer inefficiency and loss. And customers tend to learn from these experiences. They (like me) tend to shy away whenever they can from those who cause them such difficulty. Instead, they return again and again to those who are proven in mitigating their variation and providing consistency.

This is part of the tremendous appeal of Southwest Airlines. Not only are its fares remarkably low, but it is consistently among the industry's best performers in customer service. Its incidence of lost luggage is among the industry's lowest; its on-time performance frequently tops the list.[21] And the company's insistence on flying only direct routes mean no connections for customers to deal with—they get to avoid the attendant flight disruptions and gate shuffles. Overall, customers can expect a more predictable experience at a great price—a combination that keeps them coming back again and again.

This same basic effect—mitigating customer uncertainty—seems integral to Toyota's success in sustaining positive value. The company's product reliability has tremendous perceived value, something that now serves as a driving force behind its seemingly unstoppable growth:

> Consumers know that they can count on their Toyota vehicle to work right the first time and keep on working, where most U.S. and European automotive companies produce vehicles that may work when new but almost certainly will spend time in the shop in a year or so.[22]

Toyota (and its subsidiary, Lexus) routinely stands well above the rest in producing the most reliable models from any car company.[23] Its high reliability drives down loss to the corporation and to the customer from returning cars over and over again for warrantee repairs. Moreover, its high quality gives the perception that its cars last longer—that they have greater durability. This seems to be reflected in their greater resale price, a factor that might tilt the scales toward purchasing a Toyota in cases when all else seems equal.

This high reliability stands in clear contrast to warrantees offered to "protect" consumers against latent defects. Even major airlines began offering warrantees in the form of mileage points to compensate passengers for performance problems (for certain cases of late departures).[24] In the end, however, such warrantees cannot stand up to those whose strong performance gives customers what they really want: trust that they will receive what they purchased in the first place.

Fostering Trust

Jerry Grinstein, chief executive of Delta Air Lines, made a startling statement when explaining his firm's shift to a lower, simpler fare structure.
Passengers, he observed, had lost confidence that they were getting the
value they paid for; they were switching to Southwest because they did
not trust other airlines to give them a good deal:

> Passengers no longer believed they were receiving the highest
> quality at the lowest possible price. And they were right. . . .
> Southwest succeeded so well that today customers flock to the
> airline's Web site, even when Southwest's prices are higher than
> other carriers'. They simply trust Southwest to be the best value
> around. [25]

This powerful form of value—trust in the consistency of a firm's
offerings—benefits customer and corporation alike. Businesses gain
greater credibility by demonstrating that they will consistently deliver
on their promises—a powerful force in today's marketplace.

This seems central to Wal-Mart's success. Like many of today's other
discount retailers, the large size of Wal-Mart stores and out-of-the way
locations can make them less convenient to visit than small specialty
shops. This makes browsing for a just a few items very difficult—an in-
convenience that might keep shoppers away. At face value, this can be
seen as a liability; Wal-Mart, however, seems to have made this part of its
competitive advantage.

A key part of its success is Wal-Mart's "everyday low-pricing" pol-
icy. While others resort to gimmicks, rotating discounts from item to
item in order to draw in customers, Wal-Mart instead offers stability and
certainty. Shoppers determined to find bargains need not run from one
store to the next; they can now stay at Wal-Mart for *all* of their shopping
needs. Thus, stores can make the most of their already-engaged pool of
shoppers by offering them an ever-expanding range of products, reaching well beyond basic household items to include groceries and even
consumer electronics.

Wal-Mart's consistency in price and product selection has an even
broader effect, drawing people from as far as twenty miles out of their

way to do their shopping. Moreover, it means that shoppers no longer feel they must wait for sales before they buy anything.[26] Not only does this save in advertising costs and rearranging stores for special promotions, but it mitigates the demand spikes that might otherwise strain the firm's ability to perform. In effect, Wal-Mart succeeds in *optimizing customer and corporate value in concert with one another,* a phenomenon that Sam Walton described:

> ... customers will return again and again, and that is where the real profit in this business lies, not in trying to drag strangers into your stores for one-time purchases based on splashy sales or expensive advertising.[27]

Whether it is Southwest Airline's consistent service, Toyota's reliability and durability, or Wal-Mart's everyday low prices, customers have come to appreciate and even expect this new form of value. These firms have reset customer expectations across their industries; their quality and consistency have become the key ingredients that customers seek (particularly during a downturn, when customers are looking to get more for their money). And they have shown how this new customer confidence translates not only to greater sales; it enables new products and strategies that further dampen the effects of external variation.

But this phenomenon is not limited to large, established corporations; small businesses can apply this as a powerful means to gain competitive advantage as well. A great example is Hibbett Sports, a small but growing full-line sporting goods company. Its rock-solid value margin and powerful growth in an industry saturated with strong, entrenched competitors is powered by its detailed focus on the specific needs of local markets—backed by a steady means for flowing value.

Hibbett conducts a comprehensive value analysis before opening a new store, comparing the customer value it must provide with its own capability to deliver efficiently and effectively. It tailors each store to fill local need based on everything from local demographics to community sporting activities, local colleges, or professional sports teams—and offers high-end merchandise that few local competitors carry. Vendors rely on Hibbett to sell their goods in a particular market, landlords give better lease terms to fill locations that need sporting goods stores, and customers visit for its strong service and to find merchandise that might not otherwise be readily available.[28] Coupled with its powerful, lean execution, its results have been impressive: a powerful, steady value margin and spiraling growth that persists even as others are forced to downsize (its value curve and further examination are provided in Chapter 12).

A very different kind of value can be seen for the Garrity Tool Company, a small, private firm that produces complex and often critical parts for military aircraft, medical systems, and automobiles. This firm's reputation for excellence comes from its record of consistently meeting its customers' demanding requirements for low-volume manufacture of complex parts built to some of the strictest standards—a business in which others struggle. Yet this firm seems to thrive, consistently delivering high-quality items on time despite facing low volumes and widely varying demands (in Chapter 7 we will see what it does to make this possible). And the company's founder, Don Garrity, knows the importance of building customer trust; as he puts it, "I can't be a success unless my customers succeed."[29]

For large and small companies alike, creating this new form of value brings the need to create a rigorous means for measuring performance. Earlier, however, we saw the difficulty that large corporations face in measuring the relationship between their internal activities and the value these create. Doing this requires a fundamental restructuring of how measurement is performed—taking into account both today's complex dynamics of flow and this more complex view of customer value.

Integrating Measurement with Flow

A company's approach to measurement has broad implications in how it views its operations and, as we have seen, how it responds to change. It affects everything from how key information moves through the organization to who acts on it and how they make decisions, as described by Johnson and Kaplan in *Relevance Lost*:

> The organization's management accounting system serves as a vital two-way communication link between senior and subordinate managers. It is the means by which senior executives communicate the organization's goals and objectives to subordinate

and decentralized managers. In the reverse direction, the management accounting system is the channel by which information about the firm's product performance and production efficiencies is reported to upper levels of management.[30]

With a firm's measurement system so integral to its decisions and actions, it stands to reason that minimizing attendant delays or disconnects is integral to creating smooth organizational and operational flow. The best solution, it seems, is to keep measurements as close to the decision makers and to the action as possible. This, however, requires corporations to align themselves in a way that is inconsistent with a long-accepted mindset, one that is based on an age-old principle—the *scientific management* methods identified by the early twentieth-century industrial efficiency pioneer, Frederick Taylor.

Taylor indicated that managers alone must oversee work—everything from setting standards to measuring performance. He saw no role at all in this for laborers, who he explained could not grasp the underlying science implications of their efforts. In practice, this means keeping a clean split between two distinct and separate realms: that of performing work and that of its management.

But such a clean split of responsibility that worked so well a century ago creates a real dilemma within the dynamic environment firms face today. Workers are not given sufficient insight to anticipate change and avoid problems down the line. Managers must pour through masses of data before determining what problems might lay ahead. The result is a steep, sluggish organizational hierarchy that inherently lags in decision making. This creates an enormous barrier to linking cause to effect across their vast number of activities, a lag that cannot readily be overcome even using today's powerful computing capabilities.[31]

At the Toyota Motor Company there is no clean split between those who measure and those who perform work. Workers apply their own series of standardized measurements, using them to manage the flow and outcomes of their own activities. This seems to simplify the management process, not only reducing errors, but enabling high data accuracy and ensuring their proper interpretation. By intertwining its measurement with its actions and decisions, the company mitigates this key source of lag that acts as a barrier to dynamic stability.

Southwest Airlines seems to have blurred traditional lines as well, dramatically expanding the workforce's span of insight and driving down information and decision-making lag. Employees know to keep an eye on the company's goals of profit and revenue; the company trains its employees to understand how what they do impacts the company's bottom line (and helps motivate them through their profit-sharing program.) Regardless of their assigned functions, individuals keep in mind the larger objective of their work (such as ensuring on-time departures), and recognize how and when to step in to protect this overall progression of value.[32] As noted by Professor Jody Hoffer Gittell in *The Southwest Airlines Way*, Southwest draws on this *relational coordination* to expand each employee's role in facilitating positive outcomes:

> When asked what they were doing and why, American [Airlines] employees typically explained their own tasks without reference to the overall process of flight departures. For example, ramp agents explained to me that when the bell rings, it is time to go out to meet the plane.
>
> By contrast, interviews with Southwest frontline employees revealed they understood the overall work process—and the links between their own jobs and the jobs performed by their counterparts in other functions. When asked to explain what they were doing and why, the answers were typically couched in reference to the overall process. "The pilot has to do A, B, and C before he can take off, so I need to get this to him right away."[33]

Wal-Mart demonstrates another way of doing this, decentralizing decision making with its "Store within a Store" technique. Whereas other retailer stores relegate the department head to performing the types of tasks one might expect of an hourly wage earner—such as ripping open boxes and stocking shelves—Wal-Mart has turned them essentially into managers of their own businesses. The firm shares with them measurements on everything from the cost of their goods to freight costs, profit margins, and even how their store ranks with all the others.[34] This is key if they are to actively manage the flow of value within their own department, constantly assessing and correcting along the way rather than waiting until higher level managers realize corporate goals failed to reach their mark.

Building measurement right into workers' day-to-day activities provides them the right insight at the right time to mitigate many sources of lag. Workers have broader spans of insight, giving them the ability to make more decisions on their own. This, in turn, minimizes the information that must be shared across the organization, thus reducing the complexity of information flow. Managers can thus be left to manage—no longer tracking the details of day-to-day issues.

The end result is smoother flow across operations, decisions, and information, with the organization working together as a unit to optimize the firm's value-creating capability and relate this to its constantly changing environment. This enables both smoother responses to operational problems and to start-up problems often associated with the flow of innovation. And most of all it helps corporations smash through the harmful mindsets that for too long have limited their ability to respond to the reality of today's dynamic business conditions.

———■———

What seems difficult for so many to grasp is that, in today's dynamic environment, traditional measures of value no longer apply. Lowering wages does not unto itself create value; neither does firing trained personnel as a reaction to change. Creating excellence instead means looking beyond the narrow bounds of traditional measures of efficiency that have become disconnected from the realities of their surrounding dynamic environment. It means setting the new target of attaining both customer and corporate value that can be sustained and even grown over time—and then creating measurements that point everything else toward making this become a reality.

We will see in the next chapters that making this happen, however, requires implementing a broader solution that allows such a measurement system to work. As was mentioned earlier, this means standing up a very different concept of arranging the way work is done—one that dampens, or even harnesses variation that otherwise naturally expands every time the operating environment shifts. It means shifting from measuring and managing work as a disconnected series of activities, from looking at fragmented outcomes as end products even though by themselves they offer no value to the customer or to the corporation. And it means shifting to an integrated *value stream*—tying together operational, organizational, information, and innovational flow, and consistently pointing individuals in each part of the organization toward an unwavering goal of creating sustained value.

From Supply Chains
to Value Streams

The great challenge for Americans is to overcome
their 'every firm for itself' individualism in which each
organization along the value stream optimizes its
own stretch while suboptimizing the whole.
—James P. Womack and Daniel T. Jones[1]

PERHAPS THE MOST SUBSTANTIAL impact from uncertainty and
change comes from the supply chain. Henry Ford clearly recognized
this; he went to great pains to control it. Others since him have struggled
with it. Still, after nearly a century of dealing with it, the supply chain
remains one of the greatest challenges in business management.

Its answer, however, comes not in addressing those issues where
most businesses have come to focus. It cannot be solved by reducing the
tremendous distance that often separates a supply chain's parts. Nor is
the answer simply slashing a firm's number of suppliers, or making inventories move faster.

Instead, the greatest challenge lies in this concept itself.

What, then, is a *supply chain?* It is typically defined as a firm's extended enterprise—its chain of suppliers that provide the raw materials, parts, and components that progressively advance in complete-
ness to become end products and services. For many, however, it is just
what the term itself implies: *a chain of supplies*—a series of inventories
that permit suppliers to buffer their interactions with others along the

way. Yet, we know that inventories themselves create no value; they simply offer a way for bridging value-creating activities whose flow is otherwise disconnected or uncertain. Moreover, they do not come without liability. Not only do they bring the added cost of investment and warehousing, they tend to obscure variability and create lag that sets the stage for unexpected bouts of disruption (an effect that was illustrated in figure 1.2).

Why is it, then, that managers insist on focusing on this chain of supplies as their core means for bringing value to their corporations?

Many years ago I bought a motorcycle, and as part of the deal the previous owner taught me how to drive it. To me, operating all of the hand controls while shifting with my foot seemed like something of a juggling act—one in which a mistake could be quite disastrous. To get past this, my instructor told me to "drive with the clutch"; he taught me to clamp down on the clutch to disengage the engine at the first sign of trouble. I drove this way for a long time, an approach that was clearly less than efficient, but it got me where I wanted to go.

In retrospect, I was not really "driving" with the clutch, but instead was focusing on it as a means to deal with a complexity that for me seemed to be overwhelming. In a way, this is how managers have come to look at their supply chains. They do not actually *run* their business with their chains of supplies; these have, however, become the focus of their attention. Rather than tightly coordinating the progression of individual work steps, corporations tend to lean on mountains of supplies to bridge across the gaps between them. These inventories essentially serve as their "clutch"—offering businesses the means to keep driving along despite even severe disconnects between their activities.

This approach of depending on inventories to buffer disconnects in flow is fairly universal; most firms rely on their "clutch" to a large degree. Yet, doing so as a wholesale way of running their operations can create lag that, as we saw in Chapter 1, acts on environmental change and uncertainty and generates enormous waste—a condition that for many corporations is undermining their competitiveness.

Simply removing supply chain waste without first understanding the reasons why it accumulated is not the answer. Doing so can have the opposite effect firms intended, amplifying uncertainty and loss—even crippling those very operations they had targeted for improvement.[2]

Before taking such actions, corporations must fully understand the nature of variation and lag throughout their activities. They must study the effect this has on how they create value. Only then can they identify the fundamental changes they need to make that will effectively and permanently drive out loss.

The Dynamics of Supply

In his book, *Clockspeed,* Charles Fine, a professor at MIT's Sloan School of Management, identifies as *volatility amplification* the manner in which variation grows as it moves across the supply chain. In his words, "A ripple at one end of the supply chain can trigger a tidal wave at the other."[3] Industries producing everything from electronics to machine tools experience this effect, causing disruption and waste, and placing enormous strain on their suppliers.

This dynamic reaction to sudden change is characteristic of the decentralized activities that make up a supply chain. Henry Ford clearly understood this; he implemented an approach based on overarching control that, for a time, succeeded in managing his supply chain's negative effects. We saw in Chapter 2 how his focus on process control synchronized the movement of dependant activities, minimizing process variation and driving waste down to levels unheard of even today. We also saw, however, that Ford's control-based solution would not work well within the sort of complex, dynamic business environment that exists today.

Yet, many still proceed much as Henry Ford did; standing up control-based business rules or information technology systems aimed at exerting great rigidity at each point along the way. Others go in the opposite direction, delegating authority while monitoring only outcomes. Depending on how corporations implement these, their strongest efforts can backfire—increasing the lag that drives uncertainty and disruption, undermining suppliers' ability to accommodate change and promote innovation.

Understanding the Progression of Variation

To understand why, let us take a closer look at what causes this dynamic reaction, what we might call the *supply chain effect*. As was described earlier, most firms do not deliver products to their customers just as they roll off the production line. Instead, they supply them from vast stocks of inventory that buffer against the peaks and valleys that make up their incoming demand. Factories maintain their stocks by building large batches each time inventories fall to a predefined level (or when they reach a prescribed point in time) known as their *reorder point* (depicted in figure 6.1).[4]

Corporations have come to rely on these reorder points as their mechanism for advancing their progression of value across today's immense and geographically disparate supply chains. Yet, the approach is wholly dependant on inventory buffers, creating a major source of lag at every supply chain interface. And, as we have seen, although lagging systems might function smoothly during times of stability, they quickly break down when conditions shift.

FIGURE 6.1   Managing Demand through Reorder Points

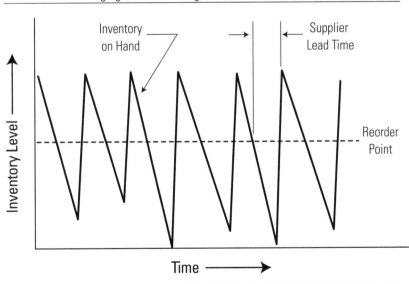

Consider how such lag disrupts information and organizational flow. Suppliers under these arrangements do not respond to actual marketplace demands; instead, they fill the needs of those firms at the next lower supply chain tier, often with little or no insight into what drives their ordering patterns. These firms, in turn, build and deplete their own inventories, creating new patterns to which their suppliers must respond. Thus, supply chains face progressively increasing disconnects in insight—demands at each tier that deviate further and further from customers' true consumption patterns (as is notionally depicted in figure 6.2).

Perhaps one of the best demonstrations of this effect comes from "the beer game," a simulation introduced by MIT's Sloan School of Management in the 1960s to illustrate how such lagging response disrupts supply chain flow.[5] Individual players are assigned to manage different links in a brewery's supply chain (the manufacturer, distributors, and retailers). Each seeks to keep sufficient stocks of beer to respond to his or her own customers' demands, placing orders to replenish supplies based on normal lead times to receive them. Things progress smoothly until demand suddenly spikes, depleting inventories and creating shortages.

With less stock to go around, distributors are forced to deliver lower quantities to retailers than they had ordered. These retailers, in turn,

FIGURE 6.2   The Progression of Variation up the Supply Chain

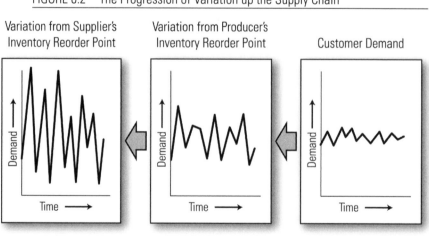

overreact to this unexplained drop in supply (just as we saw earlier with the driver's response to the sudden appearance of break lights), and begin ordering in larger and larger quantities. Their response further drains the system, increasing shortages across the supply chain and creating greater and greater uncertainty. In the end, operational flow breaks down just like we saw with the snowstorm described in Chapter 1, causing severe shortages followed by a glut of supply when conditions once again stabilize.

Corporations everywhere recognize the critical importance of resolving this devastating reaction to uncertainty and change. But they can make things worse with the supply chain actions they put into place.

Chasing Lagging Solutions

In the late 1980s and early 1990s, firms across the country embarked on an aggressive mission to downsize their supply chains. Corporations that built everything from automobiles to aircraft took drastic measures, slashing their number of suppliers and restructuring how they oversaw supply chain operations.[6]

A key goal was to develop closer working relationships with far fewer suppliers to whom they could delegate greater authority. Those who remained would assume responsibility for managing entire supply chains (for example, Ford's first-tier suppliers took charge of entire components or even major systems like whole interiors or brake systems).[7] Their rationale seems straightforward enough: Since supply chains' long sequences of disconnects amplify variation, why not just shorten them? By removing some of their links, perhaps corporations could eliminate some of these disconnects. Delegating entire processes to major suppliers and holding them accountable for their outcomes intuitively stood to slash their own management burden. It seemed that those closer to the action would somehow be able to manage these activities better, while improving supply chain oversight and reducing their potential for disconnects.

Yet corporations that do this can face sudden, unexpected consequences.[8] The reason seems fairly simple: Basing supplier arrangements mostly on outcomes leaves suppliers to operate using the same traditional approach—perhaps fine-tuning inventory and lead-time buffers to meet their particular delivery requirements. Those who delegate to them, however, likely *will* change how they operate. For instance, they may no longer hold any inventories, now instead blindly trusting in the outcomes of these new, still lagging, arrangements to support their operating needs.

The result can be devastating. Sudden surges in demand might draw down suppliers' inventories, depleting buffers intended to protect against variable demands. Customers, who see only their suppliers' outcomes, might have no insight into this declining state of their capabilities. Thus, when their suppliers finally fail, they must suddenly react to as much disruption as ever before, but now with no advance warning and without the inventories they previously held to protect their operations against such conditions (thus increasing the dynamic effect described in Chapter 2).

We see that simply increasing suppliers' responsibilities without fundamentally changing their underlying approach, in reality, is no solution at all. Real improvement instead requires transforming how business is done, from end to end across all elements of value creation. Only this will lead firms to overcome the hidden disconnects between these that amplify variation and create disruption and loss. Doing anything less only stands to worsen the situation.

Streamlining the Whole

In their book, *Lean Thinking,* James Womack and Daniel Jones describe the *value stream* as the specific sequence of all the actions required to transform a product from its basic elements to its finished state and then deliver it to the customer.[9] By laying it out using *value stream mapping,* corporations can see the wastes that traditional methods tend to promote: those long lead times, hidden inventories, and wasted activities that repeated bouts of crisis cause to accumulate over time. This offers corporations a powerful means to uncover the wastes hidden by traditional, disconnected supply chain methods.

Still, most firms seem unable to see beyond their existing structure; their lack of insight into their underlying problems causes many to fixate on portions of their value streams, or on addressing only their more superficial wastes (those visible perturbations above the "sea of buffers" depicted in figure 1.2). Others apply information technology tools aimed at bypassing disconnects across supply chains. Perhaps this is why most lean initiatives fail. Rather than addressing their underlying disconnects, corporations do what they have always done: embark on a never-ending quest to address only their visible wastes.

Preventing this means performing value stream analysis not as a static exercise, but from *a dynamic perspective.* This means looking beyond today's outcomes—those wastes that are visible at a given time. Instead, firms must assess what it is about their business that, when faced with unpredictable and widely varying conditions, causes delays, defects, inefficiencies, and loss *to accumulate in the first place.*

Firms that evaluate the value stream from this dynamic perspective can better see the underlying lag within their flow—discontinuities in operations, gaps in information, delays in decision making, and barriers to innovation—that act on variation to create the waste they can readily see. More importantly, this makes clear why simply removing this waste is not enough, why most corporations must fundamentally restructure the way they do business if they are to accommodate today's demands for frequent change and faster innovation.

Targeting Operational Lag

Most companies today focus their attention on managing aggregate activities—on maximizing their performance within processes, departments, or with suppliers that deal with a wide range of products or services. They emphasize internal measures like fully utilizing factories or equipment, optimizing production runs, or keeping the workforce busy. What they miss with this, however, is the enormous waste and vast disconnects in flow that can only be seen by tracking their build-up of individual products.

Consider, as an example, how spare parts are obtained to repair and maintain the military's fleets of aircraft. For millions of items, suppliers deliver directly to warehouses to support reorder points driven by forecasted demands or other criteria. From a traditional supply chain mindset, this looks like a textbook operation. Planning is generally suf-ficient to keep parts in stock; orders are usually filled when promised.

But from a value stream perspective, this system is riddled with lag.

How can this be? Although its aggregated elements—from demand planning to production through delivery—might individually perform like clockwork, its underlying value-added activities can progress at a snail's pace. Turning out some of the simplest of these parts from begin-ning to end *takes months or even years to accomplish.* Surprisingly, even such astronomical lag typically goes unnoticed, until its resulting supply chain effect gets out of hand and creates serious problems.

The source of most of this delay is fairly straightforward—it comes from suppliers' production lead times (the time it takes for suppliers to fabricate the parts once they receive an order). My own study of this phenomenon showed that very long delays are fairly standard—parts of-ten take six or more months to build, with many taking a year or more.[10] What I found to be especially surprising, though, is that no obvious rea-son for this is evident. Few of these parts require specialized processing; most instead are made up of widely available materials, built within tol-erances that are no more stringent than those found in widely available consumer products. Their long lead times are not generally driven by product or process complexity, or by a scarcity of their raw materials. Instead, they are simply the result of operating under a management sys-tem that, from a value stream standpoint, is designed to spend an inordi-nate amount of time *waiting.*

To better understand why, let us follow their journey from begin-ning to end. Raw materials are typically ordered in large quantities; they might spend weeks or months in storage before they can be machined into batches of identical items and then sent to storage. Days or weeks later they might be combined with other items to form batches for their next operation (such as drilling or heat treating), then are sent back to storage. Often, parts are sent to subcontractors that specialize in opera-tions like quality inspection and surface finishing—then they wait to be shipped back. Many months after beginning their journey, these com-pleted parts are finally packaged and shipped to their customers.

My research showed this to be the norm; parts typically spend only a small part of their journey engaged in value-adding activities—often with well over ninety percent of their time instead spent making no progress at all, either waiting for an operation to begin or simply sitting in storage!

This raises an obvious question. With no compelling reason for such incredible lead times to exist, why do customers so freely accept them? The answer is simple. Too often managers just do not see long production lead times as a problem. Why is this? Because orders are filled from *supply,* not production. Therefore, as long as suppliers meet their required delivery dates (preset agreements to accommodate reorder points) and customers act in the way they had forecasted, parts will be on the shelf when they are needed, and the system will operate as intended.

But what happens if, in the midst of this extended processing time, their customers' needs change? Large deviations from forecasts are not hard to envision, particularly in this case, where military customers' demands might suddenly surge. We saw the answer to this with the earlier example of a snowstorm. When precisely synchronized supply chains are abruptly subjected to major shifts in demand, inventory buffers are quickly depleted. Long lead times mean that operations cannot soon replenish depleted inventories. Thus, when conditions suddenly change, the whole system might break down.[11]

Toyota, Wal-Mart, and Southwest Airlines show that there is a better way. Each succeeds in driving out the lag that causes disruption when conditions change; they do so by applying a number of unconventional techniques for dampening the growth of variation. As a result, their operations look fundamentally different, from the size and purpose of their equipment to their factory layout. And as we will see in Chapter 7, their differences permit them to dampen this natural variation in a way that creates *dynamic stability,* smoothing out internal variation and righting themselves even when major external disruptions are thrown their way. This capability seems central to their ability to sustain steady operational flow when conditions suddenly shift.

Bridging Organizational Disconnects

Ever since Sloan's days at General Motors, managing vast, decentralized operations has brought with it an array of challenges. As we saw in Chapter 2, Sloan developed a methodology for managing organizational components by their outcomes. Later management concepts like business process reengineering seemed to build on this philosophy, holding that supply chain links should by nature be self-contained—that "good organizational boundaries should be relatively opaque. In other words, what goes on inside one organizational element should not be seen or matter very much to people outside it."[12] Yet, the disconnects this outcome-oriented mindset causes can, in today's dynamic environment, create an effect that stifles innovation and promotes lag and loss.

We saw from our earlier example that delegating to suppliers without understanding the degree to which they can respond to changing conditions only drives up uncertainty, making corporations *more* susceptible to the impact of sudden changes in demand. Thus, within a dynamic environment, gaining deep insights into a supplier's methods *does* matter. Moreover, treating suppliers as external, disconnected activities to be held at arms length leaves them reacting to problems with little means to offer feedback, and insufficient span of insight to come up with more effective ideas.

For Toyota, building a relationship with suppliers seems as important as the outcomes they produce. The company builds each relationship over time, working closely to develop individual suppliers while monitoring their progress. Only after advancing through a rigorous development process will Toyota expand the work they are permitted to perform.[13] In doing so it builds its trust that they will consistently meet the quality, cost, and delivery standards so essential to supporting its system of management. The result is a strong understanding of what to expect from them, which forms the basis for its own approach.

Take, for instance, Trim Masters (TMI), Toyota's seat supplier for its Camry and Avalon lines at its Georgetown, Kentucky plant. TMI delivers direct from its production line, holding down cycle times to only three hours from receiving an order to its delivery—even packing its shipments so its seats can be unloaded in the very sequence they will be installed.[14] Because Toyota understands TMI's approach—its ability to respond across a range of conditions—it need not maintain the large schedule buffers or extra inventories that would otherwise be necessary to protect against shortages. Instead, it relies on Trim Masters to deliver what is needed across the wide range of conditions for which the firm will need to operate.

Clearly Toyota's size and attractiveness as a partner gives it a strong position in working with its suppliers—an advantage that small firms do not have. There are, however, other ways to build needed insight. Consider Hibbett Sports, a small retailer that was briefly described in Chapter 5. Vendors rely on Hibbett as a primary means to sell their goods in the local markets it serves; the company's powerful customer relationship and rapid growth makes the firm an important partner even to much larger suppliers (like Nike). They even collaborate on its programs to train the company's employees on the often highly technical features of their products so they can better work with customers.[15]

Wal-Mart, too, bases its supplier arrangements on coordination—not isolation. In his memoir, Sam Walton described the advantages Wal-Mart gained when it "... began to turn a basically adversarial vendor/retailer relationship into one that we like to think is the wave of the future: a win–win partnership between two big companies trying to serve the same customer."[16] By working together with Proctor & Gamble to coordinate information and approaches, Wal-Mart shrank its entire supply pipeline, from suppliers' factories to its stores; it purportedly now carries buffers for only three days of operations in an industry where twenty-five to thirty days' worth is considered normal:

> Before launching the joint program, Wal-Mart would receive up to forty full truckloads of Proctor & Gamble fabric conditioner into its distribution centers on some days and none on other days. After implementation of the program, shipments stabilized at twenty-five to twenty-seven full truckloads every day. Furthermore, the inefficient practice of expediting shipments with partial truckloads at premium rates has been virtually eliminated.[17]

Achieving such powerful results requires more than tracking suppliers' outcomes; it comes from gaining a degree of trust that is only possible from breaking organizational barriers that others seem so determined to erect. It takes coordinating activities, sharing information, and collaborating through innovation on a number of levels and in a way that will advance the goals of all that work together to create common value. This creates the added benefit of helping managers, workers, and even suppliers all feel as partners—with each willing to make important contributions.

Nippondenso, a Toyota supplier for subsystems such as radiators and alternators, exemplifies such contribution with its innovation and initiative; the company is known for significant development spending well ahead of receiving a specific contract.[18] And this is not unique; a University of Michigan study showed that Toyota is able to leverage its suppliers' innovation much better than its competitors—and they can do so with less need for communication.[19]

Southwest Airlines demonstrates that such a focus is effective in overcoming traditional borders separating internal departments or processes, going as far as positioning large numbers of operations agents specifically to facilitate *boundary spanning*. Rather than having agents work remotely, relying mostly on computer interface to manage as many as fifteen departures (as is done at many other airlines), Southwest assigns a dedicated agent to each flight. This lets them personally tie together details crossing functional lines that might otherwise be missed—coordinating shifts in freight deliveries to increase capacity for standby passengers, or tracking down additional wheelchairs for handicapped passengers.[20] The benefits seem clear: Anticipating problems means workers can quickly smooth out minor issues before they escalate to a level that distracts management's attention, demands resources, and creates loss.

And Wal-Mart has taken collaboration beyond simply executing existing plans; it now gives suppliers tremendous authority in creating them. The company has gone so far as to delegate key parts of its planning to *category captains*—suppliers it gives responsibility for everything, from identifying which products should be offered, to creating marketing plans and designing shelf layouts.[21] We will see later how this philosophy acts as a powerful enabler for mitigating the effects of flow variation—a central tenet of lean dynamics.

These firms' successes show the powerful advantages when insight and responsibility are no longer compartmentalized. For them, measurement smoothly progresses to decision and then action, driving out lag and prompting the right activity at the right time. A key to doing this seems to be breaking down the organizational barriers that prevent the span of insight they need to optimize the decisions they make. Each supports this by putting in place different capabilities for creating the right flow of information—the right types and amounts—to enable their actions.

Integrating Information with Activity

In his autobiography, Sam Walton marveled at the incredible view of the business that his firm's information system achieved. His computer and satellite systems gave him the ability to know precisely how many of any given item the company had bought—and how successfully they were sold. More importantly, he could break this down by region, district, or even by store, and for different time frames. And it seems he knew just what to do with this. At Wal-Mart, the insight it creates is not used as power; it flows freely throughout the organization to executives and store managers alike. The effect has been to permit individual activities to move independently while acting together as a system—still facing the hazards of sudden changes but preventing operations from drifting apart along the way. As Walton put it, "It makes it tough for a vendor to know more about how his product is doing in our stores than we do...."[22]

Many firms today seek to follow Wal-Mart's example; thus, information technology is often the first idea they put on the table to bridge disconnects across their organizations and supply chains. Managers use this as a means for working around their problems, a tie-in between processes or divisions that otherwise do not interrelate. Yet these managers miss a key lesson: Working around a problem is never as effective as solving the problem itself. Perhaps this is why so many of these projects fail despite the vast resources and time often applied to put them in place—not to mention the incredible disruption it creates during their implementation efforts.[23]

It is hard to tell by looking at the company today, but in the beginning even Sam Walton put up a fight every time someone asked him for money to invest in such technology. It was very costly to make such an investment, and its need came at precisely the most difficult time—his company was expanding and he was taking on a lot of debt to finance it.

Walton was, by all accounts, very frugal, but as he put it, "Yes, I argued and resisted, but I eventually signed the checks."[24]

In the end, it seems that Sam Walton was right—both in his decision to move forward as well as with his strong sense of caution. Walton's scrutiny likely gave his firm greater clarity, ensuring that Wal-Mart's managers had fully thought out what their automation would achieve: creating real value rather than simply acting as a costly Band-Aid for other poor practices. For instance, if a primary goal of improvement is to minimize lag and create the flexibility to deal with uncertainty, how can standing up an enormous, rigidly coded automated system enable this? Moving forward before answering questions like this can lead one down a costly and time-consuming path that might get the firm no closer to where it needs to be—perhaps leading it to build useless "monuments" that do little to support its progress.[25]

Other lean firms proceed with much the same caution. Consider how Toyota's executives respond when they are presented a proposal to implement some new information technology system. Rather than looking over diagrams that focus on how the system itself will work, they immediately send them back to be redrawn to reflect what is really important to their firm. Their interest is simple: How will this enhance their flow of value?[26]

With lean dynamics, information technology is not used as a way to bridge disparate processes or supply chain links. Nor is it set up as a rigid system whose inflexible needs drive everything else (the way in which some apply today's information tools). Instead, it can be used as a powerful means to supporting and integrating operations, decisions, and innovation, creating value that goes well beyond what is otherwise possible.

Wal-Mart, it seems, did precisely this; the company used information to simplify its operational and organizational lines of flow, building on Walton's apparent belief that less organizational complexity was better for his stores.[27] Today, we can see the results in some of the company's most innovative practices; for instance, it was at the forefront of a method for streamlining distribution known as *cross-docking*. Rather than receiving huge batches of items from suppliers, unloading them to a warehouse only to be stocked, stored, and later retrieved—introducing work, delay, damage, and the immense cost of the storage facility itself—a researcher describes how they kept the products moving:

. . . retailers were replacing traditional warehouses with laser-guided automated systems in which goods arriving on a truck from a factory were split up and repacked on the fly to roll right into other trucks that zipped them off to stores.[28]

This sort of seamless integration of information with operations and across organizations clearly helped Wal-Mart shave its baseline loss to a fraction of its competitors. Its satellite system permits managers to communicate with stores around the country while tracking the location of the firm's trucks en route. The result, it seems, is an ability to better manage schedules and coordinate adjustments across two typically disparate business processes—supply and transportation.[29] It is not hard to see how this would substantially slash lag—shipping items with widely-ranging replenishment needs to stores from geographically dispersed suppliers without the need for stocking and then reissuing through a warehouse. By 1983, its distribution cost was less than two cents on the dollar (which it continued to drive down), as compared to five cents at Kmart (which was about average at the time)—this was clearly contributing to Wal-Mart's powerful edge.[30]

Southwest Airlines has increasingly applied information systems to streamline operational and organizational flow, from ticket purchase and check-in, to managing baggage and streamlining work flow of maintenance operations. An excellent example of its benefits can be seen from an internally created software solution it uses to tweak its schedules based on seasonal shifts of the jet stream. Southwest points out that, by shaving a few minutes off of flight times here and there, it creates huge savings overall—and frees up assets that can help offset the effects of uncertainty:

> In August . . . this seasonal optimization will save more than 90 hours of flying time each day, freeing up the equivalent of ten aircraft. Four of those ten aircraft have been assigned to scheduled flights, and the other six have been deployed as spare aircraft time at the larger stations in the system.[31]

Another way Southwest uses technology to combat lag is through its "Early Alert" system to look for "patterns and exceptions" in its operational data and give advance warning to the appropriate work groups so that proactive measures can be taken. In a current version, an alert is issued to initiate action on take off delays, or when planes are held up from the gate after landing.[32]

Turning Up the Flow of Innovation

America has long led the world in innovation. For nearly a century its basic research and new discoveries have powered its corporations to lead the world. Yet innovation does no good if it is too costly to use, or if introducing it into a new product or service causes more disruption and loss than the value it creates.[33]

Corporations tend to innovate new products and services in a disconnected manner, disengaged from the operational activities of bringing value to the customer.[34] Designers of complex products often have little insight into lessons from their own factories; most communications go through a separate group of liaison engineers. Researchers who come up with initial product ideas are even further disconnected—Alfred Sloan intentionally separated them to keep them "free of the daily distractions of commerce and able to focus on the company's long-term needs."[35] The result can be enormous loss—designs that are riddled with problems and difficult to produce, necessitating change after change, leaving factories and suppliers struggling to contain tremendous disruption when they are rolled out.

This is particularly evident in industries like aerospace that depend on turning out cutting-edge designs, as reported in my book *Breaking the Cost Barrier:*

> Low production yields, poor assembly fit-up, and high acceptance test failures can spur the need for increased inventories, production times, and labor. An inability to provide suppliers with a stable design can lead to problems with configuration control, with a direct impact on their ability to support schedules. This disruption can artificially inflate the man-hours required to assemble the first units off the production line . . . casting doubt on estimates for downstream production costs.[36]

Such turmoil has both immediate and long-term effects. Huge teams across a number of specialties must deal with crisis after crisis, debugging problems, and chasing workarounds to keep production lines moving. Defects skyrocket, with operations often taking as much as a year to regain previous quality levels.[37] Worse still, many design deficiencies are never fully corrected, since revisiting interim fixes they put in place to keep the line moving could impact everything from product configuration to development tests to tooling design (driving up costs and reintroducing even more disruption). Instead, fixes intended only as Band Aids tend to accumulate and become permanent, suboptimizing production for the life of the program.[38]

Why, then, is such an approach so common? Product development is widely seen to be separate and distinct from the supply chain. Innovation requires tremendous specialization in disciplines that are very different than those involved in routine operations—particularly for technology-driven industries. Corporations, therefore, stand up their design teams as completely separate entities. Yet developing products with very little feedback from operations or customers, rather than integrating ideas as they progress, causes enormous lag, leading to tremendous loss.

Lean dynamics solves this problem by treating product development as an integral part of the overall value stream. It goes further than simply matching designs to a factory's basic processing capability; instead, it brings to product or service development the very different goal of promoting smooth flow.

Toyota, for example, designs its products in a way that ensures they will seamlessly fit into its structure for smoothing its value stream. As we will see in the next chapter, this means maximizing parts' commonality, reducing the sequence of dependant operations, and designing for reduced set-up times, to name a few—things critical to supporting its underlying methods for mitigating the effects of variation and achieving consistently smooth flow. Chief engineers involve people from across the firm throughout their design programs (one such forum—the *obeya*—meets about every other day to work through ideas and issues with people from a range of design and manufacturing groups).

Toyota constantly injects technology to keep its offerings fresh and appealing—but it does so using a structured approach that smoothes its introduction. As James Morgan and Jeffrey Liker observed in *The Toyota Product Development System:*

> Toyota creates a set of proven technologies that are "put on the shelf" until they are needed for specific vehicle programs. The Chief Engineers decide when and whether to pull these technologies off the shelf because it is the chief engineers who thoroughly understand what customers want and how the total vehicle fits together.[39]

Engineers creating lean designs remain familiar with—and design within—the capabilities and constraints of their factories. For instance, only after rotating through different departments becoming exposed to many aspects of Toyota's business do mechanical, electrical, and materials engineers go to work as automobile designers.[40] And then they spend years on the job, training within their specific design discipline. Engineering efforts are guided by a strong project lead who ensures balanced trade-offs happen early, and that market and production considerations are made based on a broader consideration of overall value.

Yet, lean dynamics is not limited to incremental innovation. Consider how Toyota leaped ahead of the pack with its hybrid vehicles. It began by introducing its brand of hybrid technology fairly quickly— well ahead of its competitors within what might be described as a niche market. Once gaining traction, it successfully expanded the concept to a range of vehicles, adapting its value streams to satisfy a broadening customer demand.

Service-oriented firms turn out incremental and even game-changing innovation as well, stepping outside of traditional bounds farther and more frequently than their peers. Think of how Wal-Mart constantly shakes up the marketplace, expanding to entirely new types of offerings—introducing innovations like $4 prescription drugs and even moving into the area of banking.

Turning out innovation, however, does not always mean introducing something entirely new—it might simply mean applying existing technology in a way that appeals to new customer desires. Consider Toyota's approach to designing more powerful engines when their demand picked up after the gas crisis in the 1980s. Instead of standing up the new, multibillion-dollar plants that would be necessary to turn out larger engines like its American competitors, the company designed new products that took advantage of its existing small engines' capabilities, a point made by James Womack, Daniel Jones, and Daniel Roos in *The Machine that Changed the World.*

> The product-development teams turned to the advanced engineering groups, which suggested introducing every available technical feature to boost performance of the basic four-cylinder engines. These features were conceptually simple.... Even as they raised the power of the same basic engine, in some cases by a factor of two, these innovations convinced buyers, particularly in North America, that Japanese cars were now "high-tech," that they now had the most advanced features.[41]

Bridging the gaps between how firms integrate information with their operations and the dynamics of how they turn out value makes it possible for them to be more aggressive with the frequency and degree to which they introduce innovations, but with less risk than has traditionally accompanied such change. No longer will they find themselves faced with all-or-nothing decisions, choosing against innovative actions because it means driving loss to extraordinary levels. Corporations can instead make more frequent product changes while keeping costs low and quality high—a combination that turns conventional wisdom on its head.[42]

Rethinking the Buildup of Value

Changing a firm's underlying mindset from managing buffers to flowing value requires one of the greatest cultural shifts in business improvement. Perhaps this comes from letting go of one's sense of control—trading away something that is tangible in favor of techniques that are far less so. Inventory is something that has long been an underpinning of the American system of management; removing it can lend to a sense of vulnerability and concern. But with the right approach, firms will find that their risk does not increase. They can instead slash lag, improving their responsiveness to current and emerging needs.

Doing this, however, first takes overcoming a culture and an infrastructure that are based on yesterday's theory of the business. It means adopting a workflow that responds to precisely what the customer demands, delivering through a seamless flow of value rather than as a chain of dependent activities with safeguards intended to protect each from each other. It means looking for solutions as a combined value stream, understanding that the success of the whole depends on driving out the lag that crosses each of its parts.

To accomplish this, corporations must see that creating real, lasting value instead takes more than simply cutting out today's waste. It means more than speeding inventory turns or shrinking supply chains. Instead, it means mitigating the disconnects that set the stage for crisis and loss—a key condition for any gains they make to be sustained.

Corporations must break from the mindset that there exists some sort of internal competition within the supply chain; for instance, that squeezing suppliers' margins will somehow result in improving their own. By instead working toward a common goal—creating sustainable customer value—each will achieve new levels of profit and competitive advantage.

As their assurance in each others' performance and capabilities grows, they can relax their measures intended to protect against the others' uncertainty or failure. At the same time, they can increasingly work together on new practices for mitigating the effects of variation and change—those described in the next chapter—that are critical to making this work, but which they might before have deemed too risky.

Seven

Leveling Process Variation

At Toyota . . . the ends do not justify the means.
The means are the ends in the making.
—H. Thomas Johnson[1]

IN THE YEARS FOLLOWING World War II the American system was reaching its heyday; at the same time, the Toyota Motor Company was struggling against all odds. Demand was low and variable; by 1950 the company had built only 2,685 automobiles—a number that was far too low to create the economies of scale seen by American plants that turned out two to three times this number per day. Worse still, Toyota's truck sales collapsed in 1949, causing the company to fire nearly a quarter of its workforce.[2]

Forced to rebuild from scratch with little capital to work, the firm found itself deep in crisis. Remarkably, it was this very struggle against what must have seemed to be overwhelming odds that forged the keys to its future success.

Toyota's task was daunting. The company had to create a system that could thrive in the face of low, variable demand while competing with American corporations that were instead immersed within a favorable mass market—one that let them operate squarely within the *optimal zones* for which they had built their operations.

To make matters worse, Toyota also had to deal with new internal constraints. After its postwar mass layoffs, the company settled a crippling labor revolt by giving its remaining workers guarantees that went well beyond what most western unions were able to negotiate: lifetime employment, access to Toyota facilities, and their pay tied to seniority as well as to company profitability. Workers were no longer treated as disposable assets to be hired and fired when conditions changed; they now were among the firm's most-fixed assets, to be in place for the long-haul.[3]

All of this had an enormous effect on how the firm looked at creating value. For Toyota, the traditional mindset of assuming stability and then reacting to change would not work; with it, wide demand swings would probably mean constantly operating at the extremes of its value curve (far from its optimal design point where loss is controlled)—a losing proposition, especially since it could no longer use layoffs as a relief valve against the periodic spikes in costs this would bring. Still, its chief production engineer, Taiichi Ohno, persisted in looking for new ways to approach this problem. He studied Ford's methods and then scrutinized his own shops until he found the answer he knew had to exist.

Wal-Mart's early years were also marked by serious challenge. As Sam Walton later recounted, his firm's early on need for constantly "swimming upstream" forced him to look for very different ways for running his business.[4] Unlike its major competitors, Wal-Mart's limited buying power and geographic isolation made it difficult to entice distributors to supply its stores. Wal-Mart was left to fend for itself. At first it found this whole process to be cumbersome; as Walton put it, "It was expensive and inefficient."[5]

Wal-Mart was forced to create a complete distribution capability of its own. But, just like Toyota, the firm had to find a better way. It could not compete head-to-head against the likes of Kmart and Woolco; to succeed, it needed to be different. And it clearly has succeeded. From the design of its first warehouse to its substantial investment in information technology, the system it put in place has continued to thrive across a wide span of conditions, gaining momentum even during the downturns that crippled its peers.

Southwest Airlines' story began in much the same way, struggling during its formative years to overcome crisis after crisis. Its repeated bouts with challenges from large, entrenched competitors made a profound impact on how it shaped its approach. Like Toyota and Wal-Mart, Southwest looked beyond the strength that its competitors derived from their immense scale. Instead, it took on a very different structure, one that has sustained its more than thirty-year run of profitability and growth.

In retrospect, these firms' early challenges appear to have been a blessing in disguise. Had they been able to depend on the same conditions as their competitors, they might have gone down their same path. Instead, each was driven to adopt a way of doing business that made them very different from their competitors. By creating techniques for mitigating the impact of variation on critical aspects of their operations, they found a way to consistently hold loss to rock-bottom levels. This serves them well today; in an environment in which change and uncertainty have become the norm, the system they built continues to maintain order even in the face of conditions that cause others' activities to fall into disarray.

Rethinking the Foundation for Stability

In the early 1950s, Toyota's chief production engineer, Taiichi Ohno, searched for the means to stand up to America's overwhelming advantage of volume and scale. His visits to Detroit left him inspired, yet he knew that his company could never prevail by challenging the likes of GM and Ford head-on. Instead, he would take Toyota down a fundamentally different path.[6]

Much like Henry Ford, Ohno saw that the secret to minimizing loss came from creating and sustaining a predictable flow of work. Any disruption would quickly drive up loss, causing the supply chain effect—the amplification of variation from one supplier to the next as reorder points progressively obscure customer demand. And, just like Ford, he focused on smoothing variation as a means to optimizing performance. Yet, Ford had relied on high volumes to do this; Toyota would instead have to make it work without the benefits of scale. Moreover, whereas Ford had produced only one product, Toyota needed to turn out several.

Sam Walton faced much the same challenge; he needed a way to smooth out the effects of variation that might cause disruption to his system, challenging his ability to keep the right items on the shelf. (We saw what can happen at its worst with the snowstorm in Chapter 1—sudden changes in customer demand grow to the point that suppliers can no longer deliver.) Rather than building inventories as his competitors did, he worked to hold them down to the razor-thin levels to support his low-cost structure.

Southwest Airlines faced similar circumstances. It began as a tiny firm in a field of large, established airlines with the resources to sustain the adverse effect of price wars or industry downturns. With limited resources, the company could sustain head-to-head competition only if it could find a different, more effective way to operate.

Each needed a mechanism for creating stability in the midst of the constant turmoil that came from high variation, low demand, and the complexity of their businesses. And each ultimately succeeded, creating a system of dynamic stability, in which their operations would inherently right themselves even as forces constantly tried to topple them.

Mitigating the Supply Chain Effect

Key to Toyota's approach is its powerful way of smoothing operational flow. Whereas others built in large batches—fabricating great numbers of the same product before switching over and beginning the next—Ohno organized the company's assembly lines to constantly shift from product to product, changing the sequence and quantities he made of each. The result was an approach referred to as *heijunka,* or *production leveling,* which yielded a substantial smoothing of demand patterns extending to those upstream—its higher-tier shops providing parts or raw materials.[7]

How does this work? Using a technique known as *tact time*—Toyota's method for balancing work hours to support mixed-production activities—the company precisely schedules mixed-model production within its shops. James Womack and Daniel Jones describe in *Lean Thinking* how Bumper Works, one of Toyota's leading North American suppliers for truck bumpers, uses this for scheduling daily production of similar parts as a combined group:

> [Bumper Works'] production manager would take the orders for the next month, let's say 8,000 of Bumper A, 6,000 of Bumper B, 4,000 of Bumper C, and 2,000 of Bumper D. She would add

them up (to get 20,000) and divide by the number of working days in the month (say, twenty) to discover that Bumper Works would need each day to make 400 of Bumper A, 300 of Bumper B, 200 of Bumper C, and 100 of Bumper D (with a tact time of .96 minutes). This would require four changeovers of the blanking and stamping machines, totaling 88 minutes (9 percent of the 960 minutes of the two-shift working time) at the maximum allowable changeover speed of 22 minutes.[8]

Instead of producing a month's supply of Bumper A prior to switching over to Bumper B, the firm produces only the units identified in its daily schedule. Rather than sending large inventories of Bumper B to storage and then retrieving them when needed, the shop produces just what is needed to support the current requirements of the firm. This reduces waste in several of its forms (overproduction, excess inventory, excess motion, etc.)—along with substantial sources of lag.

A direct benefit from this mixed-production approach is dampening the "bullwhip" effect described in Chapter 6. Smaller lot sizes means firms do not transmit huge reorder point demands to those upstream— an approach we have seen causes demands at each tier to deviate further and further from customers' true consumption patterns. Instead, shops producing smaller quantities of items maintain a demand profile that more closely matches that drawn by the end customer. By building fewer items more frequently (as opposed to the mass-production standard of infrequently producing large batches), they prevent the traditional progressive disconnect in activities and insight. Individual production shops can progress at around the same pace as end-item consumption, thus offsetting an important form of lag.

Further smoothing this are small *supermarkets* stocked with what Toyota calls *standard inventory*—small, tightly controlled buffers that act to dampen variation across operational steps (Toyota refers to this internal variation as *mura* that might drive *muri*—or disruption that interrupts the progression of activities).[9] Because of the variation-dampening effect that comes from applying mixed production, the quantities they hold can be kept *small and visible* (far below what they would need without the effect created by applying mixed-production—a key to preventing lag that would obviate any variation-leveling benefits). And, as we shall see in Chapter 8, there are a number of proven ways to apply this supermarket concept to diverse, complex circumstances (such as fulfilling huge demand spikes for normally low-volume spare parts used for military aircraft), problems that stockpiling finished inventory cannot realistically solve.

Implementing production leveling, however, requires a substantial shift. No longer can corporations simply "drive with the clutch"; instead they must set aside their traditional workarounds, making fundamental changes that strike to the core of how they do business. Dr. Shigeo Shingo, cocreator of Toyota's Just-In-Time system, noted that any less than this can cause even the most focused initiatives to fail:

> If you merely imitate the superficial aspects of the Toyota production system and hastily apply what you see as a system for getting parts just-in-time, you will end up with the opposite of the desired result. This will not only create havoc in your own plant but also cause your suppliers a great deal of stress.[10]

Ultimately, Toyota applied this concept of production leveling across its entire business. Doing so offered a powerful way to drive down uncertainty, all but eliminating the delay and disruption so common for others. The result has been a degree of operational predictability unheard of since the days of the Model T—a key to making possible Toyota's now-famous Just-in-Time (or JIT) system.

The Concept of Variation Leveling

What seems far less recognized is the full potential for dampening uncertainty that this mixed-production technique offers. Rather than simply dampening the growth of *internal* disruption as we have seen, firms can use mixed-production to dampen the disruptive effects of operating within a dynamic *external* environment. Recognizing and drawing on this capability offers wide-ranging advantages, from improving forecasting and smoothing demand spikes, to facilitating the deployment of lean principles throughout the supplier base.

Figure 7.1 notionally illustrates this effect. On the left we see the variation in customer demands for a series of individual items that a single factory might produce. Such variation naturally occurs to different degrees, requiring buffers (either capacity or inventory, as depicted by figure 6.3) to offset its peaks and valleys. The right side of the figure illustrates what happens when this same set of items is managed very differently—combined together as a single group. We see that by commingling their production to the greatest extent possible (as would be done in a mixed-production operation), *their combined variation flattens out.*

To better understand this effect, consider how a supermarket might plan out how many of a given item it must stock on its shelves. Individual customers' demands are highly variable and unpredictable—even more sporadic than those notionally depicted on the left side of figure 7.1. Thus, a supermarket cannot efficiently base its plans on predicting the actions of individual customers. Preparing for their combined uncertainty would mean holding enormous quantities of everything all the

Figure 7.1   Flattening Variation by Combining Products into Families[11]

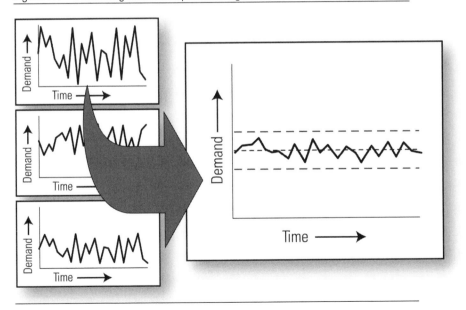

time just in case every customer buys at the same time—something that is unlikely to happen.

It makes more sense to instead plan based on aggregating customers' demands (not adding together each of their individual peaks). The result is what we see on the right side of figure 7.1—the unpredictable demands of many individuals combine to become smoother and more predictable. This means reliably meeting customers' needs while using much less inventory.

The variation-dampening effect from using a mixed-production methodology works in much the same way; by aggregating the demands—not just for different customers, but for different items that can be seamlessly managed together as a group—firms can lower variability and thus increase their overall predictability. The result is reduced uncertainty, helping firms better respond to individual changes caused by external circumstances.

Finding the means for leveling variation seems central to lean dynamics. For instance, by managing items not individually, but as combined groups sharing similar characteristics, corporations can apply a number of practices that make them effective across a wider range of conditions. With this come lower inventories, higher capacity utilization, and greater responsiveness to change—core characteristics of this very different system of management.

The Elements of Variation Leveling

Companies that seem effective at leveling variation find it possible to create value in ways never before imaginable. Toyota continuously adjusts its production to match what its customers buy (this will be further described in Chapter 8). Southwest Airlines minimizes its costs while maximizing value, pulling in customers even where others find none. And Wal-Mart reduces inventories down to almost unimaginable levels (as indicated earlier, a few days' worth in an industry where more than a month is typical), providing the variety at rock-bottom prices that customers have come to demand. Each sustains their smooth and synchronized operations during the most challenging times—even when others cannot.

But leveling variation is not something that can be directly added to traditional business operations. A number of more basic changes are needed to make it work. First and foremost, corporations' flow of activities must become steady and seamless—both step-by-step and shifting between the items within a product family. Doing so creates an array of challenges. Fortunately, we can learn much about overcoming these by taking a closer look at Toyota, Wal-Mart, and Southwest Airlines. Despite their very different businesses we shall see that they share similar techniques for overcoming the common constraints that stand in the way.

Managing by Product Family

To make this work, lean dynamics aligns work by *product families*—for manufacturers, groups of items that can share "common materials, tooling, setup procedures, labor skills, cycle time, and especially, work flow or [process] routings."[12] This differs from traditional operations, where parts are combined with others only as a means for maximizing quantities to create economies of scale for individual processing steps. Items might be combined with others for machining, then with others for drilling, then for heat treatment, and so on. Grouping by product families means parts instead share a string of common steps and can be produced end-to-end by teams working together in manufacturing *cells*—groupings of equipment, processes, and people working as teams to turn out complete end items, components, or clearly severable portions of major operations. The inherent commonality across a product family and flexibility of these cells makes it possible for them to quickly and seamlessly shift back and forth from producing one item and then to the next, combining work flow as if it were for only one item to generate the results depicted in figure 7.1.

Consider, for instance, the difference in how cells might build airplane parts fabricated out of sheet metal. Everyone in a cell would be capable of performing most or all of the tasks along the way, from trimming, forming, drilling, and reaming, to surface treatment. This permits workers to move from job to job as demands shift, creating tremendous flexibility to support mixed production and overall changing needs. Their equipment is simpler and more flexible in order to support their range of needs—and smaller to support their small-lot production (as compared to the enormous, specialized equipment that mass-production shops use to turn out huge batches of identical items). Building items from beginning to end also gives them tremendous span of insight; they learn what roadblocks exist between steps, allowing them to take measures or recommend changes that streamline overall performance.

This very different mindset—managing by product family as a means for dampening the effects of variation—is effective in sustaining smooth flow within a dynamic environment. Managing groups of common items means capacity utilization increases; the effectiveness of people and facilities increases, producing greater value in less time. Lag plummets; operations no longer depend on the "sea of buffers," as was described in Chapter 1. And this greater efficiency begins *after grouping together just a handful of items*—an effect that can be readily calculated.[13]

Southwest Airlines offers a different spin on this technique. Its use of a single family of aircraft (the Boeing 737) creates natural commonalities across everything from its training to its spare parts and even its support equipment. Training is simplified; the company need only train pilots and maintainers for one type of aircraft, and everyone is more familiar with the equipment—people can more reliably spot problems before they spiral out of control. Inventories are lower, since parts are needed to support only one type of aircraft. Record keeping is simplified, reducing the number of manuals, tools, and spare parts, making it more straightforward to substitute one plane for another in case of maintenance problems.[14] All of this helps to foster the effect shown in figure 7.1, smoothing out everything from scheduling flight crews to servicing planes.

The much greater flexibility this creates appears to be an important part of Southwest Airlines' direct flight model, holding down the immense complexity that, for others, necessitates the use of central hubs. This means fewer connections, so flights face less exposure to disruption from weather or other factors, which is a key benefit. Much like we saw with the supply chain effect, even seemingly isolated delays can drive uncertainty and loss that spreads across a network of flights, something one Southwest Airlines executive described:

When you get two airplanes that are an hour late, it's not just the 274 people that are on board those two aircraft. You potentially impact 2,500 people that day and maybe even 3,000.[15]

Dampening operational variation seems to be key to Southwest's ability to operate with lower staffing levels (twenty-five fewer when calculated as an average number per plane—a number that continues to rapidly improve),[16] while keeping a greater percentage of its aircraft in the air and consistently departing on time (overcoming the seemingly greater potential for variation that its higher number of takeoffs and landings would intuitively create).[17] Moreover, its greater efficiencies make serving out-of-the-way airports profitable, enabling the company to expand into new areas that for other airlines would not have been possible.

Wal-Mart, too, it seems has found a way to leverage its products' commonalities to engage its suppliers in streamlining activities from planning to distribution. It selects a lead supplier for families of products—*category captains*, responsible for managing the items within that family, from soft drinks to detergents. Each reviews data, determining the best way to manage the items within this group—from what products Wal-Mart should offer to the layout of shelf space. By building on a supplier's already strong insight into its constraints and opportunities, the company can optimize everything from shelf space efficiency to profitability well beyond what would be possible by managing all items individually. The concept seems to work; it purportedly gives manufacturers and retailers as much as eight and fourteen percent increases in sales, respectively.[18]

It really was not until decades later that the academic community began to report the far-reaching impact of adopting such an approach. Even then, researchers seemed to attribute it solely to the Japanese; they did not appear to recognize that a few American firms had quietly begun to apply this same basic principle:

Like the American approach to production and marketing, the Japanese approach constitutes a total system, with each part reinforcing the others. In contrast to the U.S. approach, however, the Japanese system allows manufacturers to produce a variety of models with minimal downtime and low inventory requirements, and permits fast, flexible responses to market changes.[19]

Speeding Changeovers

A central hurdle to managing in this way is overcoming the traditionally time-consuming and labor-intensive process of equipment changeovers. For example, changing over dies used for forming automobile body panels traditionally required shutting down stamping presses for an entire day. Manufacturers absorbed the cost of this downtime by producing the same item for long periods, building large *economic order quantities* (or even avoiding changeovers altogether by dedicating different equipment to producing different parts). For Ohno to realize his different vision of seamlessly switching between items within product groups, he had to come up with a way to dramatically speed this up.

Thus, while postwar America concentrated on increasing the speed and volumes produced by its equipment, Toyota instead worked on streamlining its changeover times. And this work paid off; after about a decade of trial and error, the company succeeded in driving down its major machine setups from several hours to about three minutes.[20]

Speeding changeovers requires particular emphasis on speeding *internal* setups—those activities that must occur while operations are stopped—and shifting these wherever possible to become *external* setups (those preparatory activities that can occur even while the equipment is still running).[21] In some cases, machines can be designed specifically for facilitating external setups—maximizing preconnections and preadjustments that can be made to dies or fixtures before they are attached; moreover, they might be equipped with quick-connect fasteners or clamps for speeding internal setup.

For Southwest Airlines, achieving fast, reliable changeovers is central to how the firm does businesses. The company helps speed its gate turnarounds it seems by transferring as much work as possible to external setups (preparing ground support, baggage, and other activities before its planes arrive), and then closely managing each step once planes arrive. Boeing's former president and CEO understood his firm's need to support Southwest's approach:

> The sequence with which you locate ground service equipment around the airplane has a big impact on turnaround time. What's the first thing you put against the airplane? Very frequently it's the baggage loader, because you've got to start that process first. If the baggage loader blocks access to the lav service panel, then you're going to end up with a real problem that could cost you valuable time.[22]

Perhaps just as importantly, however, is the contribution that comes from Southwest's shorter, direct routes, and its affinity for less congested airports. We have seen that this naturally minimizes the domino effect, whereby one flight delay bumps another and then the next, setting off a chain reaction that extends down the line. By thus increasing its schedule predictability, Southwest does not need to buffer its gate times or flight schedules as much to manage its departures—something that probably helps it keep more of its planes in the air.[23]

One powerful technique used for scrutinizing equipment change-overs is *kaizen*—or "continuous incremental improvement."[24] In facilitated events, employees review work procedures, equipment location, and other activities, identifying ways in which flow might be streamlined. The end result might be changed procedures, relocated equipment, or redesigned work—each helping to slash machine down time in producing items across a product family.

Unfortunately, many firms *begin* their lean transformation efforts with kaizen or similar exercises—a practice that seems at least partially to blame for today's large number of lean failures. Too often I have seen intense efforts that simply "tune-up" the status quo—speeding activities that really do nothing to create bottom-line value. Conducting such exercises seems premature if done before broadening workers' understanding of lean dynamics and the firm's underlying drivers of loss. Attaining this broader span of insight is critical if they are to keep from recommending what amounts to pockets of excellence—disconnected gains that add no benefit to the corporation's end-to-end creation of value.

Worse still, involving them and then deciding not to act on their input because of these constraints creates the real potential for turning them off, causing them to lose excitement and disengage from future efforts.

While including the workforce is a key part of lean dynamics, it makes sense for firms to proceed cautiously—perhaps first restructuring workers' jobs so they can gain the insight needed to make the most positive and meaningful impact.

Structuring the Supplier Base

Making variation leveling work requires incorporating it across the entire value stream. In Chapter 6 we saw how disruption and delay at any point sweeps across the value stream like a tidal wave, wreaking havoc on flow by the time it reaches the end of the line. Thus, fostering a smooth, reliable flow of value means dampening variation all the way back to the lowest-tier supplier. One way to do this is deliberately assigning suppliers by product family—a practice that runs counter to how many firms today do business.

Suppliers are often selected by competing to produce individual items, or combinations that do not share inherent commonalities. The result can be creating a supplier network where each provides a collection of disparate items that bear little resemblance to one another. Demand for these items can be further amplified when procurements are split between multiple sources in an attempt to mitigate risk. But as we have seen, this further complicates demand predictability by promoting *increased variation* (the opposite effect from that shown in figure 7.1).

Lean firms break from traditional methods that tend to amplify the very supply chain effect that firms so much wish to overcome, as James Morgan and Jeffrey Liker point out in *The Toyota Product Development System:*

> A lean model, on the other hand, generally works with a small stable of suppliers within the context of a broader plan. The goal is to keep these suppliers busy and competitive and to motivate them to do their best, sometimes with an eye to what they may contribute to other programs in the future.[25]

Toyota takes rigorous steps to keep from splintering demand in a way that can amplify variability across supply sources. Typically, "two or three suppliers make a given type of part and have 100 percent of the business for a given vehicle program."[26] And, unlike the wholly outcome-based approach described in Chapter 6, Toyota takes measures to understand *how* its suppliers will continue to deliver.

Consider Toyota's seat suppliers for its Camry and Avalon lines at its Georgetown, Kentucky plant. Though Toyota maintains two long-term supplier arrangements for automotive seats, both of these suppliers seem to have their own, well-defined stream of demand. In fact, each seat they produce is intended for a specific car within a given line. This arrangement clearly prevents variation buildup, while maintaining competitive pressures across Toyota's automotive seat supplier family.[27]

Let us take this concept a step further. Suppose companies structure their supplier arrangements in a deliberate manner to apply the principles of variation leveling. Managing together items that share similar materials and sizes, for instance, might let suppliers aggregate their combined material needs, giving suppliers a more refined picture of the actual demands they will face (just as was described in the earlier analogy of stocking supermarket shelves). Combining what were once individual, sporadic demands causes variation spikes to smooth out (as we saw in figure 7.1). The result should be lower lead times, greater responsiveness to change, and reduced cost.

This is precisely the result I demonstrated in a project for the Defense Department aimed at improving reliability in obtaining aircraft spare parts suffering some of the worst lead times (some as long as five hundred days). By shifting from traditional methods, instead procuring items based on product family-based groupings, suppliers slashed their lead times by hundreds of days—as much as two-thirds—while dramatically increasing their ability to respond to unexpected demand surges.

Backorders for one traditionally problematic group of items (hydraulic tubes for fighter jets) nearly disappeared—in one case even when experiencing an unexplained demand spike of nearly one-thousand percent. And this greater responsiveness did not cost more, as one might expect. Rather, prices *dropped*—not just in aggregate, but individually—by as much as thirty percent for individual items across the family![28]

Broadening Workers' Responsibilities

We have seen that a critical need exists to broaden workers' span of insight. Fortunately, gaining this insight is natural fallout of shifting from traditional, compartmentalized operations to managing by product family. Under this construct, workers must take on a greater role; they must make the shift from efficiently producing individual items to flexibly turning out entire families of products. This means their jobs become much more expansive; rather than focusing on discrete steps, individuals must now take charge of producing parts from beginning to end.

For example, a machinist who traditionally would have performed repetitive grinding steps for large batches of parts now might become part of a manufacturing cell, responsible for the range of activities to turn out an entire family of machined parts. These workers now make decisions to adjust equipment, resources, and even suppliers' deliveries to ensure their work can efficiently meet the needs of the overall system.

Flexible work rules, broad-based skills, and a culture of working across functional boundaries are central to promoting the variation-dampening effect depicted in figure 7.1. And creating these further contributes to smoothing the flow of value—across operations, decision making, information, and even innovation—driving out lag and speeding the corporation's responsiveness to change. Toyota, Wal-Mart, and Southwest Airlines and others show this to be important for operations of all types—not only for manufacturing but for service as well. A ramp manager explained how this works at Southwest Airlines:

> Maintenance has helped us load bags, push planes out. All we have to do is call them. . . . We'll get help [from maintenance] disassembling a wheelchair [even though] it's not in their job description. What's really strange about the whole thing— these guys are represented by Teamsters. Teamsters seem to be a national labor organization that's the most traditional kind. Still, I've never seen one guy in maintenance hide behind a job responsibility title.[29]

It is important to recognize, however, that such arrangements no doubt have an impact on individuals' perceived workload. Responding to real demands, rather than simply creating inventory, means workers see a greater urgency for what they produce. Still, the higher responsibility can have a positive impact on workers' outlook. More clearly seeing the impact of the work they perform can make it more fulfilling, giving them a greater sense of purpose for what they do.

Fostering such a perspective requires that managers' mindsets shift as well, away from rewarding and prizing last minute saves to instead recognizing the much greater value of creating and sustaining smooth flow. Under lean dynamics, managing for crises becomes a thing of the past; all eyes instead focus on prevention. This holds true not only for those within the company itself, but for its suppliers as well.

Designing Products and Services to Foster Smooth Flow

We have seen that firms can realize tremendous benefits by implementing the product family concept, from better utilizing resources and capacity, to driving down loss and increasing flexibility—all keys to flattening a company's value curve. Achieving this, however, requires designing products for value streams to take greatest advantage of imbedded commonalities.

It is widely recognized that firms can achieve a number of advantages by designing products with certain outcomes in mind. Reducing the number of parts that go into a product, for instance, will drive down complexity and thus simplify assembly. Ensuring that fabrication processes are capable of producing to blueprint tolerances increases product quality and drives up production yields. The result is a greater capability to consistently produce what engineering has designed, thus mitigating loss throughout a product's life cycle.

These, however, all represent a *static* view of manufacturability; lean dynamics adds a *dynamic* perspective as well. Simply ensuring that parts *can* be made is not enough; firms need to engineer products so that they can be *smoothly and flexibly* introduced into existing operations. This means maximizing commonalities between component items (similar sizes, dimensional details, etc.), always with setup-time reduction in mind. How products will be assembled becomes a primary consideration; we saw in Chapter 6 that simplifying the progression of dependant steps mitigates the amplification of variation and the supply chain effect.[30]

Still, how products are designed is only part of the answer. Firms must design factories, equipment, and tooling very differently as well to make this flow-based approach work. Doing so means equipment is smaller, simpler, and not as single focused, requiring less worker sophistication and specialization for workers to operate. This permits a single worker to operate one machine for a variety of tasks, creating the flexibility needed to seamlessly produce across product families.

Toyota takes this concept of dynamic manufacturability still further. As one observer noted, ". . . if there is any chance it may adversely disrupt stability, reliability, and flexibility, Toyota will reject the technology or at least delay adopting it until the problems can be resolved."[31] This gives it an edge in maintaining a "fresh" range of product offerings; its much faster product-development time and lower disruption to production seems to lead it to be less averse to expanding and changing designs.

Rethinking the Constraints of Business

We have seen throughout this book that lean dynamics offers a better way. Not only does it prevent the need for corporations to depend on workarounds that run counter to creating value, but it gives firms the underlying capabilities needed to take advantage of the range of opportunities that today's uncertain business environment brings. We saw the need for this in the cases of Toyota, Wal-Mart, and Southwest Airlines; they demonstrate that true leadership does not come about by simply surviving the crisis, but by applying these new tools and techniques to help in looking ahead to new opportunities.

Leveling variation introduces a game-changing capability that corporations can draw upon to create widely ranging opportunities—from creating a niche within a business area that others find too demanding, to slashing costs well beyond what conventional wisdom dictates. Regardless of the business or place in the value stream, however, creating this type of value is central to implementing lean dynamics. There are many ways firms can do this. Let us look at two examples showing different ways to break through today's mindset to realize the opportunities that exist.

Harnessing Customer Uncertainty

The Garrity Tool Company is a small, private manufacturing firm in Indianapolis with a reputation for excellence. What makes this firm stand out is its uncanny ability for producing complex and often critical items for military aircraft and medical systems, built to some of the strictest standards. It consistently delivers high-quality parts and tooling on time in the face of low, variable, and uncertain demands. Don Garrity, the company's founder and president, acknowledges his business niche as "a challenging marketplace that minimizes our competition—nobody else wants it."[32]

What is this firm's secret? It truly represents a laboratory for the principles of lean dynamics—and it appears to have successfully applied these with a focus that is very different from that of traditional lean initiatives.

Don Garrity's insights into lean techniques did not come from formal training or class work, but from years of experience, initiative, and innovation. His hands-on experience in fabricating metal parts and components made him an important member of my study team exploring lean lessons from aerospace. What is astonishing is the innovative ways he later found to apply the lessons on lean methods and constraints he apparently learned—what works and what does not—within his own firm's unique circumstances to achieve great success.

Walking through his shops and then talking to the company's general manager, John Entwistle, it became clear how its operations support the concept of variation leveling. Flexibility is built into everything the firm does—from planning, to managing suppliers, tracking performance, and building the workforce. Its equipment is highly flexible; each of its automated tools can be used to turn out nearly any part that the firm produces. The company's workers are similarly adaptive. Most are certified to operate each piece of the firm's equipment and trained to program and set up any of the dozens of his computerized multipalleted, multiaxis machines—each of which can be used to manufacture as much as two-thirds of the items the company produces. This interchangeability of people and equipment greatly simplifies the job of scheduling work, for instance making it possible to schedule in last-minute orders or urgent customer requests.

The company's work is broken into four distinct product families (gauges, prototypes, cylindrical machined parts, and noncylindrical parts). Within these, product teams manage production from beginning to end: ordering materials from suppliers, machining the parts, and over-seeing other activities, from surface finishing and quality inspection to customer acceptance, with almost no management intervention.

The firm's emphasis on mitigating lag from unneeded complexity can be seen in its approach to applying information technology. Rather than fielding a large, rigid system requiring extensive tailoring and up-keep, the firm operates off of a basic software solution that it extends through the use of linked databases. The result is an example of the power of simplicity; the system is easy to use and data are consistently kept up to date (supported by solid processes and built-in reminders), ensuring the right information is delivered to the right people to support their decision making.

It appears that this firm's selection of work supports its application of variation leveling as well. The company carefully pursues new busi-ness to take advantage of its flexibility to manufacture a wide range of items as combined product families—and thus level-loading its facilities despite widely varying quantities, lead times, product complexities, and other constraints (the effect depicted in figure 7.1). Its resulting ability to adjust to surges in demand without affecting quality and delivery has led to high satisfaction and trust that keeps customers returning again and again. Moreover, its approach of pursuing highly diversified business seems to have the added benefit of smoothing out the boom-and-bust cycles that might otherwise come from supporting customers within in-dividual industries. As Don Garrity puts it, "this lets us shoehorn work into voids to keep everyone working and equipment utilized."[33]

Customers seem to trust that with the Garrity Tool Company they will receive the right part at the right time and at the highest quality against stringent requirements (its quality, growth, and innovation has repeatedly won city and state business awards). Quality is built in; everything is laid out to support this result—from the layout of work to the positioning of equipment. For instance, surface plates, dial indicators, and other various gauges are located at each machine so that dimensions can be closely monitored during each step of each operation. The result seems clear from its bottom line: the company has rapidly grown year after year, thriving amid the pressures of operating in this variable, uncertain environment.[34]

This demonstrates an important lesson: Lean transformation need not be driven by assemblers or others at the pace-setting end of the value stream. Variation leveling offers suppliers a significant ability to take the lead in implementing their own lean shift. The Garrity Tool Company did not depend on others to create stability first. Instead, it took on work that is by nature unstable—building prototypes, small lots of items, and filling last-minute orders—jobs of varying complexity and urgency. And it uses its internal flexibility to create a stabilizing effect on the firm's workload.

Improving Value Stream Predictability

For most corporations, uncertainty and spikes in demand drive a certain way of thinking. Managers seem to resign themselves to operating in a disconnected manner, running their business as a series of activities and buffers tied together with some overarching set of controls. When waste is found, they feel they must apply the same tired solutions that do not necessarily get at the root of the problem.

One firm I visited sought to slash costs by reducing its inventories by more than twenty percent. Unfortunately, it did so without first understanding the reason those inventories existed—the uncertainty they had been put in place to offset. The result? Stockouts skyrocketed; large teams of expediters struggled to keep operations in control. Conditions once again stabilized only after its inventories were restored.

Consider a different problem. A recent study by the Automobile Aftermarket Suppliers Association (AASA) estimated that many of the items supplied by the automotive aftermarket business are rarely used—in fact, around six billion dollars of inventory is for parts that have not moved in a year or more. The recommended solution? Come up with new ways to forecast customer demand.[35]

While this intuitively seems to be a reasonable course of action, it is important to understand that these "slow moving" items offer little demand history data on which to run statistical forecasting models. Without sufficient data, firms are left with little on which to base projections. This is not uncommon; methods for optimizing inventory levels face serious limits—whether because demand is too weak, or because conditions are simply too variable to count on the results.

Consider an alternate approach. Instead of relying on individual forecasts (subject to these serious limitations), what if the industry shifted from managing vast inventories of individual items to aligning suppliers by product family? Perhaps some could become category captains, permitting them to more precisely analyze and adjust to the needs of more manageable product groupings. Slow-moving items might be combined with fast-moving items to enhance the variation-leveling effect, thereby reducing lag and much more effectively slashing inventory buffers. And rather than scrambling to respond each time demands change, their smoother overall demand might instead bolster suppliers' abilities to consistently respond to even widely changing customer needs.

We shall see in the next chapter that improving value stream predictability in this way "that fundamentally changes established practices" has enormous implications.[36] For instance, creating a flow that at each point more closely matches actual customer demand factors into another key, yet controversial, consideration: how firms choose to synchronize their flow of work.

Eight

To Push or to Pull?

And this is a very important point: without the computer,
Sam Walton could not have done what he's done.
—Abe Marks, First President, NMRI[1]

IN 1959 THE COLD WAR was in full swing. Soviet Premier Nikita Khrushchev was visiting the United States for a historic meeting with the President. As the story goes, he broke away to make an unscheduled visit to a supermarket—and was astounded by what he saw. Shelf after shelf was stacked with packaged goods, fresh produce—any type of groceries a consumer could want or need.

How could this be?

Clearly this must be a staged event. How else could this supermarket stock so many items in one place at one time—and keep them looking so fresh? Still, since this was a random visit, how did they know to which store they were to divert all of these supplies?[2]

The American supermarket came to capture the fascination of the world; it represented a shining example of America's incredible bounty and its tremendous know-how. For Khrushchev, the sight must have been extraordinary: shelves bursting with a spectrum of products, their availability seemingly unaffected by customers who took as much as they could want. This had to be shocking to a man leading a country where supplies were scarce and shortages common.

For American corporations, this served as just one more proof that size *is* the answer; that the economies of scale from such massive operations was what created its tremendous value. And there appeared good reason for this belief; in America, scale dominated everything, and excellence seemed always to result.

For Toyota, however, the American supermarket demonstrated something quite different. Its innovative production engineer, Taiichi Ohno, saw more than simply another demonstration of the need for scale; instead, he found in it a different lesson: its application of self-service for regulating operational flow. Its success proved that top-down controls were not needed to keep every aspect of operations flowing smoothly. Instead, it showed that a flexible solution could more precisely accommodate varying demands.

By letting actual demands *pull* operations rather than have average forecasts *push* them forward, he saw that overall flow could be stream-lined, minimizing lag and waste within the dynamic environment his firm faced.

The success that Toyota has since gained from applying this philosophy demonstrates the validity of Ohno's observation. Yet, his pull-based approach is hard for many to accept; it represents a radical shift from traditional thinking—a direct affront to the mindset that has guided American business since the days of Henry Ford.[3] And the implications of this thinking are far from trivial; where a firm comes down on this has widespread and dramatic implications to the potential for success of its business.

The Growth of Rigid Solutions

As we saw in Chapter 2, Henry Ford's moving assembly line revolutionized the management of factory operations. Most people can see how this directly reduced assembly times by bringing vehicles to his workers. However, we also saw in Chapter 2 that its real power came from slashing the variability between assembly steps, *synchronizing his operations in a way that virtually eliminated variation from disrupting his progression of activities.*

Eliyahu Goldratt's classic book, *The Goal*, shows the need for such synchronization, using as an example a line of boy scouts marching down a trail. He shows how the troop's leader tries again and again to keep this column of hikers from stretching out as their journey progresses. Still, despite his best efforts, he found himself constantly stopping to pull the line back together:

> Our hike is a set of dependent events . . . in combination with statistical fluctuations. Each of us is fluctuating in speed, faster and slower. But the ability to go faster is restricted. It depends upon all the others ahead of me in the line, so even if I could walk five miles per hour, I couldn't do it if the boy in front of me could only walk two miles per hour. And even if the kid directly in front of me could walk that fast, neither of us could do it unless all the boys in the line were moving at five miles per hour at the same time.[4]

This same tendency to spread out is inherent in any chain of dependent activities, whether it is automobile production, flight schedules, or replenishing supermarket shelves. Just as with the scouts, some amount of variation between each activity is natural. Yet, their potential to "spread" can be far greater; their complex webs of dependent activities can create many more paths for variation to build up than for a single line of hikers. Any slowdown in a manufacturing operation can impact other work stations, sending delays up and down the line and out to the supply chain. A single late departure within an airline's complex sequences of interconnecting routes can trigger a domino effect, creating widespread schedule disruptions throughout its network of flights. And we already saw the impact that such disruption can have to a supermarket in the examples of the snowstorm and the beer game.

Thus, just as Henry Ford showed, some sort of system is needed to regulate the movement of operations; keeping dependent activities marching together in lock-step is critical to preventing the growth of disruption and waste that would otherwise result.

Applying Top-Down Controls

Because Ford produced only one product, he was able to sequence his operations so that each task directly tied to the next—so much so that visitors thought "that Ford's factory was really one vast machine with each production step tightly linked to the next."[5] This had to create the same problems as the scout leader encountered; any delay at one station would have a direct impact on the entire line and had to be tightly controlled.

To understand how the company dealt with this, let us look again to Goldratt's analogy of the Boy Scout troop:

> Let's say the demand on us is to walk two miles every hour—no more, no less. Could I adjust the capacity of each kid so he would be able to walk two miles per hour and no faster? If I could, I'd simply keep everyone moving constantly at the pace he should go—by yelling, whip-cracking, money, whatever—and everything would be perfectly balanced. . . . Maybe I could tie each one's ankles with pieces of rope so that each would only take the same size step. . . . But that isn't practical . . .[6]

We saw in Chapter 2 that Ford kept his long sequences of activities moving in unison using tight management control—very much like the scout leader's "whip-cracking" idea. His moving assembly line led the way; it forced a constant rate of flow that all had to follow. By imposing tight controls over work flow throughout his operations, from assembly to component fabrication shops, and all the way back to his suppliers, he found it possible to keep much of this "spreading" from occurring.

Ford's intensive oversight must have created a tremendous management burden; corporations everywhere adopted Sloan's less intrusive philosophy as the better alternative. Instead of controlling individual perturbations as they occurred, managers now focused on regulating their overall *outcomes*. They created top-down controls—overarching schedules that paced their suppliers and individual work stations, essentially "pushing" them at a predefined pace, balancing their lines to meet average forecasted demands.

This, however, brought an increased potential for waste. With companies' attention diverted from the individual perturbations between the steps along the way, the natural result was for activities to spread out. Individual activities that made up their operations became less and less tied to what the customer demanded; instead, they focused on satisfying internal goals and schedules (leading to the disconnects described in Chapter 6). They began balancing their activities with buffers to wash out the immediate impact of variations that occurred between them.

Unfortunately, along with these buffers came lag. And over time this led to a tremendous accumulation of waste.

Today, American corporations have become all too aware of the impact this has on their bottom line—the waste that is a result of the spreading between their activities that has grown over time. And many came to believe that information technology offers the top-down control they feel they need to remedy this.

Scheduling through Automation

Today, companies apply extensive automated systems for the purpose of tying together today's sprawling operations. They seek to push every major activity across their businesses to move at a scheduled pace. Through tight control of schedules, corporations hope to create enormous efficiencies—driving out defects, delays, and other contributors to uncertainty and loss just as Henry Ford had done early last century.

But is automation the answer? To answer this, let us look at what happened when this mindset was taken to its extreme limits two decades ago with the advent of completely automated factories (known as Flexible Manufacturing Systems or "factories of the future"). Advanced information technology guided everything, from signaling work to managing production, using specialized robots for cutting and forming materials, to automated guided vehicles for moving it across the factory, to automated storage and retrieval systems for managing inventory.

Today, these systems have largely disappeared. The reason? Their tremendous rigidity and inflexibility made responding to normal variations exceedingly difficult—just as we saw with Ford's Model T production line.[7] What many once saw as the ultimate factory solution, in reality, was not.

Today's technology systems—from MRP to ERP—often seem to be put in place for much the same reason; managers see their strict scheduling and ability to disseminate information as a means for bridging operational and organizational gaps. Yet, in reality, these often fall short. Why is this? For the same reasons we have seen so far. If a primary goal of improvement is minimizing lag and creating the flexibility to deal with uncertainty, how can standing up enormous, rigidly coded automated systems enable this?

This, it appears, is what makes Wal-Mart's automation stand out. Sam Walton seemed to sense that his firm's long-term success would depend not just on its ability to grow, but on maintaining the small business feel that had given it his early edge. This brought with it a key challenge: how to tightly synchronize work steps and decision making without stifling creativity and innovation. His solution? Become "the best utilizer of information to control absentee ownerships that there's ever been."[8]

In doing so, Walton created a new paradigm in decentralization that was not based on creating rigid controls or managing by the averages. His information systems let him follow the impact of activities and decisions across his entire enterprise, almost in real time. With this, he was no longer limited to looking at how his stores performed in retrospect—a view to which Ford and Sloan's approach was largely relegated. Moreover, his decentralized decision-making structure let stores quickly respond to changing needs, keeping the right items on the shelf while minimizing costs, thus serving the corporation's broader objectives.

Wal-Mart does not rely on automation to bridge disconnects in flow—an approach that we have seen does not work well within an environment of uncertainty and change. Instead, it applies automation in conjunction with its approach of synchronizing its internal activities to those of the customer at each step along the way. Not only does this minimize lag and loss during times of stability, but the responsiveness it creates contributes to its stable value margin even as conditions change.

A Shift to "Pull"

Michael Cullen has been described as "the father of the modern supermarket."[9] In 1930 he introduced the concept of "'monstrous' stores, three to four times the size of standard grocery stores," leading the way for the supermarkets we see today. To drive down staffing and costs, Cullen championed a key innovation: He shifted from holding items behind counters to placing them out for all to see. No longer limited by a clerk's ability to retrieve items, his shift eliminated a key choke point that otherwise would constrain his stores' business.

It was this same concept that Taiichi Ohno took back to Japan, setting the stage for a key aspect of Toyota's world renowned "Just-In-Time" system. Much like one might see on a supermarket's shelves, Ohno stationed small bins of the supplies needed to support his operations from which workers could take whatever they needed to keep their work moving. Each time workers removed an item, they would detach its *kanban* card, placing it in a bin to indicate how many they consumed.[10] This served to signal to upstream fabrication stations to produce more of the item. In essence, this system *pulled* production at each step to match the pace of demand.[11]

This visual replenishment approach for signaling work flow is critical to Toyota's way of synchronizing what it builds to match those quantities that are sold. Operating under this system means that work at each step along the way moves at precisely the pace needed to support current needs. Inventories of all types are held to rock-bottom levels (including *work-in-progress,* or items in a partially built state)—with only enough to offset their very small variability. Lag is virtually eliminated; waste in overproduction, waiting time, and product defects are almost nonexistent.

A critical part of making this work goes back to Ohno's approach of grouping together common items into product families (items that can be made using the flexible equipment and skill sets within a manufacturing cell). As described in Chapter 7, Toyota uses product families that create a production-leveling effect, extending from the assembly line all the way back through upstream activities. Other efforts, such as shortening lead times, slashing setup times, and reducing travel distances, further contribute to making this work.[12]

The end effect is to dampen the supply chain effect (described in Chapter 6), preventing huge demand swings at upstream work stations that could overwhelm their ability to keep up. This result was described by Kiyoshi Suzaki in *The New Manufacturing Challenge:*

> The more parts one pulls at a time, the bigger the impact on the upstream processes. The same situation applies to subassembly,

fabrication, and suppliers' processes, all the way through the linkage of the production processes. The steadier the flow of materials with leveled/mixed production, the less disruption there will be in upstream processes.[13]

Thus, Toyota's ability to tightly synchronize its activities is not the result of one particular action; instead, its success is inextricably tied to how it manages the many elements we have discussed. Like Wal-Mart and Southwest Airlines, it relies on everything from leveling variation to decentralized decision making, even on coordinating new ideas and product innovations across the business. And making this all work depends on applying his very different concept to how it synchronizes activities at each step along the way.

Toyota, Southwest Airlines, and Wal-Mart have each created this capability to regulate flow, scheduling activities across their value streams in a way that smoothly delivers just what their customers want. And, despite the enormity that each of these firms have since come to represent, they continue to flow smoothly and effortlessly—creating that small-business feel despite their enormous size.

This seamless synchronization of value is one of the most fundamental attributes of lean dynamics. Firms that have succeeded in doing this share a number of common characteristics, including those discussed in the following paragraphs.

Predictability: Dampening Schedule Uncertainty

One lesson we can learn from Toyota's method of scheduling production activities is the great benefit of level-loading its individual workstations. Constantly shuffling what it produces as a routine part of its day-to-day work schedules (as was described in Chapter 7) creates a powerful effect in driving lag, and thus unpredictability, from its buildup of value.

By continuously changing up the sequence and mix of what their shops produce, firms can leverage the power of mixed-production for maintaining level shop scheduling despite varying item demands. And as we saw in figure 7.1, this can be used to make resources much more effective—for results we can calculate. By mixing the production of just a handful of items, a company can substantially increase its capacity while slashing the need to hold buffer inventory and improving its responsiveness to changing demands.[14]

Reliably scheduling activities without depending on traditional buffers is central to the concept of lean dynamics. By minimizing these buffers, firms drive down operational lag, dampening the spread of activities across the value stream. Perhaps its greatest benefit, however, is how it enables these firms to synchronize each of their activities with the actual demands of the customer, rather than to some internal goals or objectives (like inventory reorder points). This way, when their needs change, these companies seamlessly continue flowing fresh value to the customer (as was described in Chapter 5).

Simplicity: Letting Flow Drive the Solution

From our discussion so far, we have seen that "pulling" operations—prompting activity based on actual customer demands—offers a powerful means for mitigating the dreaded "spreading" effect, and the loss that goes with it. But what happens when such an approach is not practical? Consider an airline; it clearly cannot accommodate changes in passengers' volumes by continuously altering its flight schedules. Moreover, passengers need to plan their travel arrangements in advance, and regulations (like filing flight plans in advance) and operational realities make "pushing" preset schedules a key part of their business.

Southwest's answer comes in the way it structures activities based on what amounts to a master schedule (its flight schedule), while still benefiting from flexibility within local work activities that adjust as they need to in order to support it. This is much like the *hybrid approach* to regulating flow that my study of aerospace showed works well within a factory environment:

> At the fabrication shop level. . . . operations are often set up such that they can be controlled through direct visual and verbal cues. These shops are left to operate autonomously, using a variety of approaches . . . as a mechanism to fill orders. . . . What is different here is that this local system is effectively a component of a larger production and inventory system, with the orders that it fills driven by an overarching MRP II system governing the operations of the overall factory.[15]

Firms that do this seek to apply the simplest means available to mitigate spread from occurring within their flow of value. Using a range of simple cues or techniques, they create the capability to synchronize not just their operational flow (the visible effects that most firms seek to improve), but to intertwine efficiencies gained here with improvements in the other forms of flow as well. The result is optimizing how operational steps, organizational activities, flow of information, and even innovation work together to create steady and consistent value.

Consider Southwest Airlines' flexible approach to turning around airplanes at the gate. Rather than assigning seats when passengers make their reservations (as others do), Southwest ties its boarding and seat selection to passengers' arrival at the terminal—motivating them to arrive early and streamlining their plane boarding. Similarly, its use of direct, personal information exchange streamlines other key functions as well. Operations agents, for instance, coordinate information on incoming flights (such as what it is carrying, who and what will come off, and how much fuel it will need) with everyone from boarding agents, freight crews, and ticket agents. They, in turn, back each other up to meet the company's requirements for speedy gate turnarounds.[16]

It seems that, in different ways, Southwest, Wal-Mart, and Toyota apply aspects of this hybrid philosophy. Each operates using some sort of overarching schedules for planning their capacity and work flow across their span of activities. Yet, they do not configure rigid systems to control every aspect of their daily work. Instead, their local activities are structured to remain simple and largely autonomous. This lets them efficiently and effectively compensate for day-to-day variations across operational, information, and organizational flows—keeping even complex operations in lock-step without the need for intrusive controls.[17]

Mistake Proofing: Catching Defects Before They Spread

Flowing operations without traditional buffers requires taking on a completely different mindset. Since any delay at one work station will be quickly felt at the next, equipment breakdowns, quality defects, supplier problems, and even worker absenteeism can have an immediate impact on corporations' well-synchronized schedules. Inaccurate information can drive faulty decisions, creating a similar effect. Companies that apply lean dynamics must therefore take great pains to isolate and prevent such potential for disruption.

Toyota was clearly aware that it had to address this if level scheduling was to become a reality. It focused great attention on addressing and mitigating every potential vulnerability, honing the reliability of equipment and other resources so that unforeseen breakdowns did not occur. There was no alternative; anything else would require large buffers—driving up lag and breaking down the ability for this way of business to operate.

Among its solutions was *poka-yoke,* or mistake- proofing—making people or even machines capable of monitoring their own work, catching defects before they are sent down the line.[18] This is central to lean today; as was described earlier, the Garrity Tool Company locates surface plates, dial indicators, and other various gauges at each machine so that dimensions can be closely monitored during each step of each operation. This prevents operators from building in defects, and keeps defects from being sent down the line.

Another solution was to institute something known as *Total Productive Maintenance* (or TPM).[19] By proactively avoiding sudden breakdowns of production equipment, the company avoids the introduction of defects into its system as its precision drifts:

> The TPM concept embraces not only the concept of routine maintenance, but also that of predictive maintenance. While routine maintenance must be performed to fulfill the basic servicing needs . . . (such as checking and filling lubrication oil receptacles and identifying warning signs of impending machine trouble), predictive maintenance is intended to anticipate and actively manage the time that this equipment would otherwise be down for unscheduled, corrective maintenance. Feedback from routine maintenance . . . can reveal minute changes in equipment performance that can be used to predict the need for maintenance actions well before processing capabilities are degraded to unacceptable levels. With this information, requirements for special maintenance actions can be forecasted and scheduled with sufficient lead time such that work-arounds

can be planned. Often, equipment is scheduled to build temporary buffer stocks of inventory to support production operations during the period in which this equipment maintenance is performed.[20]

Wal-Mart realized the importance of mistake proofing early on, standing up an SKU (stock keeping unit—a unique identifier for tracking items) and bar coding system (something that Walton acknowledged was expensive and difficult to put in place). "But we got it working, and now, of course, everybody has one."[21] Its ease of use led it to become the standard for the fast-moving operations of the grocery industry, something that Bob Ortega observed in *In Sam We Trust* gave Wal-Mart a distinct advantage:

> But, unlike the fancier goods at department stores, nearly a third of the merchandise Wal-Mart and other discounters carried—toiletries, paper products, cleaners, etc.—also was carried by grocery stores, which meant manufacturers were going to slap on a bar code anyway. Shewmaker rightly assumed that improvements would take care of the capacity problem. Then, too, 80 percent of Wal-Mart's goods went through its distribution centers (compared to less than 30 percent at Kmart). Because workers at the centers already were putting tickets on clothing, towels, sheets, and other soft goods, Shewmaker knew it would be simple to have them attach bar codes to those items, too.[22]

Wal-Mart continues this path of minimizing information errors by implementing what appears to be the next generation of the bar code: the Radio Frequency Identification Tag (or RFID tag). The firm applies tiny tags not only to track items as they check into and out of a location, but also to track them along the way without the need to individually rescan piles of items. Using a handheld scanner, an associate can push a button and find out what is loaded in a container or even a truck without opening it. This offers great potential to further streamline flow by increasing visibility at each point along the way, particularly for bridging gaps across diverse processes where different people take ownership at different points along the way.

The impact of Wal-Mart's approach is clearly evident today. With it, workers can more reliably enter data to support the firm's information flow, preventing defects before they are sent down the line. This is a critical element to variation leveling—preventing a key source of variation from entering the system.

Prevention: Building In Mechanisms to Mitigate Vulnerabilities

Still, some sources of imbedded lag and uncertainty can be particularly hard to correct. Consider an area previously discussed: the business of obtaining spare parts to support maintenance or repair of aging military systems. Very low demand—often nearly nonexistent—for many of these items can cause skills to dwindle and needed equipment to deteriorate. Technological constraints might make lead times for components extraordinarily long. Moreover, high costs and insufficient demand for accurate forecasting means traditional supply chain measures often can do little to help. Despite this, their criticality dictates that orders must be filled quickly when demand suddenly surges without notice.

One answer is finding and addressing those systemic hot spots causing uncertainty across product families, and then tailoring actions to address them—an approach that I demonstrated through a program aimed at ensuring availability of critical Defense supplies, from spare parts to medical items and pharmaceuticals.[23] My team's efforts in isolating their underlying causes and then taking such actions as adding surge capacity or infusing partially completed components drove down lead times for critical items from months to days, assuring the availability of critical items during unforeseen demand spikes. Moreover, these actions cost a fraction of what traditional solutions cost—compounding to eliminate the need to hold as much as a billion dollars of inventory.[24]

Corporations that apply lean dynamics take similar actions. Toyota, for instance, strategically applies inventories to hot spots that might disrupt its flow of value—but just enough to protect against disruption. Southwest Airlines does this for mitigating its most critical hot spot, the variation it sees in attaining aircraft fuel. Recognizing fuel prices as a critical area of vulnerability, the company employed a practice known as *fuel hedging*—locking in long-term arrangements to guard against instability. When fuel prices skyrocketed (which has shaken the airline industry since 2004), Southwest did not seem affected at all—the company continued generating a powerful value margin despite circumstances that seriously impacted its competitors.[25]

To make lean dynamics work, unforeseen disruption must be prevented; firms must become persistent in uncovering potential hot spots that leave them vulnerable when conditions shift—such as materiel shortages, shipping constraints, long lead times, and many others—and become innovative in how they address them. Aligning suppliers by product family so they can take advantage of underlying similarities shared by different items (such as common materials and manufacturing requirements) can make it easier to apply just one solution to address common issues affecting a larger group. It is more likely, for instance, that a supplier will pre-position long-lead materials if they can be used to shorten lead times for a range of items rather than just one. This way, firms can maximize the payoff and minimize the cost of actions reducing delivery delays, quality defects, or other problems that would otherwise reduce predictability and reliability of flow.

Resilience: Optimizing Responsiveness to Customers' Changes

"Sam never did *anything* in size or volume until he actually had to," recounted Bob Thornton, a Wal-Mart executive, regarding Walton's resistance to investing in large equipment that ultimately proved invaluable to the firm's operational success.[26] Perhaps it was his aversion to tying up capital without clearly seeing a return, or perhaps he had an innate sense that scale brings with it an inherent inflexibility to change—whatever the reason, his constant resistance to accepting conventional solutions at face value protected his firm from investing in inflexible "monuments" that might have cut it off from achieving the sustained value margin it sees today.

This aversion to creating rigidity within its value streams—from its shops to its suppliers—appears central to Wal-Mart's powerful value-creating capability. Moreover, this philosophy seems to flow from the highest levels of its management planning. The advantage is clear. Wal-Mart's apparently tight synchronization between planning and execution seems to have powered its tremendous expansion, both in its size and in the breadth of its business. Wal-Mart meets with overwhelming success in virtually every direction it moves, challenging and defeating entrenched rivals across a range of retail businesses—from food to consumer electronics and even toys. And each move only seems to bolster its resilience, further stabilizing its value creation and enabling its growth.

Another striking example can be seen in Southwest Airline's response following the tragedy of September 11th. As noted earlier, while others were grounding their aircraft because they could not fill them, Southwest found a way to keep virtually all of its planes in the air. By rebalancing its routes and even expanding to new ones (it was during this time that it added cross-country flights from Baltimore to Los Angeles), Southwest achieved results that were remarkable. While others suffered losses that ran into the billions of dollars, Southwest sustained its solid value margin.

Toyota sees similar benefits. Unlike others, it did not become trapped by sudden shifts in customer demand (producing too many SUVs when fuel prices jump, or taking extreme measures to clear our last-year's model that did not sell).[27] It does not seek to make gains against simplified outcomes like increasing overall market share (as others seem to do). Instead it increasingly tailors its product offerings to local markets; the resilience in which it creates its operations makes possible the flexibility to shift focus to match customers' shifting demands, but without undermining the economies of its operations.

Toyota continues to make this a major focus. Rather than avoiding the forces of change and uncertainty, it apparently seeks to harness them by building a global system for production and supply for the expressed purpose of extending its tremendous flexibility to change across its global operations.[28]

Firms practicing lean dynamics bridge the gap between strategy and execution, recapturing a synergy not seen since Ford's special case in producing the Model T. Their stable value margins power a steady flow of product innovation, offering the greater choices for customers that further enhance these margins. The result is sustained value and growth, thriving amid conditions that conventional wisdom dictates should undermine their performance.

Dynamic Leaps to Excellence

We have seen that customers are becoming increasingly dissatisfied with static offerings that do not meet their dynamic needs. They expect better quality, reliable service, and more for their money. They expect tailored solutions that more precisely meet their specific needs—not one-size-fits-all. And they expect companies to better anticipate their changing needs, ensuring that what they are looking for is delivered at the highest quality, when they want it, with no surprises.

Toyota, Wal-Mart, and Southwest Airlines have demonstrated a remarkable feat in doing so: Each operate under a flat value curve, an indication that their *customer value is precisely synchronized with a dynamic capability to consistently produce it.* Fueled by their system of management's ability to mitigate the negative effects of uncertainty, they operate seemingly unconstrained by the traditional limitations others must face. The result is a powerful advantage in turning out the fresh, new offerings that customers have come to demand, while sustaining tremendous operational efficiency—giving them the quality, speed, and low pricing customers have come to expect.

Where can they go from here? Toyota, Wal-Mart, and Southwest Airlines all seem to be moving in the same direction—on a never-ending journey to attaining greater and greater value. By constantly expanding their innovation and improving their ability to anticipate and operate effectively in times of change, they seem well on their way to achieving an ultimate objective of *pull*—a sustained ability for synchronizing corporate and customer value despite the constant forces of uncertainty and change.

This constant advancement, however, does not seem to occur in a way that causes constant drift across their value streams—the preferred approach of American corporations (we see this from their widespread acceptance of the "learning curve," which actually plans for such a drift through a product's life cycle).[29] Toyota instead introduces major changes as a series of leaps. This prevents disruption to its tightly synchronized operations (a key to mitigating loss and maximizing value), while enabling the firm to incorporate its lessons and new innovations to periodically leap to the next level of performance.

FIGURE 8.1   Toyota's Leaps toward Perfection[30]

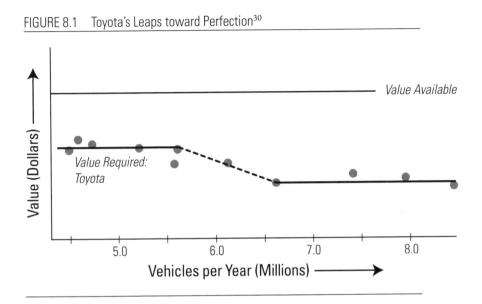

We can see this same effect on a much broader level, clearly depicted in its value curve. The left side of figure 8.1 shows that Toyota's value margin remains stable up until the year 2002 despite the dynamic nature of its operating environment. Yet, from 2003 to the present we see that a substantial change occurs—a sudden leap to a new, much greater value margin.

Why such an orderly shift? Consider the magnitude of what Toyota is in the midst of changing—implementing a range of highly complex efforts on a global scale, each one tightly interrelated with the next as well as with current operations. It continues to broadly globalize its operations, expanding production to new facilities and enhancing its flexibility by leveling variation not just within individual workstations, but across its global enterprise.

Tightly synchronizing all of these changes seems particularly critical, in light of the immense challenge of simultaneously maintaining rigorous synchronization across it's "globally balanced operations and a full product lineup."[31]

Toyota's cost-reduction programs seem to have contributed to this downward shift. For instance, it has made substantial progress toward "the reduction of the line for 1.6- and 1.8-liter Corolla ZZ engines to one-third and the 3.0- and 4.0-liter V6 engine production line to one-sixth of their original lengths. . ."[32] But its objectives—and thus its measurements—go beyond simply cutting costs; the firm focuses on enhancing its product value, something it pointed out in its 2005 annual report:

> We return the benefits of cost reductions to customers by ploughing the freed-up resources back into product upgrades or price repositioning . . . converting savings into higher quality enables us to offer new models with markedly improved functionality and performance at prices that are the same or lower than before.[33]

For corporations to succeed in emulating these leaps in value, they must adopt a similar mindset. They must understand that the goal of "pull" goes far beyond tying demand to operational execution for the purpose of removing inventory. Instead, it is the perfect synchronization between strategy and execution, fostering coordinated leaps in creating greater margins of customer and corporate value.

Implementing
Lean
Dynamics

W|E HAVE SEEN THAT TOYOTA, Southwest Airlines, and Wal-Mart have done something quite extraordinary. Each of these firms has turned conventional wisdom on its head, creating agile operations that remain strikingly unaffected during normal conditions, or even in downturns that traditionally cause corporations great difficulty. Fueled by their ability to mitigate the normal effects of uncertainty, they find themselves largely unconstrained by a number of operational limitations others must face. This enables internal and external objectives to work together in unison, transforming negative forces into a positive result that enhances their competitiveness.

As with any fundamental change, however, the real challenge lies in its implementation. What is needed, therefore, is a structure for transformation—a plan that will help corporations apply the principles and practices described herein to their different businesses or industries and the range of circumstances they face.

Chapter 9 proposes the top level elements of such a structure—from its vision and case for change, to the activities for managing their transformation. Chapter 10 describes key parts of a successful implementation plan. Chapter 11 explores the common pitfalls that can derail its progress along the way. Finally, Chapter 12 concludes this book by showing why firms must act now; it gives a glimpse into the tremendous promise that exists for those who embark on this journey—if they are only willing to see the way.

Nine

A Plan for Action

... in an evolving environment, it is important that
we distinguish clearly between the things that must
be changed and things that must not and have the
courage to make the necessary changes.
—Katsuaki Watanabe, President of Toyota[1]

IN 1991, MICHAEL O'LEARY, the deputy chief executive of a small,
Irish airline, was in search of a new vision. His company was struggling—"on the verge of collapse."[2] Aware of Southwest Airline's tremendous track record, he flew to Texas to meet with the man at its helm at
the time, Mr. Herb Kelleher. The visit began one of today's most remarkable turnaround stories: In just over a decade, Ryanair emerged as the
world's most profitable airline.

Ryanair's remarkable journey began with a simple but powerful step.
Unlike so many others in this industry, this company saw the need to
change—*really* change. Its visionary leader apparently recognized that
true success could not be found by following conventional wisdom; instead, achieving the fundamentally different result it needed to thrive in
its chaotic environment meant embracing a very different way of doing
business, and then finding a way to put it in place.

Ryanair's example shows us much about the journey to excellence.
This company did not blindly march forward as so many others have
done, nor did it simply add on to what it already had in place. Instead,
Ryanair's journey began by first taking a step back—developing a deep

understanding of the change it had to make, guided by Southwest Airlines' clear example of sustained excellence. The company quickly shifted from a failing approach to a new system of management that continues to reach new heights.

Ryanair's path to excellence strikes to the core of what is described throughout this book. Transforming to lean dynamics requires coming to see that uncertainty and change are now the norm, and that succeeding in this dynamic environment requires making a fundamental change. It takes building an underlying capability for dampening the effects of variation before it takes hold, preventing the need for workarounds long before a crisis ever unfolds. And in doing so, it means mitigating the tremendous risk that most face but have not learned to see. It means adopting those characteristics described in Chapter 4 that distinguish those who manage using lean dynamics from all the rest.

But setting out on this course requires more than simply learning the basics. It requires fact finding and research—hard analysis that leads corporations to understand what is wrong now and what it will take to make it right. From this, managers can build a plan of action for transforming their business, making change and uncertainty the conditions on which they will thrive.

Building the Case for Change

The prospect of fundamentally changing how a firm does business raises great concern. It is not hard to understand why: Change is synonymous with risk, since it traditionally leads to disruption and loss. Unfortunately, this mindset stands as perhaps the greatest barrier to implementing lean dynamics.

Corporations tend to minimize change, introducing it in small measures within isolated pockets, often within the bounds of the structures that already exist within their businesses. This is what marks many of today's lean transformations; teams move equipment closer together, eliminate obsolete processing steps, remove buffer inventories—actions that seek to create improvement but only so far as is possible without disturbing the core of how they work today. Such an emphasis—seeking to remove visible waste—is not enough; in fact, it can drive rigid solutions that further steepen firms' value curves. Gains might be short-lived; variation can grow, causing loss to skyrocket when conditions once again shift.

Achieving lasting success instead begins with building the confidence to change—really change. Corporations must come to see that their greatest risk lies not in pursuing change, but in their unwillingness to do so. They must develop a case to help managers and workers see this—to understand that they cannot succeed by making small shifts around the edges, but instead through real and radical transformation that strikes to the core of how they do business.

Assessing the Challenge

Crafting this case for change is not something that should be taken lightly. It will serve as a guiding light throughout a firm's transformation, providing a succinct and compelling argument for why the corporation must step off into what will likely seem to be tremendous risk. It must be sufficiently clear and compelling to ensure management and workers at all levels fully understand and embrace it, and to keep them focused on this as the way ahead throughout the transformation.

At its foundation is an honest and specific assessment of the corporation, showing why it can no longer continue to do business the way it has in the past. This must be sufficiently convincing to overcome preconceived notions held by workers and managers across the corporation. Workers must see from this why it is in their best interest to take on new activities, gain new skills, and accept the much broader responsibilities that this new way of doing business will require. For managers, this case must be particularly compelling: It must convince them to cease "driving with the clutch" and embrace a new way of operating that at first will seem uncertain and dangerous.

Many of the facts used to build this case will not be new; they will simply be presented in a way that makes clear the underlying cause of those challenges they already see.[3] Much of the workforce will already be aware of their periodic outbreaks of expediting and workarounds. What they need to understand, however, is how the firm's narrowly optimized approach causes these to occur, how disconnects across flow—not only operational, but organizational, information, and innovation—create an inflexibility to customer change that leads to these crises.

Moreover, workers and managers need to see the full extent of the consequences. Loss extends well beyond what they typically see—those disruptions and workarounds many of them frequently face. They must see the impact outside the corporation as well—from suppliers it cannot develop, to customers it cannot satisfy, to opportunities it cannot pursue. These can have a lasting effect on the bottom line to workers and managers alike—the consequences will affect the firm's profitability, their jobs, and the company's future.

The value curve provides a powerful backdrop for conducting such an assessment (figure 9.1). A steep value curve makes clear that *a problem does exist.* It forces a realistic look at the firm's success in creating strong, steady, measurable value, getting past many of the typical excuses that cause complacency and inaction. It shows if the firm is not well-equipped for responding to change, if sudden shifts in volume will cause crisis and workarounds, poor quality, and resistance to new innovation.

FIGURE 9.1   Assessing the Dynamics of the Business

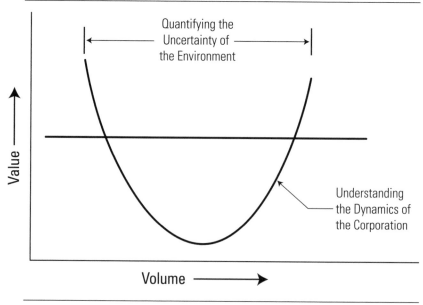

It shows how change drives up loss, reducing value to the customer, which creates the further potential that customers will look elsewhere, thus diminishing both current and future business.

The first step is taking a hard look *outside the business*—gaining a quantifiable grasp of the dynamics of the environment. What are the challenges the firm is likely to face? Will it continue to gain the steady, high volumes on which its efficiencies depend? What disruption might affect the resources it needs—from labor to materials to energy? Will it need to introduce new innovations into production? Answering these questions will provide objective information showing the range of conditions that the firm must prepare to deal with as it sets its course. Essentially, it describes the range across which the corporation must prepare to operate (the span across the curve depicted in figure 9.1).

One way for assessing such external forces is through the use of business scenarios. Scenario planning offers to identify disconnects that no one had previously known existed, so that action can be taken to mitigate their potential effects, as Bill Ralston and Ian Wilson point out in *The Scenario Planning Handbook:*

> We can speculate about not just "the future," but a range of possible futures that might arise from the uncertain course of the forces of change. And then, within the boundaries of these alternative possibilities, we can develop a strategy that is focused but resilient, specific but flexible. . .[4]

A second perspective comes from taking a hard and specific look *inside the business.* By walking step-by-step through the progression of their value-creating activities, managers can see the impact of external forces on how they do business—how shifting further and further from "normal" conditions will quickly and dramatically increase loss and drive down the firm's competitiveness.

An automaker, for instance, might ask how it would respond if gasoline prices rose beyond four dollars per gallon (not a far stretch today). Could it shift to produce more of its smaller, more fuel-efficient vehicles whose demand might increase, while reducing its output of gas-burning SUVs? How would such spikes in energy prices affect an airline, or even a company like Wal-Mart aimed at holding down costs while depending on an enormous fleet of trucks to supply its stores?

One way to assess the impact of such sudden change is to map out the firm's cycle time variation, or the swings in the time needed to turn out each successive unit. As we saw in figure 2.3, cycle time variation can be enormous for a traditionally managed corporation, spanning as much as thirty percent from the nominal. Starting by mapping the variation and hidden waste that already exists can paint a powerful picture of the inflexibility to change that has already left its mark on the business, pointing to how much improvement is needed and the severity of lag that must be corrected.

Together, these hard looks will make clear the corporation's vulnerability to the changing conditions it will likely be forced to face. This forms a critical first step to identifying that it must indeed shift its approach—and quantifying the dire consequences if it does not.

Choosing the Path

It is not enough for a firm simply to decide *that* it must change; stopping here can leave it in a precarious situation. The second and equally critical element is determining its path—what direction the corporation must take to improve its situation. This is perhaps the most important step in the transformation—and the one where many corporations seem to fall short.

Managers seem ready to jump onto new ideas; too often they end up juggling an array of initiatives with no real understanding of their individual contributions or how they fit together. Often, the goal *seems* clear—but in the end, achieving it does not necessarily help them increase their competitiveness. Consider Ford's focus on cost reduction as described in the company's 2002 annual report:

> Ford is the first and only automaker to deploy 6-Sigma throughout all of its operations. Our 6-Sigma projects have saved us more than $675 million worldwide since we began using it in 2000. [5]

Yet, despite Ford's 6-Sigma success, figure 9.2 indicates that this had little effect on shifting Ford's value curve (the black data points

FIGURE 9.2   Ford's Value Curve[6]

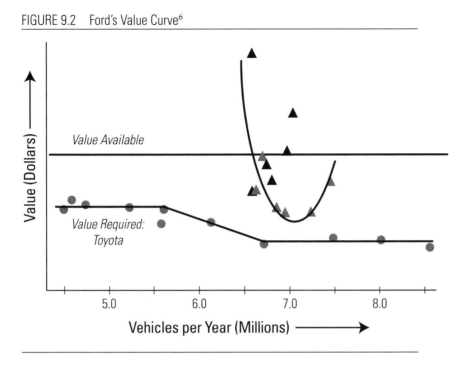

depict Ford's performance since the company purportedly began seeing results from its 6-Sigma efforts). Its swings from the center during
this time seem to follow much the same curve, corresponding to an
even greater loss (most clearly depicted by the point at the upper-left
side of its curve).

How could this be? Although it is unclear what happened at Ford,
we have seen in general that targeting visible waste alone is not the answer. While necessary to deal with the firm's current operating realities,
such initiatives might do little to shift a firm's underlying system for creating value. We saw in Chapter 2 that, if companies do not make their
business more flexible, they might find themselves only saving money
at one point—their optimal volume—at which they are likely to operate fairly infrequently in today's uncertain environment. Worse yet,
workarounds creating rampant violation of standards might cause loss
to spring back once conditions change and variation reemerges. Only by
making more fundamental shifts can corporations address those factors
undermining their ability to accommodate change and promote much-
needed innovation.

What, then, should be the focus of a firm's improvement efforts? Corporations must address those factors that cause their cycle of loss—the lag that stands in the way of shifting to a new, flatter curve that is better suited to competing across the range of circumstances they will likely face. They must accept the reality of their uncertain circumstances they face, taking steps to eliminate the lag in all aspects of their business that amplifies operational variation and creates loss.

Developing the case for change is a particularly critical step for beginning the transformation. Without this, managers and workers will see no compelling reason for shifting from the course to which they have grown accustomed. Its importance continues throughout the life of the transformation, serving to focus the firm's improvement activities, keeping managers and workers from continuously revisiting their decision when difficulties present themselves (as too often occurs). A well-built case will set the direction for all that must follow, particularly the future vision for the corporation that will make clear the destination and keep them on a steady path for the long journey ahead.

Creating a Dynamic Vision

Just about any goal in life can be difficult to achieve it if you are not first able to clearly describe what it is that you seek. Experts warn us about this for everything from fitness to finance—visualizing the result is the first step to achieving sound results. Just as a roadmap does for a railroad company constructing new tracks, this is critical to making all the different parts connect together in the end so that trains can run smoothly. It will serve as the compass to keep its next steps from running adrift, ensuring it develops a path that is well thought out, measurable, and achievable.

This is particularly true for business transformation. Shifting the direction of a vast corporation can seem like a monstrous task—like turning an aircraft carrier. It requires redirecting the momentum of people, processes, and infrastructures steaming ahead one way into an entirely different direction. And just as with a giant ship, it means carefully executing a coordinated turn, guiding it by a clear point on the horizon toward which all efforts will lead.

An effective vision must not only acknowledge the firm's surrounding dynamics, but it must embrace this, addressing the challenges of uncertainty head on. It must tie in its internal capabilities as an integral part of its plans for delivering these solutions. Finally, it must begin with the customers, understanding that what they value today may be quite different from what they valued in the past. Thus, a vision must be *transformational*—changing the basis for competition across the industry.[7]

A Focus on the Customer

The year 2007 marked a profound shift in the automotive industry. During the first quarter, the Toyota Motor Company edged out Ford, Chrysler, and even GM in worldwide automobile sales. Just two years earlier, Toyota became Japan's first company to earn more than a trillion yen in a year—a profit twice that of General Motors and Ford combined, despite unfavorable exchange rates.[8] Perhaps even more surprising is that analysts had come to report Toyota's move as "inevitable," something that little more than a decade ago would have been shocking.[9]

Toyota's historic advance came in no small part from its ability to focus all that it does on creating precisely the value its customers want. It gradually transformed its image from one of just another Japanese manufacturer that turned out low-quality knockoffs, to a powerful force known for innovation and "Toyota quality." In doing so, the company changed how customers across its industry perceive value; many now see Toyota as the leading producer of quality vehicles—one of the top attributes they have come to prize.

Southwest Airlines has done much the same. This firm does not simply lie in wait of what its environment will bring; instead, it reaches out beyond preconceived expectations—for instance, drawing new customers from other forms of transportation to greatly expand airline passenger traffic in the regions it services (by a minimum of thirty percent and as much as five hundred percent).[10] Others attempt to emulate it, but generally without success.

Like Toyota and Southwest Airlines, Wal-Mart's clear focus on everyday low prices and tremendous product selection has an even broader effect, drawing people from as far as twenty miles out of their way to do their shopping. This focus on consistently giving customers what they want, when they want it, creates a powerful, positive disruptive effect on customers' expectations, and is clearly the centerpiece around which any firm's vision for lean dynamics must be based.

Integrating Execution with Innovation and Strategy

A firm's vision must make clear that lean dynamics is very different from other improvement efforts. Lean dynamics does not simply seek to improve static efficiency; such an emphasis would be a throwback to Henry Ford's narrowly targeted focus of cost reduction that ultimately failed him. Instead, it means creating the capability for sustaining value even in the face of rapid change and uncertain market conditions. This means providing the needed foundation for striking out in new directions and with new innovations, avoiding the spike in loss they create, and thus ensuring more and more of them find their way into the marketplace. It means rethinking *everything*—beginning at a very basic level.

We saw in Chapter 6 an example of such integration between production and innovation—how in the 1980s Toyota's ability to cost-effectively produce highly reliable engines formed the basis for adding technology that increased their complexity without compromising their quality (and how Detroit's methods made it difficult to follow). Today, this same integration means Toyota need not shy away from releasing new innovations that multiply its vehicles' complexity—technologies ranging from computer-controlled engines to hybrid technology. Instead, the company turns out some of the most advanced products that its customers increasingly demand.

Toyota's annual report makes clear its vision for delivering such continuous change and innovation—not by simply reducing costs, but by applying the techniques this book describes. In fact, because of its flexible capability for turning out value, it seems, customer change and market uncertainty are not simply hazards for the firm to overcome; they serve as the basis for opportunity and the means for sustaining its growth into the future.[11]

We saw much the same with Wal-Mart and Southwest Airlines; these firms, too, seem to look to times of uncertainty and crisis as if they are opportunities. Their ability to seamlessly flow new value even as other firms struggle against turmoil and crisis gives them a powerful edge. Maintaining this steady foundation for promoting constant innovation—particularly when competition is diminished—seems to be a central part of their lean dynamics vision.

An Eye on Dynamic Constraints

When managers evaluate plans for transforming their organizations, their thoughts seem constrained by the context of today's environment—on how their firms are prepared to face what they know currently exists. Rather than planning for conditions that can cause them sudden disruption, they seem to assume that conditions will remain the same, or perhaps gradually shift over time.

Yet what happens if these assumptions are wrong? We have seen that large deviations from current expectations have today become the norm; formally addressing their likelihood within the vision can lead corporations to think in different directions, creating entirely different solutions.

For Toyota, Wal-Mart, and Southwest Airlines, such a mindset is clearly central to their thinking, as they routinely articulate to their stakeholders (we can see this from their websites and in their annual reports). And the results are clear: They look quite different than those of their competitors—more forward-thinking and less prone to disruption and misdirection. By keeping these dynamic constraints always in the foreground, they seem more aware of what their businesses must achieve, and more aggressive in their focus on the new opportunities these dynamic conditions create.[12]

Guiding the Vision

In many ways, the process of transforming to lean dynamics is like that of redesigning an aircraft. It begins by describing what result the end user envisions, and then developing design specifications for the final product. It requires identifying a leader who can integrate the many complex but intertwined elements that must form a part of the effort. And it takes extensive coordination across groups that represent many distinct functional disciplines, striking a balance that meets their individual needs while optimizing the whole.

Thus, running successful development efforts of all types requires extensive coordination that goes well beyond the drawing board. This is not unique to lean dynamics; this has been a common theme across many business-improvement efforts attempted over recent years. Let us now review some of the many lessons, from the standpoint of guiding the lean dynamics' vision.

Developing Executive Ownership

The most basic step that must be taken at the outset of any major transformation is for leaders to gain strong ownership for what lies ahead. This takes more than gaining buy-in from a few middle-managers; it means securing real commitment for this transformation all the way at the top of the corporation. Those at the helm must build an understanding that goes beyond the information presented in the case for change. They must develop a deep sense for how this will work, and for why this is the way that business must be done—something important for *any* transformational activity. Consider what Larry Bossidy wrote (with Ram Charan) in *Execution: The Discipline of Getting Things Done:*

> In the mid-1990s, a friend told Jack Welch about a new methodology for making quantum increases in inventory turns in manufacturing operations. Relatively few business leaders back then understood what a powerful tool faster inventory turnover was for generating cash and increasing return on investment. . . . Welch was excited about the idea, but he was not content to get just the concept—he wanted to understand the workings personally. . . . Didn't the chairman of GE have better things to do with his time? Absolutely not! By involving himself deeply and personally with the subject, Welch learned what it would take to execute such an initiative at GE. . . . By the time Welch retired in 2001, inventory turns had doubled, to 8.5.[13]

Such detailed management scrutiny is particularly critical for firms that embark on the long-term, counterintuitive journey it takes to implement lean dynamics. Sam Walton's in-depth involvement seems to have been pivotal to his firm's success. He asked the right questions, challenged his people, and made the right decisions that helped make Wal-Mart what it has become today. We have seen that Herb Kelleher did the same for Southwest Airlines, as did Toyota's top managers in giving clear support for Ohno's very different methods.

This really sets the pace for everything that follows. How can managers lead the way if, in the heat of the crisis, they continue to fall back to their old mindset? Without developing a clear understanding of its foundation, their decisions will be no different than those of the past. Like Jack Welch, they must themselves gain a thorough understanding of what their firm will look like—how and why it will do business in this new manner, and what it will take along the way. Only after gaining this understanding can they begin to make decisions within a context that will not undermine their firm's progress, giving their change agents the "top cover" to sustain progress, particularly at its early junctures.

Assigning Leadership

A firm must identify clear leadership for its transformation—a senior-level manager who takes ownership for leading all that is involved. To set and maintain the course, this leader must be well-versed in the corporation's business, but must also possess strong expertise in lean dynamics. This is critical if he or she is to sustain the vision despite the challenges the firm will face, keeping the many aspects of the transformation from becoming derailed.

It is important to note that the effort need not necessarily originate nor be led by the firm's top executives. Instead, with top-level support, a change agent who reports to them can make the necessary actions occur. This was clearly the case with Toyota; his leadership's support permitted Taiichi Ohno to stay the course despite hearing what probably seemed to be credible pleas to stop his unproven changes that defied conventional wisdom:

In the beginning, everyone resisted kanban [Toyota's visual technique for synchronizing production] because it seemed to contradict conventional wisdom.... When I was—rather forcefully—urging foremen in the production plant to understand kanban, my boss received a number of complaints. They voiced the feeling that this fellow Ohno was doing something utterly ridiculous and should be stopped.[14]

It is this same challenge that leaders today will undoubtedly face. Lean dynamics looks very different from how workers and managers are accustomed to doing business; its methods will undoubtedly draw strong, convincing criticism at each step along the way. For this reason, its initial steps might be largely directive in nature (its widely known collaborative features can be phased in as the transformation matures). Leading such an effort requires a strong, well-informed leader with the necessary insights and top cover to drive actions forward.

Structuring for Results

To make a challenging vision succeed, corporations need to create clear ownership of the effort at the ground level, beginning with those individuals who lead, track, and report its progress. Activities should be broken down in such a way to give those in charge sufficient span of insight and responsibility to act; in other words, their roles must be structured in a way that does not compartmentalize their ability to manage the flow of value.

This represents a major departure from what happens in some of today's transformation efforts. Some, for instance, align their activities by major business processes. In doing this, firms tend to cling to their traditional ways of doing business; they tend to structure processes in a way that mimics traditional departments rather than reflecting the creation of value. Tracking their progress might therefore reveal little with regard to the state of the firm's value margin.

To understand why, let us take order fulfillment as an example—a process encompassing all the steps involved in converting a customer's order into a delivered product. Depending on how it is structured, this process' success might depend on other processes, which depend on others still. For instance, orders cannot be fulfilled if supplies run short; any breakdown in forecasting and managing inventories (perhaps a separate process) or in supplier deliveries (yet another process) will make it impossible for order fulfillment to meet its objectives. Such fragmentation of work can cause lag of all sorts—operational, organization, information, and innovation—which clearly can undermine results.

It is not hard to see why the greatest struggle can be overcoming *cross-process issues*—steps that do not fall within the realm of a defined process, yet are important to supporting the overall flow of value. Where areas or interfaces exist for which no process owner has been made accountable, corporations can run into enormous turmoil in everything from identifying metrics, to evaluating and acting on problems.

Such disconnects can be overcome by assigning *a product family owner*—an individual responsible for the value produced for each distinct area of business that contributes to the bottom-line value created by the corporation. This person's authority must span the entire value stream, encompassing all actions affecting value: Not cost reduction, not increased efficiency or greater market share—but *value creation as defined in tangible terms* by the value curve. Rather than focusing on internal measures such as inventory turns or stock availability, he or she would track those more meaningful to the customer and corporation: timeliness of delivery, product cost, customer satisfaction and loyalty, and sales demand. Only by taking ownership for these bottom-line measures of value can this manager guide the company to look end to end and across the horizon and track, beyond static goals to those dynamic forces that will ultimately drive the business.[15]

Fostering Stakeholder Ownership

Another lesson that we can take from today's major business-improvement projects is the benefit that comes from including key stakeholders in guiding the effort. One proven practice is to create a *steering committee*—a group of executives from across the enterprise that approves the vision, objectives, and implementation plan, meeting regularly to assess progress and identify its direction at major decision points.[16] Standing up a steering committee solves several traditional problems at once. It engages decision makers from the outset to set the direction. It gains their buy in and hones their understanding as the journey progresses. And the committee members can apply their insights to solving real-world issues that are bound to arise along the way.

Structuring this committee, however, requires great caution; how firms do this can make the difference between bringing great benefit or serious liability. The committee, for instance, must guide the transformation *without shifting from the vision or the structure needed to implement lean dynamics* (a propensity that is the Achilles' heel of a leadership panel, and as such must be strongly avoided). A clear charter can help to resolve this; it should set specific limits to the decisions that steering committee members can make, such as avoiding revisiting previous decisions (which, for instance, might require a decision from the company president).

What, then, should be the makeup of this committee? When deciding this, it is important to think beyond the insights these individuals might bring to the group and consider what they will bring back to the organizations they represent. Clearly, each major function, from design to production and distribution, should be represented. But why not include labor leaders as well? And perhaps major suppliers? Exposing them to the concepts, measurements, and issues from the outset might equip them to lead the way within their own organizational elements, giving them the confidence and expertise in lean dynamics that will set them up to sustain the direction. Each of their perspectives—and increased span of insight—will help to make the corporation's end-to-end transformation most effective.

Building a solid plan for action provides the needed foundation upon which an orderly transformation can proceed. This plan's powerful rationale for change, thoughtful vision for the future, and engaged leadership structure are critical prerequisites to moving forward. Clearly, a firm should not roll out the details of the transformation or involve the broader organization until these are fully worked out. Otherwise, this might create the most damaging form of lag—causing false starts and misdirection, and undermining the confidence of the workforce that is so critical to making these efforts succeed.

Structuring the Transformation

Best efforts and hard work, not guided by knowledge,
only dig deeper the pit that we are in.
—W. Edwards Deming[1]

ONCE THEIR PLAN OF ACTION is completed, companies need to identify a specific, actionable methodology for moving forward with this new direction. Unfortunately, this is an area where many seem to fall short. Perhaps this is because so many take aim at improving discrete functionalities; clearly if no broad-based solution is envisioned, no overarching plan is needed.

Lean dynamics is different in that it does involve broad-based transformation. It requires standing up a broad array of complex, interrelated actions such as restructuring work by product families; sequencing how work, information, and decisions flow to support this; and integrating across divisional boundaries in such a way as to optimize the result while minimizing the disruption created. Leading all of this demands much of the same rigor as managing a major development project—and for many of the same reasons: Mapping this all with a structured approach will go a long way to keeping it on track.

This approach must support the vision; it must successively roll out all of its parts in a way that mitigates perceived risk, but without compromising the integrity of the approach. Doing so assures that people are trained, suppliers selected, tooling and equipment developed, and organizations are stood up in a way so that they all support a consistent set of goals. Moreover, the approach should seek to create near-term, tangible progress, but without taking direct aim at discrete outcomes. Finally, it must refocus the firm's actions toward smoothing internal disconnects, thus mitigating the magnitude and effects of variation and driving down loss.

There are many paths a firm could take—it might begin with a single product family, or by realigning work organization-wide (as is often done in reengineering efforts), or perhaps by making an initial shift and then introducing refinements in phases. Thus, it would be impossible to precisely prescribe each turn to take along the way. Individual firms must make this determination for themselves, first examining their own starting points and the challenges they face within the environment in which they operate. Still, their path should be guided by a common set of logic that can be derived from what we have seen so far.

Laying a Foundation for Success

It is only natural for managers who have learned about the powerful techniques that make up lean dynamics to want to quickly put them into place. But succeeding with these individual elements requires first building a sturdy foundation—an underlying structure that supports them all.

What makes up this foundation? At its base are those elements that logically span the transformation as a whole. Since these support the next parts of the structure, they cannot be phased in or broken apart— either of which can create unfortunate results. Instead, putting these in place will set a solid foundation for other elements that follow.

Quantifying the Objectives

A vision is only powerful if it is achievable. Alfred Sloan clearly recognized this; he put in place clear objectives and supporting standards to achieve his results. We saw that Sam Walton refused to step into major projects without pressing for a clear explanation of why it was needed. The same was true for Herb Kelleher and Taiichi Ohno. Their up-front rigor seems to have paved the way for each of their firms' tremendous successes despite facing enormous challenges along the way.

Still, managers often prefer to err on the side of immediate action, implementing whatever seems to make sense and only later attempting to tie what they have done to a broader plan. Some do this intentionally, seeking to "learn" more clearly what outcomes they should seek as their efforts progress. They might use measurements more as an afterthought—as a means for justifying what they have done rather than for evaluating their incremental progress as they take each step forward. Proceeding in the absence of an overarching direction can cause companies to become lost along the way, succumbing to the trap of *following the problem*—chasing those issues most evident to them while missing the real target they set out to achieve in the first place.

Another major problem comes when firms lose track of what success really means. Many companies declare victory too soon, thinking that they have succeeded based on achieving intermediate goals (such as removing visible waste like inventories) without addressing their underlying causes so they can stand on their own—causing years of work to later unravel.[2] Others may apply flawed measurements—leading them to falsely conclude that their efforts have hit the mark. Internally focused metrics, for instance, can be a poor guide without a solid link to bottom-line value. Without setting their sights on clear objectives designed to create tangible value over a broad range of conditions, corporations' improvement efforts can easily become misdirected. Without these objectives, there is no way to know whether they should press forward, or whether their efforts are instead causing deeper problems and should be discontinued.

To avoid such hazards, it is critical for those embarking on lean initiatives to make clear their objectives *before* they begin their journey. Such objectives should tie directly to their vision and be sufficiently clear to guide their accurate measure of progress along the way. This will help them not only to avoid common traps, but also to turn their conceptual image into something that seems much more real and achievable, perhaps making their vision for the future easier for the workforce to embrace.

Moreover, their objectives must go beyond simply measuring outcomes (a traditional problem described in Chapter 5). Managers must identify real linkages between internal flow and end results if they are to avoid creating "islands of excellence" with no real improvement to bottom-line value. They must not lose sight of the bottom line they seek for their actions: moving the corporation from a steep value curve to one that is flat across the range of possible environments it might face.

Finally, firms' objectives must guide their efforts through that awkward period during the beginning part of their journey. Such transition metrics can be challenging to create, but they are particularly critical to keeping transformation efforts on track. They make it possible for all involved to see the less-visible changes—stabilizing variation and mitigating the causes for lag by adjusting how work flows and how decisions are made—that must precede the more tangible parts of their transformation, like speeding delivery times and slashing inventories. This helps clarify expectations for each step, showing how seemingly unimportant steps contribute to achieving their end goals. These transition metrics identify the limits of what should be expected, keeping all from losing track of what success means at each step along the way.

As lean dynamics is very different from what most managers have learned about managing the business, the same goes for creating and tracking its objectives. With so many more possibilities to explore, lean objectives should reach beyond traditional measures, stretching to achieve outcomes that are more challenging than ever before—and more exciting as well.

Building the Knowledge Base

Building the requisite knowledge to proceed will probably require the services of a *sensei*—someone who has had previous success in rolling out the elements of lean dynamics. Although today there are many consultants to choose from, firms must take great caution when making this selection. Some may put the firm on a very different course than the one described herein. Selecting someone with the right background therefore requires firms to first build a solid understanding of what they wish to achieve.

Even then, it is critical to guard against building too much dependence on an outsider; the greatest successes seem to come when managers and workers have themselves internalized these principles and practices. The sensei's primary mission therefore should not be to *lead* the effort; instead it should be to *impart knowledge*—to offer guidance to companies as they manage their own transformation, ultimately to help those across the corporation learn to apply it on their own.

As we saw in the previous chapter, creating this strong base of knowledge within the corporation must be the first order of business; this should not be delayed until new capabilities are ready to be deployed, as is so often done. Leaders must quickly gain the knowledge they need to lead their own transformation. Involving workers along the way will show that corporate leadership embraces them as the firm's most valuable assets. Doing this should help keep from alienating them from the effort, avoiding a key hazard that so often seems to derail otherwise promising improvement efforts.

Attaining a Baseline of Stability

When a ship encounters a major storm, its first order of business is to stabilize its situation. Any efforts to refine its heading will likely be wasted—the ship will inevitably be blown back off course as it maneuvers to preserve its safety. This is much the same with a firm's implementation plan. Taking direct aim at the end goals of lean dynamics while struggling against serious crises will likely only lead to misdirection and further loss. Instead, a company, it seems, must first focus on stabilizing its situation.

My study of aerospace manufacturers' lean transformation efforts highlighted this need to first attain a basic degree of stability.

Surprisingly, my study showed that more recognizable "lean" activities produce little benefit if done first—that trimming suppliers (and working more closely with those who remain), implementing statistical methods for tracking quality variations, and even aligning shops into manufacturing "cells," do little good until these more basic stabilization improvements have been made.

Rather than jumping head-first into higher-order initiatives like automation and quick equipment changeovers, those who made the most progress began by taking measures that preempted their need for many of their workarounds. Advancing up a framework that progressively increased their operational predictability (depicted in figure 4.4) helped them drive down workarounds and slash their cycle time variation, correlating to a cost savings of as much as twenty-five percent.[3]

For aerospace manufacturing, this began by stabilizing inventories and production operations—creating an ability to closely account for and regulate everything that already exists (warehoused and work-in-process inventories and existing production activities).

Taking such initial actions seems critical to jump-starting a lean transformation. Corporations' improvements in tracking and stabilizing cycle time variation offers to form the needed foundation upon which deeper changes can better succeed. They will also introduce to individuals across the corporation a key concept critical to what they face ahead—the need to smooth cycle time variation. And doing this will create tangible benefits—creating momentum and buy in to the transformation effort.

At the same time, however, attaining these early results can create a different kind of hazard. Finding and removing pockets of waste can lead managers to shift their emphasis to seeking more of the same. Those leading the way must understand the great risk that comes from slashing buffers before they fully understand the broader dynamics that caused them to accumulate (effects that become more apparent in the next phase). It is widely understood that a company's motivation for transformation is best driven by the existence of a crisis; with this now gone (albeit only temporarily), pressure may build to prematurely truncate these efforts.

Once a company attains this basic degree of stability, it can begin to address its deeper problems with embedded lag (such as using massive inventories as a "clutch" to fill orders, and disconnects in information, decision making, and other forms of flow as described in Chapter 6). This, however, is far from simple. Managers face the enormous job of correcting myriad sources of lag across their enterprises, simultaneously smoothing out gaps across all forms of flow, from end to end and across the value stream. Worse still, they must begin by finding these disconnects—the same gaps they and their workforces have learned not to see.

Realigning for Value Stream Flow

We saw in Chapter 6 that the way in which a company constructs its value streams lays the foundation for its ability to create and sustain customer and corporate value. Disconnects in operational flow lead to gaps in responsibilities, metrics, and ultimately in their insights — all of which sets the stage for lag in their decision making. And this breakdown in insight makes loss difficult to correct.

It therefore stands to reason that the next step must be to restructure the firm's value streams in order to correct this disconnect. But corporations must take care to do this in a way that supports their predefined vision and objectives for their transformation — in particular, mitigating the effects of uncertainty.

Identifying Product Families

As described in Chapter 7, shifting from managing products as individual items to combined groups creates tremendous resilience to change, permitting companies to more precisely anticipate smoother demands across a wider range of conditions. From this comes greater flexibility, lower operating costs, higher quality, and an ability to more frequently introduce new innovations — the underlying foundation for managing in the face of change and uncertainty.

How a company identifies its product families is therefore a critical starting point. Their selection must foster the firm's ability for driving out lag and in doing so helping to create a sort of dynamic stability. It is important to note, however, that a firm's product families will not necessarily be based on the end product the customer sees — they might be an end product, or even a component. The definition of a product family will vary from business to business, and depend on where it falls within the overarching value stream.

An aircraft assembler, for instance, might logically base its families on its different platforms. Its suppliers, however, might find that it makes more sense to align product families around major components, grouping together common items that span different vehicles. Engine blades might make up a family; machined aluminum parts within a certain size range and of similar geometric complexity might make up another. Distributors might follow a similar path, basing their families on shared characteristics that enable their suppliers to smooth out forecasts and deliver even items with variable demands more smoothly (rather than the usual breakouts by price, volumes, or end products that do nothing to support this).

Figure 10.1 shows how the product families for an aircraft might look when viewed from the perspective of the individual suppliers that contribute to its construction. The aircraft is made up of a wide range of component products, each of which supports other types of aircraft—possibly produced by different end manufacturers. Yet each of these shares inherent commonalities that permit those who produce them to create efficiencies and the sort of variation dampening we saw in Chapter 7. And mapping out subordinate product families in this manner (each of the blocks circled in the figure might represent a product family to a given supplier or business element) can be particularly helpful in aligning suppliers in a manner that optimally supports the variation leveling effect of figure 7.1—targeting *systematic opportunities* to mitigate lag, smooth out flow, and drive out loss, facilitating the underlying objectives of lean dynamics.[4]

Where, then, should a firm begin for identifying its particular families? Probably with its *customers*. What change and uncertainty do key customers face (perhaps an event like a snowstorm leads them to buy in droves, or spiking fuel prices cause them to shift from previous

FIGURE 10.1   Identifying Product Familes across the Value Stream

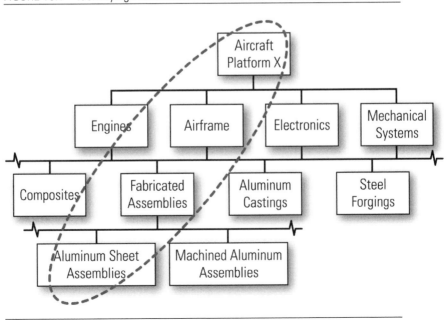

car-buying behaviors), and what volatility does that create for the company? What are the firm's constraints in supporting these needs? Does the difficulty in forecasting customers' demands resulting from this make it difficult to meet customers' needs? Do frequent demands for expedited deliveries place undue burdens or costs on the firm's delivery system? My experience has shown that asking these types of questions can help hone in on what sources of variation contribute most to loss, thus pointing to the most important variation-leveling areas that aligning by product family should aim to achieve.

Fortunately, the variation-leveling effect that firms can derive by leveraging mixed production within these product families opens the doors for initiating improvements at any point along the value stream. Lean efforts need not be led by those at the end of the line—the final assembler in manufacturing value streams. Instead, suppliers can gain the advantages we saw in Chapter 7, creating stability even in challenging environments. We saw this with the Garrity Tool Company: producing a complex mix of prototypes, small one-time production lots, and expedited orders, and still delivering on time and at the high quality its customers require. This advantage is far from trivial; it eliminates the need for some sort of overarching control—an approach we have repeatedly seen brings lag and loss.

Structuring Value Streams

How a firm defines its value stream strikes to the core of what lean dynamics is all about. Doing so should break down the traditional compartmentalization between the steps that form a firm's buildup of value. The end goal should be perfect alignment between attaining customers' objectives and the actions of the corporation.

From this it seems that the first step is to perform a value analysis *from the perspective of the customer.* We saw in Chapter 7 that this means going beyond targeting visible waste or even greater market share. Instead, the goal must be creating real value—value as defined by its customers. A firm might begin by identifying what it is that customers find the most valuable. Proven techniques like customer surveys or focus groups can reveal which attributes customers value the most. Actively seeking this insight can go a long way to preventing an Edsel—producing a product or service that simply does not fit the needs of the customers.

Part of this assessment might be to define the elements that make up the *customer's* value—taking inventory of everything from beginning to end included in the value he or she seeks. For instance, an airline customer might begin by planning his or her destination and then booking a flight, then traveling to the airport, checking in, boarding the flight, and so on. This constitutes the customer's continuum of needs—the entire sequence of activities involved in moving from his or her starting point to a final destination (illustrated in figure 10.2). The airline's challenge is to identify what portion of the whole that *intersects its own capabilities*—where it can contribute by improving the customer's experience while creating strong corporate value.

How should a firm approach this? As we have seen, it all begins with its product families—focusing on aligning what the firm does to dampen internal variation, thus mitigating the effects of external uncertainty and driving down loss to itself and its customers. The firm can thus design its offerings around that portion of the customers' overall continuum of needs in a way that takes greatest advantage of all the variation-leveling capabilities it can offer.

Consider how Southwest Airlines does this. We have seen how its use of common aircraft (the company only flies Boeing 737s) makes possible all kinds of smoothing effects that focus its personnel, facilities, equipment, and even its routes on maximizing value to the customer and corporation alike. Some of its visible outcomes are point-to-point flights that depart and arrive at their destination airports on time, while more reliably delivering customers' baggage to their destinations. By thus applying variation-leveling effects within its portion of the value continuum, Southwest creates a positive effect on the customers' overall travel experience.

A machined part supplier to an automobile producer might draw on its product families to drive down uncertainty that might otherwise increase loss to customers and corporations contributing along the way. For instance, by managing as a combined group those items it manufactures from the same base material, it can aggregate orders from its suppliers, reducing uncertainty (as illustrated in figure 7.1) and loss for

FIGURE 10.2   Intersection of Customers' Needs and Corporations' Value Creation

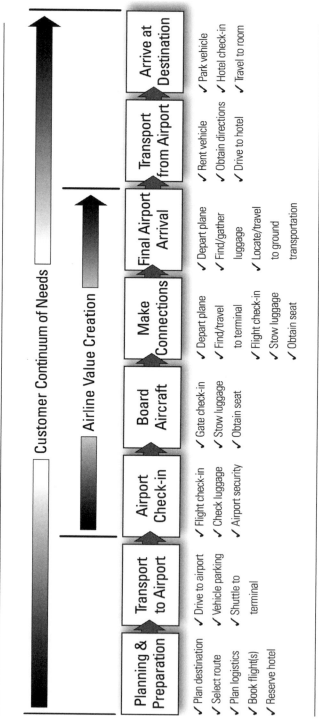

themselves, their customers, and suppliers by smoothing value stream uncertainty.

While there are many ways to approach this, one thing seems certain: Restructuring work does no good if the result does not help sustain a strong value margin. It stands to reason, therefore, that companies should focus on those activities that cut to the core of their business (rather than on activities that are only peripheral to their results, as so many firms seem to insist). This would more likely yield tangible improvement to the corporation's creation of value—improving its value curve—rather than offering uncertain progress against internal metrics.

What actions might companies take to drive down lag and loss? Restructuring by product families, it seems, should be aimed at gaining the variation leveling effect from mixed model production. Companies might take this further still, procuring similar items using long-term contracts take advantage of the demand-leveling effect of figure 7.1 (working with suppliers to adapt their production plans, or even adjusting the layout of their facilities to support mixed-production flow). A manufacturer might leverage product families to maximize its use of mixed-model production for the same general effect. By making fundamental changes in how they manage work, each can dramatically improve their planning, reduce the quantities of what they need to stock, and dramatically increase their support to their customers.

Moreover, this will help keep everyone's focus where it should be: away from internally oriented goals and instead on creating real customer value.

Mitigating Vulnerabilities

We saw in Chapter 7 how combining common items into long-term agreements based on suppliers' core capabilities can help their suppliers leverage commonalities inherent in their product families. This can enable other actions, like slashing the need to buffer problems with hard-to-get materials or those suffering persistent delivery delays or shortages. By instead building in carefully targeted variation-dampening measures that draw on their product family structure (like prestaging partially completed components in the manner described in Chapter 8), firms can streamline their flow of value while dramatically reducing their risks.

Six Sigma skills can be useful here in identifying and driving down variation at these hot spots, improving a wide range of outcomes on everything from improved product quality to faster delivery times. Such measures can make possible smoother, more predictable flow and create the necessary conditions for tight synchronization for attaining initial leaps to greater value (as depicted in figure 9.2). As the lean transformation matures, such measures can be scrutinized in an integrated fashion to further lessen their lag, driving the value stream to achieving further leaps in value.

As other work stations are added, the impact of making incremental improvements will become more and more evident. Operational flow will become smoother and more predictable. Organizational flow will level out as well. Changes in production volumes will no longer create the crises and workarounds that must be elevated up the chain to resolve. Managers can focus on broader objectives, leaving workers to manage day-to-day activities. Without the need to deal with workarounds, information flow will improve. And with value streams now realigned around product families, redesigning products and tooling will now offer their greatest benefits, further advancing the variation-leveling effect while smoothing their introduction into existing flow. Innovation need no longer be viewed as a necessary evil; its introduction can become a natural extension of day-to-day business.

Measuring Results

It is important to note that substantial benefits can begin right away; simply taking on a product-family mindset—managing to optimize the end-to-end production of groups of items instead of targeting efficiencies of individual processing steps—is itself a powerful catalyst for improvement. Measuring and adjusting based on initial results is critical; validating against preset objectives (particularly transition metrics aimed at improving foundational capabilities, like creating greater internal predictability by stabilizing production and inventory activities) will help to ensure that things remain on course. Moreover, such measurements make it possible to credibly report on early success, if for no other reason but to reinforce the validity and criticality of case for change that had been decreed to the workforce.

Still, these results can create a real risk that firms will suffer a hazard described earlier: becoming too satisfied with initial gains. One factory I encountered showed that it had driven its wait time to value-creating ratio down from 40:1 to 9:1—a great accomplishment until one realizes that this means items still spend ninety percent of their time waiting to be processed. Despite strong initial results, much more work clearly remained. This makes it clearer why progress must be tracked against underlying objectives to keep accomplishments in context.[5]

Constant communication must help all understand that achieving strong initial results is only the beginning of what lean dynamics holds for them. It means more than simply achieving a near-term shift in cost structure, or getting past some immediate crisis. It will instead put them on track for achieving their vision for the future—becoming a powerhouse in the global marketplace, creating ever-increasing benefits to the customer, the corporation, and even the workforce!

———■———

Clearly, there exists no cookbook for implementing lean dynamics. Every situation is different; a wide range of approaches based on the themes presented here stand to yield tremendous outcomes. At the same time, however, significant deviations from the tried and true can lead firms down paths to those hazards we have seen to this point. The next chapter identifies some of these that must be avoided as a firm sets out on its lean journey.

Eleven

Making Lean Dynamics Succeed

A smart man learns from his own mistakes.
A truly wise man learns from the mistakes of others.
—Anonymous

FOR MANY YEARS I have observed different types of organizations pursue business excellence. Just as business literature points out, these often end up the same way; despite tremendous effort and enormous expense, firms too often fail to achieve anything close to what they set out to accomplish

Still, even these experiences offer tremendous value. I first came to this realization when I visited a firm whose managers described to me their initial failure in putting in place a major information technology solution for managing production activities and controlling inventories. What really caught my attention was what they did next. Rather than becoming discouraged and giving up, they reinitiated their efforts, applying their newfound insights to achieve truly powerful results—much as Ford had done after it missed the mark with its Edsel (as is described in Chapter 5).

It stands to reason that, while the examples of excellence we have studied help mark the path to success, understanding the hazards as well can help corporations avoid stumbling along the way. The following are some of the most common missteps, and what firms might do to avoid them.

Avoiding the Problem

One particularly daunting barrier to improvement is the attitude of denial that pervades some organizations. Rather than focusing on the art of the possible, they take a defensive view of their situation. Some point out that there is no need to significantly change—explaining that their problems are much simpler; if only they could reduce their operating costs, or shrink their supplier base, or cut their overhead costs, all their problems would shrink away.

In doing so, they choose to avoid the problem.

Perhaps those with this mindset should instead begin by asking themselves a few simple questions. Regardless of their present circumstances or the business they are in, wouldn't they be better off if they could find a way to better deal with the uncertainty that surrounds them? Couldn't they achieve more if they were not driven to react using workarounds each time conditions shifted outside of the narrow range for which their business is prepared? Wouldn't a stronger, sustained value margin give them more money for investment, tie fewer people up in crisis management, and better support the innovations they need to win out over their competitors?

While the answer might seem clear to those who have read this book—something different is needed—coming to this conclusion can be one of the most critical parts of this process for those mired in immediate crisis—and perhaps the most difficult one to achieve.

Chasing Symptoms Rather than Pursuing Sustainable Value

I often ask people for their definition of *lean,* to which many respond with something like: "getting the fat out." This answer seems to reflect a widespread focus on directly targeting visible waste rather than pursuing the fundamental principles that should underlie a firm's improvement efforts—*transformational* shifts that mitigate their sources of lag. Without making a fundamental change in approach, it stands to reason that little chance exists for achieving the fundamentally different results they seek.

We have seen that taking direct aim at desired outcomes like removing inventories can create enormous problems. We saw in Chapter 5 that even firms like Toyota—a benchmark for lean—keep some of this "fat" in place to offset variable conditions, an important element to its system for creating strong customer and corporate value. Lean dynamics instead focuses on putting in place a carefully structured system that mitigates the causes of waste. Visible wastes are not looked at as the target, but as a *symptom* whose cause must be understood before taking action. Following this mindset creates deeper, sustainable results, and helps prevent the "tampering" described in Chapter 1, along with its many unintended consequences that can undermine a firm's journey to achieving its goals.

Corporations must make clear from their plan of action—extending from their case for change to their vision and objectives—that their lean transformation is not simply about chasing symptoms. Instead, lean dynamics is about transforming to a new way of doing business that is more suitable to today's dynamic business needs. Perhaps, then, a more suitable slogan than "getting the fat out" would be *getting the lag out*—eliminating gaps in operations, decision making, information, and in rolling out innovations across all forms of flow to drive down loss and promote value in a sustainable manner, and thus keeping customers coming back again and again.

Focusing on Velocity Rather than Dynamic Flow

A similar hazard for many firms' improvement initiatives is adopting a narrow focus on increasing operational speed. While this, at face value, might seem to be the same as lean dynamics (after all, a well-documented lean benefit is speedier flow of everything from supply to new designs), targeting this in isolation can suboptimize results.

My study of aerospace called this practice into question—it showed that the best gains did not come from simply speeding the progression of work. Surprisingly, even large increases in speed (as measured by major cycle time reductions) by themselves had little effect on costs. Major gains were *only produced when firms' faster speeds were accompanied by a substantial reduction in cycle time variation*. Smoothing their flow of value seems to have achieved faster speeds—along with greater bottom-line value.

How does this compare to today's popular methods? Consider the approach used by Dell, a leading producer of personal computers. Dell is widely recognized for its operational speed; by eliminating retail links (using its "direct model") it moves finished inventory more quickly than others do. As a result, Dell holds very few inventories, producing a high inventory *velocity*.[1] But Dell's approach purportedly is limited to its own inventories—not those of its suppliers, as authors Jeffrey Liker and David Meier explain:

> Unfortunately, what is good for the assembler is not always good for the supplier. Dell expects suppliers to keep a considerable amount of inventory that the supplier is paying for in warehouses near Dell's assembly plant.[2]

Lean dynamics is different in that it eliminates the sources of lag *wherever they reside* across the continuum of the value stream. Since a chain is only as strong as its weakest link, disruption seen by upstream suppliers can still throw even the most compressed customer chain into crisis—driving up variation and loss across the *entire* value stream. Lean dynamics' success instead depends on eliminating gaps and disconnects across all forms of flow from the lowest-tier supplier all the way to the customer.

Pursuing a Single, Narrow Model

A common barrier is the belief that lean practices must look precisely like those at Toyota. Firms everywhere are trying to *directly* apply techniques popularized by the world's most visible example of lean success. This potentially locks out key opportunities offered by lean dynamics.

Consider the use of product families for leveling variation, or the benefits of measuring and tracking cycle time variation—each of which can help increase operational predictability and reduce lag and loss. These concepts are often neglected—frequently absent from lean initiatives (and even from much of today's literature). Yet, we saw how the

Garrity Tool Company, a small manufacturer of machined parts, applies variation-leveling techniques to build a business amid uncertain, low-volume, highly variable demands for complex parts, and how retailers have turned traditional constraints to their advantage.

Their real lesson is that firms must recognize the wide-ranging opportunities and solutions offered by implementing the underlying principles of lean dynamics.

Depending on Outsiders to Lead the Way

Because lean dynamics represents such a radical departure, companies may find it necessary to bring in outside expertise. This is not uncommon today; many of today's business-transformation projects (particularly those related to information technology) depend on outside specialists to guide their efforts. Yet, managers must be cautious; they must recognize that employing outsiders to *lead* the steps of their lean implementation is not the answer.

Asking outsiders to stand up new processes and then turn them over like keys to a car will mean missing an irreplaceable opportunity for broadening their own span of insight—a key to continuing their journey to excellence. Instead, the company's own executives must gain the knowledge to take charge of its transformation. They will need to create their own skills: First, to select the right sensei or other outside expertise to help guide their journey, and later to sustain the new practices they put into place.

Failing to Gain Workforce Buy In

Jack Welch observed that "only satisfied customers can give people job security. Not companies."[3] Achieving this requires the buy in and participation of the workforce; their fate and that of the corporation lies in how everyone works together toward achieving this. All must see that nothing short of a strong partnership can lead to the profitability and customer value that is important to fending off their competition.

Still, simply condensing the message down to sound bites and slogans is not the answer; this stands to trivialize the effort and erode the workforce's belief that there is, in fact, a credible plan. Corporate leaders must instead demonstrate that they do understand and believe in the specifics of lean dynamics. Creating a strong plan of action and sharing their case for change will go a long way in demonstrating this. Furthermore, early successes as they roll out their carefully structured implementation plan will only feed their own commitment and resolve. Great success occurs when their excitement infects the entire workforce.

The workforce's involvement (which we have seen should progressively increase over time) will likely help by making them feel more like partners than employees, involved in solving problems and creating solutions that have a broad influence across the business.[4] In theory, this should appeal to their pride of workmanship as well as their feeling of ownership—permitting and empowering them to attack the waste that has no doubt been frustrating to them as well.[5]

This focus appears to be a major contributor to the Garrity Tool Company's success (a firm that was described in Chapter 7). What is particularly impressive is how the company develops its workforce to increase everyone's span of insight and involvement. The firm's president, Don Garrity, describes his workers as the firm's most valuable asset, investing heavily in their training and offering superior benefits, a combination that has resulted in enviable retention rates. He drives their active participation in managing day-to-day work—for instance, seeking their feedback for most of the equipment the firm buys (the firm continues to expand the span of activities they are involved in, thus increasing their span of insight). Don Entwistle, the company's general manager, noted that a tangible result is helping to ensure sound returns from the company's investments.

> An example is back in our shipping department. We just bought a new bagging machine. My Shipping Coordinator took the time to analyze the current process and develop a time frame for when we would begin seeing a return on our investment. The Parlec Tool Pre-Setter was a collaborative effort with Dwight and several machinists. That also has been a time saver, not necessarily with regard to a reduction in set-up time, but more

along the line that the quality has improved first time out, and tool life has been increased.[6]

Corporations cannot afford to let their people become discouraged; they will end up simply going through the motions, waiting until this management initiative is replaced by the next. Instead, firms must somehow find a way to engage their workforce, encouraging them to take on the new activities, gain the new skills, and accept the much broader responsibility that this new way of doing business will require.

Extending Lean Tools to Beyond Their Demonstrated Scope

Firms that get serious about taking on new improvement methods seem ready to apply them to everything that they do. Rather than focusing initiatives on the creation of tangible, bottom-line value, they focus on individual aspects of the business, presumably driven by the sense that removing inefficiency and waste will logically translate to improvement in outcome. But, as we saw in Chapter 5, this is a faulty presumption within today's complex business world.

For instance, it is hard to see how operational improvement techniques can be applied directly to the steps for *creating* new discoveries. Consider what happened when 3M applied GE's Six Sigma methods to its process for discovering new technologies. It purportedly succeeded in slashing its operating costs—but apparently not without adversely impacting the company's new inventions. Since 2000, the company's percentage of sales from new products purportedly dropped from one-third to only one-quarter; moreover, the company's reputation for innovation has tumbled to Number 7 from its previous position at the top of the list.[7]

Applying business-improvement techniques to areas in which there is no reasonable precedence brings significant risk; its experimental nature creates a greater likelihood of failure. This can undermine management's credibility with the workforce, making lean much more difficult to implement even in the lower risk areas in which its benefits have truly been demonstrated.

Thinking that Lean Dynamics Is Easy

Another critical pitfall is the converse of avoiding the problem: thinking that making the needed changes will be easy. This seems to pervade today's business mindset; managers everywhere seem determined to find the silver bullet—the easy, surefire fix to all that ails them. Although lean dynamics does offer a powerful approach to achieving sustained excellence, it is hardly a quick, easy fix. And approaching it as such will almost certainly guarantee its failure.

Companies must understand that implementing lean dynamics is a complex and challenging undertaking. It requires them to shift everything from how they structure work to how they measure its progress. It means changing how they work with information and who can make decisions. It even means changing how they think about introducing innovations. Adopting these lean ways of dong business takes time and patience; it took Toyota, Wal-Mart, and Southwest Airlines decades to get to the point we see them at today.

Those who see lean dynamics as nothing more than adding new features to their existing system of management—like adding options onto a car—run the risk of misjudging what they are getting themselves into and misunderstanding what it really takes to succeed. This describes all too well what someone I know found when visiting a "lean" hospital. Doctors were given overly rigid work rules that made no sense—requiring them to return staplers to outlined spots on their desks after each use, and issuing Band Aids to physicians only a few at a time (requiring doctors to formally request replacements for those they consumed, using a kanban-like system).

Too often shallow interpretations of techniques like these trivialize what they must do, causing great damage to the credibility of their efforts. Worse still, they represent serious underestimations of what transforming to lean will take. Each of these can undermine a firm's ability to make the more challenging shifts they need, perhaps even dooming their efforts from the outset.

A similar hazard comes from underestimating what is required for sustaining a firm's gains. This is an easy trap in which to fall for those accustomed to drawing conclusions from visible outcomes. And what is visible can seem remarkable: virtually no unplanned activity means that traditional crisis management shrinks away. From this managers could easily conclude that day-to-day work becomes easier. Instead, a lean firm's dramatically reduced lag means that work becomes more intense. Frantic activity is replaced by *precise action*—real-time response to actual demands, smoothly adjusting to changes at all levels to fill orders without lag.

The bottom line is fairly straightforward. Transformation takes time, great focus, and tremendous commitment to stay the course for the long haul. With lean dynamics, the need for frantic activity is replaced by *ongoing vigilance*—hard work that leads to much greater value.

———■———

These are just some of the many hazards that corporations will face as they set out on their journey to lean dynamics. Others lessons have been noted; they will more likely become clearer as firms seek to apply these new principles and practices to their own particular circumstances. Yet, with strong top-management support, solid expertise (even if initially brought in through a sensei), and a rigorous plan for action, firms can steer clear of many of the worst, learning their lessons from those who preceded them rather than struggling through these themselves. With any luck, they will face only small bumps in the road—minor inconveniences in comparison to the vast benefits the corporation will reap from this transformation.

Twelve

Conquering the Crisis

Managers who can get better at managing
this external uncertainty . . . can start to harvest
that half of the company's value that is otherwise
left to the whim of the environment.
—Paul J. H. Shoemaker[1]

EXCELLENCE OFTEN REQUIRES CHANGE. For many firms today it requires people to shift from something with which they have become familiar to something with which they are not. It runs counter to their deeply entrenched need for stability, and thus it causes many to stay close to what has worked well enough in the past.

Such inaction almost surely guarantees a crisis.

During one of his famous seminars, Dr. Edwards Deming faced a question that highlights this dilemma: For a firm that seems to be doing well with no impending threats on the horizon, why change at all? Why go through all the turmoil and churn of making the changes he suggested if there is no immediate cause?

"Where is the crisis?" the man asked. "We and our competitors in the United States have 70 percent of the world's market for aeroplanes." With an unquestioned lead in technology and with so many barriers that would block the advance of competitors, it did seem at the time as though America's hold was truly invincible.[2]

In retrospect, the threat was real. Only two decades later, many of these unquestioned leaders no longer exist. In 2004, Airbus had taken the lead over Boeing—the only remaining U.S. producer of commercial jet airliners. For the second year in a row, it sold more planes to airlines around the world.[3] The crisis, in fact, is upon us now; even once-dominant juggernauts of American business are no longer safe.

But today this threat extends far beyond aerospace. Cheap, overseas labor is now undercutting the price that American factories can ask for all sorts of goods. Globalization and the information age have made mass markets a thing of the past. Customers demand greater innovation, near-perfect quality, increased customization to meet their particular needs—and they want it all faster and cheaper. Together, these demands challenge corporations' traditional presumptions. Uncertainty and change are now everywhere—something that many corporations are ill-equipped to handle.

Some have already suggested that the crisis has come too far, that American labor is just too expensive, that sustaining a competitive edge now requires firms to surrender as much work as possible to other parts of the world. Firms seem to focus on labor, from workers' healthcare costs to even product-quality problems. One major consulting firm purportedly concluded that American labor no longer can compete head-to-head with low-cost countries (or LCCs); that other countries' educated workforces coupled with their lower wages and their ability to produce equivalent or higher quality makes them better suited to performing a wide range of functions.[4]

Yet, this book demonstrates that targeting individual costs is often not enough; neither is resorting to gimmicks like sales promotions and warrantees aimed at extending the status quo. Warrantees are no substitute for turning out high quality, nor are cash incentives of billions of dollars to consumers a solution to turning out too many products (expenses that can dwarf other costs). Customers no longer want workarounds; excuses no longer substitute for producing the value that customers want.

Those who resign themselves to such a philosophy might find themselves accelerating in the downward spiral of loss that they seek to avoid.

How, then, can corporations meet this impending crisis? The answer is clear: They must move from their obsolete practices formulated in the early twentieth century. They must cease relying on methods that were designed for much different times. They must see that competing with others using the same tired approach offers no superior value; history shows that competitors will eventually discover how to mimic technologies, challenge existing product lines, and match economies of scale.

Nowhere is this need to change more evident than in American aerospace. For more than a century, this industry has captured our dreams of the future, expanding the bounds of reality to turn what was once only fantasy into what is now almost commonplace. It continues to bring capabilities that transform society—even recreational space flight now seems close to becoming a reality. Yet, despite its powerful innovation, aerospace today faces real threats that just two decades ago no one would have believed would come.

Those who have read this book understand that there is a better way. Innovation and execution can work hand-in-hand, creating tremendous, sustainable value rather than compete with each other as has so long been the case. Together they can promote stable, expanding margins of value that anticipate and capitalize on the growing change and uncertainty throughout their environment.

Yet, none of this is possible without first adopting a radical change in mindset. Just as the Wright brothers first suspended their disbelief that man could learn to fly, corporations must now suspend their disbelief in the enormous potential that exists if they make the leap to lean dynamics. And the benefits will similarly extend well beyond the immediate target—extending to yet-unimagined forms of value to humankind.

Think back to the earlier analogy of a fighter plane. After cruising much of last century through skies that were clear and safe, many firms have come to see their value margins evaporate as, faced with overseas competition and uncertain conditions, they are forced to frequently maneuver at the outskirts of their value curve. They find themselves repeatedly thrust into combat, but with value margins that leave them virtually unable to maneuver.

Competing on Dynamic Value

In order to capture the competitive edge, corporations must learn from those who have done well in this hostile, dynamic environment. By incorporating those features that work best in crisis, they, too, will be better prepared to compete and win. And with such crisis now becoming the norm, it no longer appears that they have a choice.

There are a growing number of firms that seem to have done precisely this. We saw in Chapter 7 how the Garrity Tool Company, a small manufacturer of machined parts, applies variation-leveling techniques to succeed in an environment too challenging for many others, creating internal stability and consistent results amid uncertain, low-volume, highly variable demands for complex parts. We learned that Ryanair transformed itself to dominate the European airline industry. And there are others, too, who seem to be quietly implementing many of the tools and practices of this new system of management based on their individual assimilations of these lessons.

Adapting the Model

Consider Hibbett, the small but growing sporting goods apparel retail chain briefly described in Chapter 5. For years this company appears to have quietly applied much of what this book has described. And its results have been impressive; Hibbett generates industry-leading operating margins and staggering growth—increasing from 67 stores in 1996 to 620 stores today. Its sustained success has thrust the firm into the spotlight; it is consistently featured as one of Forbes magazine's 200 Best Small Companies.[5]

A quick glance at its value curve (depicted in figure 12.1) is all that it takes to show that Hibbett is different. For more than a decade, the company has sustained a rock-solid value margin—a real feat in an industry saturated with strong, entrenched competitors.

Powering the firm's success seems to be its clear vision for value, aligned with its lean system for smoothly and efficiently delivering value over time—not only benefiting the customer, but its suppliers as well. As the company's president, Mickey Newsome, put it, "due to our small market strategy and consistent sales growth, we have become more important to our vendors and are getting additional shipments of allocated merchandise. This enables us to enhance our importance to the end customer."[6]

Each Hibbett store develops a relationship with its community, understanding its needs and honing its methods to meet them. Its infor-

FIGURE 12.1   Value Curve of Hibbett Sports[7]

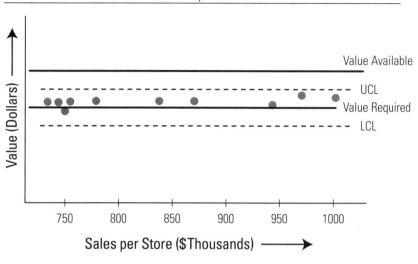

Note: Data shown from FY 1995–2004; value required for FY 2005 and beyond appears to have shifted to lower line representing a greater, still stable value margin. Data was adjusted to account for extraordinary item per criteria described in Appendix.

mation systems support stores' ability to make available just what they want while minimizing inventories that drive up costs and maximizing stock availability. The insight it gains from this information supports its rigorous management of goods from supplies to stores—from the efforts of its "talented group of planners" that work closely with its buyers, to facilitating its cross-docking that helps to maintain low overhead and fast turnaround. To further hold down costs, the company uses its own fleet of trucks to deliver to its stores.[8]

Part of Hibbett's success seems to come from its emphasis on robust organizational flow. The company actively invests in its workforce to maximize workers' span of insight—a key, as we saw earlier, to minimizing organizational lag. In order to help its staff provide top customer assistance on products that are often highly technical, the company developed a program to coordinate with vendors to educate staff on products and trends. Merchandising monitors competing stores, maintains close relationships with its vendors, and coordinates with stores and other staff.[9] New store managers attend Hibbett University (HU), gaining the depth of knowledge to provide the level of service expected within this company.

With this solid foundation, coordination between the company's stores and organizational elements seems effective using only simple, intuitive methods: coordinated meetings and emails within and between divisions, with the president, and the stores. Schedules posted on a shared drive help keep all informed on company activities; stores are kept informed through a weekly memo system.

Hibbett's results are truly astounding. According to one analyst, "Hibbett is the only major sporting goods retailer that has developed a successful 'small box' format that can profitably operate in secondary markets."[10] And this success—as well as that of the Garrity Tool Company—helps to demonstrate a key feature of lean dynamics: Its principles enable firms to thrive in markets not typically considered to be in the realm of "lean" methods.

Breaking the Traditional Mindset

Together these cases teach us an important lesson: Firms that apply the principles and practices of lean dynamics need not follow a preset mold. They can be different sizes, have different strategies, and pursue different niches. Perhaps most of all, how they apply lean dynamics differs widely. It takes more than a superficial look to identify these firms: It takes a deeper analysis of their creation of value—something that can be seen from a value curve.

These firms offer excellent examples of applying lean dynamics' underlying principles and practices without trying to become the firms from whom they originated. Take the Garrity Tool Company, for instance—no one would possibly confuse this firm with Toyota. Yet, its formula seems very successful; the company has successfully adapted this methodology to create a niche within an area that otherwise might go largely unserved.

And Hibbett is no Wal-Mart. Despite applying similar principles and practices—from information technology to cross-docking—the customer value it offers is substantially different. It is so different, in fact, that it sees having a Wal-Mart nearby not as a liability, but as a *benefit*. Wal-Mart's low-price focus does not compete head-to-head with Hibbett's higher-end merchandise, and it tends to increase sales by drawing in greater traffic volume. As the company's president, Michael Newsome, put it, "we love being in a shopping center with Wal-Mart. We consider them more of an ally than a competitor because they bring us a lot more business than they ever get from us."[11]

This fact points to perhaps the largest pitfall for firms pursuing this path today: Too often they try to become just like Toyota or Southwest or Wal-Mart. What they miss, it seems, is first developing an understanding of the real goal—not implementing Toyota's Kaizen, cutting gate time (like Southwest), or implementing information technology solutions (in an attempt to be like Wal-Mart) but understanding their underlying mechanisms for creating dynamic value. The answer they must see lies not in *becoming* those firms they wish to emulate, but taking their underlying lessons and creating the unique form of value that differentiates them within their industry or specific competitive area.

A Caution Against Complacency

It should be clear from the data and examples throughout this book that Toyota, Wal-Mart, and Southwest Airlines have raised the bar for corporations everywhere, changing the rules of business forever. Their application of lean dynamics principles and practices have shown it possible to achieve something entirely new: the ability to thrive across a broad span of conditions that most corporations simply seek to avoid. Others have followed; we see that they, too, are achieving great success. From this, it would be too easy to believe that their story has been told; that their current success can only give way to more success. Yet, history shows that such a mindset is what paves the way to decline.

Consider GM, once the mightiest manufacturer in the world. Anyone who would have foretold its current situation at its peak in the 1960s would have been dismissed as utterly crazy. Yet, GM's decline has today put it at risk of falling to second place behind Toyota, a company that, until fairly recently, was hardly recognized as a real competitor. But the world changed, and GM did not; it failed to abandon a system proven to succeed for a business environment that had long since changed. And today we see the results: plummeting market share and skyrocketing costs with no definite end in sight.

This fate is not unique to GM; today Ford and Chrysler seem to be struggling, as are major airlines, retailers, and many others. Even "lean" firms are not immune; as tremendous as their results have been to date, Toyota, Wal-Mart, and Southwest Airlines, as well as the others we have seen, face serious challenges ahead. Wal-Mart, for instance, must prepare to compete head-to-head with another lean retailer, Tesco, as it expands its reach into this country (much can probably be learned from the results as these lean firms prepare to collide in the near future). Toyota must deal with its own rapid expansion, sustaining its reputation for quality while keeping activities in lock-step as it develops differentiated products and produces them for global markets within factories around the world.[12] And Southwest Airlines must continuously adapt its strategies in conjunction with its lean system of management to accommodate its rapid pace of expansion and new operating constraints—from environmental issues to the cost of fueling its planes.

Firms everywhere must realize that the only thing that remains constant is the need to change. Even those who are "lean" cannot rest—globalization, new environmental realities, challenges from lean competitors, and other changing realities stand to derail their progress. This is particularly true for the small firms described herein; they remain vulnerable to these and other forces as they advance. For them and others, keeping on track is not a given; it requires constant vigilance and remaining grounded in the concepts described herein.

Success in business is about the survival of the fittest, within the environment that presents itself. Lean dynamics offers a proven approach for thriving amid some of the most extreme of these conditions. But even this powerful approach requires tailoring, strategy, and continued vigilance.

Constructing
the Value Curve

W E CALCULATE A FIRM'S VALUE CURVE by plotting its two measures of value (*value available* and *value required*) against its measure
of the flow of value (created by the company for the customer over time).
The following apply:

- A firm's *value available* is a tangible measure of the *value* its output represents as assessed by those who buy it. This is measured
  simply as the dollars its customer exchanged in return for a measure of output these activities produce; specifically, the net sales
  for the products or services it turns out during the measured
  time frame. These are depicted as successive measurements of
  the value the firm creates from normal activities over a period
  of time.

- *Value required* is defined as the sum-total *cost* of creating what
  the firm produces for its customers during the measured time
  frame; this includes all of the activities, expenditures, and even
  wastes resulting from the company's execution in turning out
  this value. It is measured as net sales minus the net income for
  its output during the measured time frame, presented as a series
  of successive snapshots taken of normal activities over a period
  of time. Thus, value required should not include large investments or gains unrelated to normal business activities (e.g., revenues gained from the sale of a corporate division, an unusual
  investment in modernizing facilities).

- The measure of *flow* (the horizontal axis) is represented by successive measurements of output volumes, depicting the flow of these outputs to the customer over time. The measure of volumes must relate to the way in which value is delivered to the customer (as a product, through a store, etc.) and will vary depending on which is suitable for the industry the company operates in. For instance, volume for an automobile manufacturer can be depicted by the number of vehicles it sells to its customers. Volume for a retailer can be described as its sales per store. Volume for an airline is described as the volume of passengers it transports per flight (or its load factor).
- The difference between value required and value available, when plotted against this volume measure, defines the firm's *value margin*—how well its activities will sustain its competitive strength as conditions vary over time.

The value curve is intended as a means to understand the *relationship* between value available and value required. For clarity, these have been displayed in a way that makes their proportional relationship clear. Because value available and value required are both functions of net sales for the same system—its variance affects both of these data in a proportional manner—we can accomplish this by depicting value available and value required as a ratio (holding value required as a constant and then displaying value available in its calculated proportion).

The construction and interpretation of the value curve must take into account key considerations.

- Interrogating a firm's performance means pressing the system to its limits; this means drawing on data from a range of sequential years during which the firm is subjected to nearly the full range of conditions it might see throughout its operation (just as we saw with the example of GM during the years from market peak to depression).
- The corporation's methodology for creating value must remain somewhat stable during this sequence of years. Significant changes in approach, such as a corporate merger or suddenly introducing advanced manufacturing equipment, can cause

changes in output that would disrupt our ability to interpret results. Permanent changes in capacity can be readily accounted for as long as the general methodology has not shifted (e.g., Southwest increases its sales by growing its fleet of aircraft— but its methodology remains the same—to include the type of aircraft it uses).

To demonstrate the construction of the value curve, we will construct the value curve depicted in figure 3.2. Data to construct this curve can be found in Alfred Sloan's autobiography, *My Years With General Motors.*[1] The span of time depicted is from 1926 and 1936, during which time automotive demand swung dramatically from one extreme to another (as was described in Chapter 3)—but its methodology remained fairly stable (with exceptions that could readily be accommodated).[2] The following outlines the calculations of the value curve.

For the purpose of constructing a value curve, *value available* is nothing more than the income from the sale of each vehicle, or:

Value Available = Vehicle price = (Net sales $/Unit sales)

Value required is calculated as the sale price per vehicle less the profit made for each unit:

Value Required = [(Vehicle price) − (Net income per vehicle)]

The *x*-axis of the value curve represents the business' measure of *volume* (or flow). In this case, volume is represented by the number of vehicles the company sells:

Volume = Unit Sales of Cars and Trucks

The results of these calculations are plotted in figure A.1. The dotted lines depict the value margin that exists at each volume; however, it is difficult to visualize the trend that exists here.

FIGURE A.1   Value Available versus Value Required

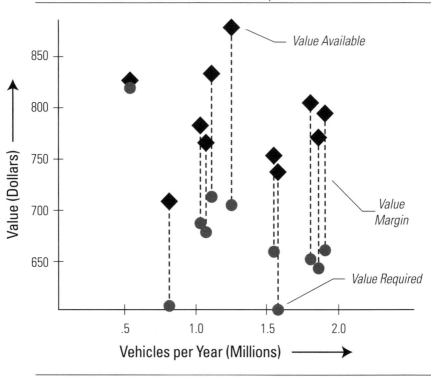

For clarity, the value curve depicts these data in a way that better illustrates the proportional dependencies between these pairs of data points across these data sets. For this reason, *value available* is set as a constant; we can then calculate and display its proportional relationship with a proportionally adjusted *value required,* showing this relationship between value available and value required, while making clear the trends that would otherwise be difficult to see (depicted in figure A.2)

It is interesting to note that the adjusted value required curve displays a shape that is remarkably similar to the Long Run Average Cost (LRAC) curves as applied in managerial economics. Setting value available as constant causes this to fit the pattern of profit maximization curves under perfect competition, where price is seen as a constant (*value available* here is analogous to their application of price).[3]

The curves displayed in this book for Southwest and for Wal-Mart were developed in a similar manner. Southwest's measure of volume is

FIGURE A.2   Depicting the Value Curve

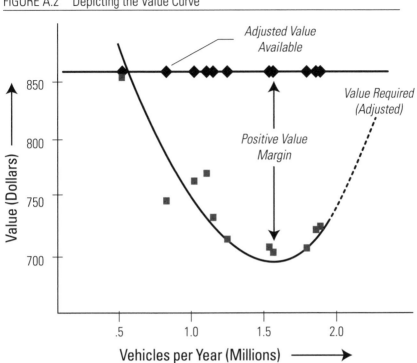

TABLE A.1   Value Calculations

Year	Volume	Value Available ($)	Value Required ($)	Proportional Value Required	Factor
1926	1234850	856.9084002	706.0956035	706.0886817	1
1927	1562748	812.3636524	661.9204421	698.2090166	1.055
1928	1810806	806.1398659	653.4630424	694.6095892	1.063
1929	1899267	792.0974102	661.3720999	715.4798704	1.082
1930	1158293	848.9865146	718.5367994	725.2343504	1.009
1931	1033518	782.6092269	688.8739393	754.2666995	1.095
1932	525727	822.3124702	821.998659	856.5729895	1.042
1933	802104	709.3974622	605.6532145	731.5845731	1.208
1934	1128326	764.5597726	680.5688595	762.7650272	1.121
1935	1564252	738.7821854	599.9129303	695.8280805	1.16
1936	1866589	771.0802646	643.3165067	714.9163841	1.111

load factor, since it represents changes in unit of output delivered to its customer—or passenger volume per flight. For Wal-Mart, volume is calculated as total sales/number of stores (with output thus broken down by the point at which customers select and draw what they want from the value stream). For simplicity, value is calculated for the corporation as a whole (rather than by unit).

As was stated earlier, the approach used herein depends on the ability to measure a stable system over time; it therefore applies only for those periods when no major shift in approach is introduced. Thus, comparisons to Kmart, as well as Southwest Airline's competitors, were restricted to those time periods before these firms fell into bankruptcy (subsequent restructuring would certainly represent a sufficient shift to invalidate this approach). Moreover, it was stated that value required should not include large investments or gains unrelated to normal business activities; thus, in some cases adjustments were made (which have been identified) to account for these effects (e.g., adjustments for Kmart from liquidating major parts of the corporation; Ford from selling off a major component.)

Finally, it is interesting to note that the *value required* curves representing Southwest, Toyota, and Wal-Mart are more consistent with the Long-Run Average Cost curves of firms with "constant returns to scale."[4] This should be expected, since their way of doing business permits them to rapidly and continuously readjust to external changes.

Glossary

Buffers—The use of inventories, extended lead times, or other methods intended as a means for preventing schedule delays from impacting adjacent processing steps or customers. Buffers act as a significant source of lag.

Changeovers—Shifting equipment from performing one activity to another. In production, this means switching cutting tools, forming dies, and making other changes that typically require production to temporarily stop.

Common causes—Normal deviations from intended outcomes or objectives that should be expected and planned for as part of doing business (the converse of *special causes*).

Cross-process—Activities or measurements that do not fall within a firm's formally identified processes, requiring special attention to manage and track their performance.

Cycle time—The time it takes to complete the steps for one processing cycle within a given operation.

Cycle time variation—A measure of deviations from intended cycle times for successive units produced by a given operation; large cycle time variation is a negative indication of smooth flow.

Division of labor—A methodology that divides up the individual steps that go into producing a product among many specialized workers, each performing only a small part of the overall operation. This approach makes possible the efficiencies of mass production.

Dynamic effect—Overreactions from the uncertainty caused by deviations from intended outcomes, causing a chain reaction across a factory and its suppliers that can be complex and widespread.

Dynamic flow—The progression of value creating steps when pressed to operate across a broad range of conditions.

Dynamic stability—Corporations' ability to right themselves without the need for expediting or deviating from normal processes when subjected to external sources of disruption.

ERP (Enterprise Resource Planning)—An information system used to provide overarching structure and control of activities, intended to extend to all information and processes across a corporation.

Expediting—Reactive actions once a crisis emerges; creating workarounds to overcome disruption and achieve the firm's schedule goals.

Flow—The buildup of value as it progresses through the value stream. Smooth flow is indicated by the absence of defects, out-of-station work, and other delays; it is indicated by low cycle time variation.

Information flow—The movement of accurate, timely information to the right people at all levels and points across the value stream.

Innovation flow—The progression of improvements and new technologies into products and services.

JIT (Just-in-Time)—A way of doing business in which items are produced and then delivered just when they are required and in only the quantities needed to support current demand. This approach differs from traditional factory or supply chain management where items are produced in large batches and then issued from accumulated inventories.

Kaizen—A methodology for fostering continuous improvement of activities, typically involving participants from the workforce.

Kanban—A methodology used by Toyota for fostering pull between workstations.

Lag—Disconnects within a firm that cause its actions to amplify variation and increase its disruptive outcomes. Lag can come from a range of sources: from gaps between measurement and outcome, to discontinuities within flow of information, activities, or decisions.

Lean dynamics—A system of management, based on the principles and practices of lean manufacturing, proven to create strong, steady, tangible value for corporations and their customers across today's broad range of changing conditions. Lean dynamics is transformational; its principles and techniques let firms adapt to shifts in their environments to sustain effective operations, decision making, information, and innovation. And, unlike many other business improvement approaches, lean dynamics is measurable, offering a clear means for firms of all types to track their progress toward achieving sustainable excellence.

Lean manufacturing—A way of maximizing business results by optimizing the buildup of customer value from its basic elements to customer delivery. A central focus is avoiding wasteful activities, delays, and inventories that consume resources but do not add to customer value. Its counterintuitive techniques of managing by product families (in which people, equipment, and processes work together to produce groups of common products or components from beginning to end) and building fewer items more frequently represent a distinct shift from the mass-production standard of producing identical items in large batches. The end result is turning out greater quality at higher speeds using less of everything, from factory space to labor hours and inventories.

Lead time—The total time from customer order to delivery of a product.

Load factor—A measure of how full an airline's planes are when they fly (i.e., their percent passenger volume per flight).

Loss—The adverse outcome of everything that can lead to lower bottom-line value.

Manufacturing cell—The grouping of people, equipment, and processes, producing complete end items, components, or clearly severable portions of major operations from beginning to end. They draw on the inherent commonality between items across a product family so that workers and equipment can quickly and seamlessly shift back and forth from producing one item and then to the next, combining work flow as if it were for only one item.

Material Requirements Planning (MRP)—An information system (computer program) used to provide overarching control of production schedules, inventory management, and planning activities within a factory. Often used as a module within a broader MRP II (Manufacturing Resources Planning) system that includes other modules for such activities as overall capacity planning.

Mixed production—Producing a group of items within a product family, drawing on their inherent commonality to quickly and seamlessly shift back and forth from producing one item and then to the next from beginning to end. This creates efficiencies even when producing lower quantities, eliminating the need to build in large batches and supporting the goals of production leveling and variation leveling.

Operational flow—The progression of those activities involved in transforming products or services from their basic elements to their finished state, delivered into the hands of the customer. This is this physical flow that we most often think of when we picture the buildup of value—and the most visible casualty when operating conditions shift.

Organizational flow—The timely progression of decision making by people at levels and points across the value stream to mitigate misdirection or lag. Smooth organizational flow is promoted by an organizational structure in which decision making remains consistent even when a firm's "normal" conditions break down.

Overhead—A method of accounting for those costs companies have not directly attributed to the products or services they sell.

Process—A set of operations necessary to complete a major element of work.

Product family—A groups of items that share significant commonalities, facilitating rapid changeovers that make it possible for manufacturing cells to quickly and seamlessly shift back and forth from producing one item and then to the next, combining work flow as if it were for only one item.

Production leveling (heijunka)—A technique for building fewer items more frequently (as opposed to the mass-production standard of infrequently producing large batches) so that individual production shops can progress at a pace similar to end-item consumption, thus offsetting an important form of lag.

Pull—Synchronizing activities engaged in creating value with actual customer demand at each step along the way—even as customers' demands continue to change (the converse of push).

Push—A way of synchronizing work using a top-down system for schedule control (see MRP).

Scientific management—A system introduced by the early twentieth-century industrial efficiency pioneer, Frederick Taylor, based on the premise that careful identification and control of the individual tasks that make up each job can generate greater productivity and workforce morale.

Sensei—A guide or a teacher with extensive knowledge (in this book, of lean dynamics principles and practices).

Span of insight—The degree to which workers (and managers) understand the broader reasons and impact of their actions and decisions. Organizations structured based on division of labor tend to have narrow spans of insight, in which people respond to the outputs of other departments—often without understanding their cause.

Special causes—Deviations in performing operational steps that are the result of some extraordinary outside influence and that cause results to fall outside of the system's statistical control limits.

Standard volume—An approach introduced by Alfred Sloan under which managers report their results based on their *average* production levels.

Statistical control limits—Statistically determined thresholds (upper and lower control limits) between which results are expected for operations not experiencing unusual circumstances (see *special causes*).

Supply chain effect—A chain reaction in which unexpected changes in customer demand are amplified up the chain, growing in magnitude at each work station or supplier further from the source.

Total Productive Maintenance (TPM)—A proactive approach to tracking and performing maintenance on equipment before its performance begins to degrade. It is intended to prevent sudden failures that can contribute to variation and uncertainty.

Value—A product or service that satisfies a customer need or desire even as it changes over time.

Value available—A tangible measure of the *value* a firm's output represents as assessed by those who buy it. This is measured simply as the dollars its customer exchanged in return for a measure of output these activities produce; specifically, the net sales for the products or services it turns out during the measured time frame.

Value curve—A graphical means of portraying how much value a company creates at each point across the range of conditions that its activities must perform.

Value margin—The difference between value required and value available, when plotted against a volume measure, indicating how well a firm's activities will sustain its competitive strength as conditions vary over time.

Value required—The sum-total *cost* of creating what the firm produces for its customers during the measured time frame; this includes all of the activities, expenditures, and even wastes resulting from the company's execution in turning out this value. It is measured as net sales minus the net income for its output during the measured timeframe, presented as series of successive snapshots taken of normal activities over a period of time.

Value stream—The sequence of activities that work together to produce and deliver products and services ordered by the customer, from end to end, beginning with their most basic elements.

Variation—Deviations from intended objectives or outcomes, causing difficulty in forecasting and disruption in activities—driving a cycle of uncertainty, disruption, and loss.

Variation leveling—A less-recognized potential for dampening uncertainty made possible by the mixed-production technique. Rather than simply dampening the growth of *internal* disruption (production leveling), firms can use mixed-production to dampen the effects of operating in an uncertain environment.

Waste—Activities, delays, or materials that consume resources but do not contribute value to the end result. Toyota identified the existence of seven common forms of waste, which it constantly seeks to eliminate.

Workarounds—The use of extra inventories, padded lead times, out-of-sequence work, and expediting that violates set work standards or procedures to overcome current schedule risks, delays, or disruptions within a firm.

Notes

Introduction

1. The findings of this study were documented in *The Manufacturing Afford-ability Development Program: A Structured Approach to Rapidly Improved Affordability*, Final Report, Washington, DC: The Naval Air Systems Command and The Joint Strike Fighter Program Office, July 1996. These results are further explored in S. A. Ruffa and M. J. Perozziello, *Breaking the Cost Barrier: A Proven Approach to Managing and Implementing Lean Manufacturing*, New York: John Wiley & Sons, Inc., 2000.

2. An excellent summary of this project and its initial results can be found in "Part Grouping: Angioplasty for the Supply Chain" by Colonel Michael C. Yusi, USAF, *Air Force Journal of Logistics*, Spring 2003, 15–26. It describes the present author's government-industry collaborative initiative in which Boeing slashed the time to produce and deliver a family of tactical aircraft spare parts while providing much greater capability to respond to sudden surges in demand.

3. The savings from taking these actions were estimated to be as much as a billion dollars if other costs beyond one-time inventory savings are included, such as periodic disposal and replacement of shelf-life limited items.

4. J. P. Womack, D. T. Jones, and D. Roos, *The Machine that Changed The World* (New York: Rawson Associates, Macmillan Publishing Co., 1990), 28. This compares lean production to mass (traditional) production, indicating it takes half the human effort, manufacturing space, investment tools, engineering hours, and half the product-development time.

5. Taiichi Ohno, *The Toyota Production System: Beyond Large Scale Production*

(Portland, OR: Productivity Press, 1988), 38. Ohno states that "After the oil crisis, people started paying attention to the Toyota production system." He also states that "by 1974, Japan's economy had collapsed to a state of zero growth and many companies were suffering." At the Toyota Motor Company, "the widening gap between it and other companies made people wonder what was happening at Toyota" (1).

6. Kevin Freiberg and Jackie Freiberg, *Nuts! Southwest Airlines' Crazy Recipe for Business and Personal Success* (New York: Broadway Books, 1996), 84. Kelleher's complete statement is: "Reality is chaotic; planning is orderly and logical. The two don't square with each other."

7. Michael Barbaro and Justin Gillis, "Wal-Mart at Forefront of Hurricane Relief," *The Washington Post* (September 6, 2005): D1. Mr. Broussard's complete statement: "If the American government would have responded like Wal-Mart has responded, we wouldn't be in this crisis."

Chapter One

1. Peter M. Senge *The Fifth Discipline: The Art & Practice of The Learning Organization* (New York: Doubleday, 1990), 57.

2. Peter Drucker, *Managing in a Time of Great Change* (New York: Truman Talley Books/Dutton, 1995), 21–22. Drucker observes that corporations are increasingly finding themselves in the midst of unmanageable crises—but not because things are being done poorly or that the wrong things are being done. "What accounts for this apparent paradox?" he asked. "The assumptions on which the organization has been built and is being run no longer fit reality."

3. Jody Hoffer Gittell, *The Southwest Airlines Way: Using the Power of Relationships to Achieve High Performance* (New York: McGraw-Hill Companies, Inc., 2003), 236–39. Gittell describes the airline industry's response after September 11th, showing that US Airways suffered the greatest flight reductions among major U.S. airlines, and the largest layoffs in the industry (at twenty-four percent). Gittell also discusses employees' grievances, giving an indication of some of the disruption this must have caused among the workforce.

4. Sholnn Freeman, "Truck and SUV Sales Plunge as Gas Prices Rise: GM, Ford Hit Hardest in September," *The Washington Post* (October 4, 2005): D1. Freeman describes the impact of spiking gasoline prices. The article paints a particularly painful picture for Ford, where trucks and SUVs are "the backbone of the company's sales and profits . . ." During September

2005, the company's sales of F-Series pickup trucks dropped by thirty percent, and sales of its large SUVs—including the Explorer, Expedition, and Lincoln Navigator—each fell by fifty-five percent.

5. Michael Hammer, *The Agenda: What Every Business Must Do to Dominate the Decade* (New York: Crown Business, 2001), 79.

6. These wastes are described in a number of sources, including Kiyoshi Suzaki, *The New Manufacturing Challenge: Techniques for Continuous Improvement* (New York: The Free Press, 1987), 12–18.

7. J. Welch and J. A. Byrne, *Jack: Straight from the Gut* (New York: Warner Books, 2001), 337.

8. Ibid. They further elaborate on the criticality of shifting focus from averages to span, in which the authors state, "We were three years into Six Sigma before we 'got it.'"

9. This is an overview of the experiment described in W. Edwards Deming, *The New Economics: For Industry, Government, Education* (Cambridge, MA: MIT CAES, 1993) 194–209.

10. Ibid, 204–5. Deming describes "tampering" as making a change simply in response to a "faulty" outcome, causing a different result from our actions than we seek.

11. Peter M. Senge, *The Fifth Discipline: The Art & Practice of The Learning Organization,* 89–91.

12. Adam Smith, *The Wealth of Nations* (New York: Alfred A. Knopf, 1991), 5. Smith describes division of labor within the pin factory, 7, Smith makes this statement.

13. *The Manufacturing Affordability Development Program: A Structured Approach to Rapidly Improved Affordability* provides this statistic.

14. This analogy—applied here to show the effects of buffers on variation— has been widely used within the context of quality improvement, as it was by Thomas J. Cartin in *Principles & Practices of TQM* (USA: ASQC, 1993), 108.

15. Gabriel Szulanski and Sydney Winter, "Getting It Right the Second Time," *Harvard Business Review* (January 2002): 62–65. The article describes this study and its results.

16. Richard Foster and Sara Kaplan, *Creative Destruction: Why Companies that Are Built to Last Underperform the Market—And How to Successfully Transform Them* (Doubleday, a Division of Random House, USA, 2001, McKinsey & Company, Inc.), 1.

17. Robert Slater, *Jack Welch and the GE Way: Management Insights and Leadership Secrets of the Legendary CEO* (New York: McGraw-Hill), 233. The

concept of "work outs" is described in D. Ulrich, S. Kerr, and R. Asakenas, *GE Work-Out* (New York: McGraw Hill, 2002).

18. Peter Senge, *The Fifth Discipline: The Art & Practice of The Learning Organization,* 23. Senge describes this learning dilemma and makes this statement.

Chapter Two

1. Walton and Huey, *Sam Walton: Made in America,* 184.
2. James C. Collins and Jerry I. Porras, *Built to Last: Successful Habits of Visionary Companies* (New York: HarperBusiness, 1994, 1997), 27. Collins and Porras state that "Ford was one of 502 firms founded in the United States between 1900 and 1908 to make automobiles." J. P. Womack, D. Jones, and D. Roos, *The Machine that Changed the World* (New York: Rawson Associates, Macmillan Publishing Co., 1990), 28. Womack, Jones, and Roos state that Ford's Model T was "his twentieth design over a five-year period."
3. Womack, Jones, and Roos, *The Machine that Changed the World,* 27–28. The authors describe how interchangeability, simplicity, and ease of attachment enabled workers to quickly perform specialized tasks, reducing the assembly time from 514 to 2.3 minutes.
4. Womack, Jones, and Roos, *The Machine that Changed the World,* 31. The authors state, "with this separation of labor, the assembler required only a few minutes of training."
5. Ruffa and Perozziello, in *Breaking the Cost Barrier,* provide data and analysis supporting this conclusion.
6. Womack, Jones, and Roos — *The Machine that Changed the World,* 27 — provide these facts.
7. Womack, Jones, and Roos — in *The Machine that Changed the World,* 170 — describe the relationship between Henry Ford and his network of dealers.
8. David Halberstam *The Reckoning* (New York: William Morrow & Co., 1986), 68.
9. Womack, Jones, and Roos — in *The Machine that Changed the World,* 29 — state that "By the time Ford reached peak production volume of 2 million identical vehicles a year in the early 1920s, he had cut the real cost to the customer by an additional two-thirds."
10. James P. Womack and Daniel T. Jones, *Lean Thinking: Banish Waste and Create Wealth in Your Corporation* (New York: Simon & Schuster Inc., 1996), 22–23. The authors make this observation.

11. Alfred P. Sloan Jr., *My Years with General Motors* (New York: Macfadden Books, McFadden-Bartell Corporation, 1963, 1965), 162. Sloan describes that "not many observers expected so catastrophic and almost whimsical a fall as Mr. Ford chose to take in May 1927 when he shut down his great River Rouge plant completely and kept it shut down for nearly a year to retool, leaving the field to Chevrolet unopposed and opening it up for Mr. Chrysler's Plymouth."

12. Ibid., 150.

13. Ibid., 139.

14. The discussions of this and the prior paragraph draw on descriptions of "standard volume" from Sloan, *My Years with General Motors*, 142–48. Using "standard volume," unit costs (or the actual cost of building a vehicle) could now become a direct measure of performance. Previously the company had to include a varying percentage of fixed overhead costs—since facilities, equipment, and other costs had to be recovered by the different numbers of vehicles produced and sold during a given month. Under Sloan's approach they no longer varied substantially as production volume increased or decreased.

15. Womack, Jones, and Roos, *The Machine that Changed the World*, 36. The authors state that for Ford's factories ". . . each manufacturing step led immediately to the next."

16. Sloan, *My Years with General Motors*, 138. Sloan describes why varying production to match changing demands was not optimal: "Such a practice would have reduced the risk of obsolescence and the cost of storing finished products for both dealer and manufacturer. On the other hand, absolutely level production—or the nearest to it that could be attained—was ideal from the standpoint of efficient utilization of plant and labor and from the standpoint of the employee's welfare." He then concludes with the need to find a reasonable balance between them.

17. Sloan, *My Years with General Motors*, 136. Sloan describes the importance of forecasting, indicating that, while some changes could be made during the model year, key aspects were "unalterably settled ahead of time."

18. Maryann N. Keller, "Dull at Any Speed: GM Never Learned to Shift Gears," *The Washington Post* (June 12, 2005): B1. Keller makes this statement. Joann Muller—in "Why Detroit Can't Compete," *Forbes* (November 27, 2006): 48—provides a breakdown of the higher health care costs and other benefits Detroit pays, as well as other areas that Toyota's costs are much lower. Included in this is a substantial per-vehicle cost that is caused by carrying excess capacity—a waste that Toyota minimizes.

19. By the 1970s, U.S. firms had really begun to feel the effects of the shrinking and splintering mass market. Collins and Porras—in *Built to Last*, 211—describe this timeframe as one during which "... the 'learning curve/market-share' theory of corporate strategy swept American business. Touted by prestigious management consulting firms and taught at top-flight business schools, it became a pervasive management tool adopted by thousands of executives across the corporate landscape. Operating under the theory that greater market share leads to lower costs and eventually greater profits, managers at a wide range of companies began cutting prices in order to gain market share."

20. This quote is found in Kevin and Jackie Freiberg, *Nuts! Southwest Airlines' Crazy Recipe for Business and Personal Success*, 49.

21. A number of sources describe this story of tolerance buildup in Ford's transmissions; for example, Henry R. Neave, *The Deming Dimension* (Knoxville, TN: SPC Press, Inc. 1990), 159–61. Neave provides a detailed account, showing that the Mazda-produced parts had such low variability that it caused the inspector who investigated the phenomenon to wonder if his gauge was working correctly. Thomas J. Cartin—in *Principles & Practices of TQM* (USA: ASQC Quality Press, 1993), 12–14—also describes this, extending the discussion to a description of Taguchi's loss function.

22. Edwards W. Deming, *Out of the Crisis* (USA: Massachusetts Institute of Technology, 1982), 143. Deming uses Taguchi's loss function to argue the "fallacy of zero defects," stating that there is "minimum loss at the nominal value."

23. Ruffa and Perozziello, in *Breaking the Cost Barrier*, provide analysis of the relationship between cycle time variation and the proliferation of workarounds.

24. Based on a similar figure from *The Manufacturing Affordability Development Program: A Structured Approach to Rapidly Improved Affordability*, Final Report.

25. Dertouzos, Lester, and Solow—in *Made in America*, 121—describe that the aerospace approach of introducing new technology is to "buy its way onto the plane."

26. This analogy was originated by Ruffa and Perozziello, in *Breaking the Cost Barrier*, 74.

27. *The Manufacturing Affordability Development Program: A Structured Approach to Rapidly Improved Affordability*, Final Report, reported dramatic drops in cycle time, inventory and cost with variation reductions of around twenty-five percent.

28. Mikel, Harry, and Richard Schroeder. *Six Sigma: The Breakthrough Man-*

agement Strategy Revolutionizing the World's Top Corporations (New York: Doubleday, 2000), 11. Harry and Schroeder describe such savings.

29. Peter F. Drucker, *Managing in a Time of Great Change* (New York: The Penguin Group, 1995), 49. Drucker states that, "All one can get by 'problem solving' is damage containment. Only opportunities produce results and growth."

30. From Clayton M. Christensen, *The Innovator's Dilemma: When New Technologies Cause Great Firms to Fail* (Harvard Business School Press, 1997, 2000 by President and Fellows of Harvard College), 168).

Chapter Three

1. Hammer, *The Agenda*, 249.

2. Robert J. Serling, *Legend and Legacy: The Story of Boeing and Its People* (New York: St. Martin's Press, 1992), 94. Serling states, "The early jet engines like the J-47 were notoriously slow to spool up—that is, to accelerate from low to full thrust." The author goes on to discuss the perils of test flying the B-47 aircraft: "So hazardous were the test flights in the early phases of the program that Boeing paid a bonus to those who flew them; some pilots were really afraid of this radically different airplane."

3. An excellent description of the construction and use of a power curve can be found in John D. Anderson, *Introduction to Flight* (USA: McGraw-Hill, Inc., 1978).

4. The data to support this figure were derived from the table on pages 214–15 in Sloan, *My Years with General Motors*. Its construction is outlined in the Appendix of the present book.

5. It is important to note that falling behind the value curve is not necessarily cause for immediate panic. Much as an aircraft uses its altitude to regain momentum, a company can sustain itself using the resources it has built up—using its cash reserves or selling off assets. However, these reserves can quickly dwindle; occurrences that are too frequent will leave insufficient "altitude" to recover.

6. The LRAC curves described in Michael Baye, *Managerial Economics and Business Strategy*, 4th ed. (Columbus, OH: McGraw Hill/Irwin, 2002), 187, which are widely accepted in management economics, look remarkably like the value curve described herein. Corporations use these to determine actions in response to changes in their operating environments, such as when it is most economical to shut down a factory's production or park an airline's planes. They are generally viewed as fairly rigid; management solutions do not generally aim to change their shape.

7. Clayton M. Christensen, *The Innovator's Dilemma: When New Technologies Cause Great Firms to Fail*, 163–64.

8. Womack and Jones, *Lean Thinking*, 20, describe the importance of making value-creating steps *flow*.

9. This is, for the most part, consistent with the three critical management tasks described by Womack and Jones, *Lean Thinking*, 19. *Operational flow* and *information flow* described herein relate very closely to Womack and Jones' "physical transformation task" and "information management task," respectively. The *flow of innovation* relates in part to their description of the "problem-solving task." Only *organizational flow* appears to be entirely new, although it is really an extension of the progression of the problem-solving task, as applied to those decision-making activities necessary to keep everyday activities on track.

10. Ford avoided substantial change until he was absolutely forced to because consumers were no longer interested in his open body design, as described in Sloan, *My Years with General Motors*, 162).

11. Keith L. Alexander, "US Airways' Call to Arms," *The Washington Post* (March 25, 2004): E1. Alexander quotes David N. Siegel, US Airways president and chief executive officer as saying, "the enemy is Southwest and that's who we have to focus on . . ." (on Southwest's impending entrance to the company's Philadelphia hub). Keith L. Alexander, "Southwest to Give US Airways Competition in Philadelphia," *The Washington Post* (October 29, 2003): E1. Alexander states that US Airways "generates about 25 percent of its revenue from operations at the [Philadelphia] airport."

12. Keith L. Alexander, "Southwest Enters US Airways Hub," *The Washington Post* (May 11, 2004): E1 and E5. Alexander identifies that US Airways began slashing prices from the first day Southwest began its Philadelphia operations. Fares to Chicago O'Hare that previously stood at $740 dropped to match Southwest's rates; a one-way walkup fare was now priced at $140, while this same ticket cost only $94 with fourteen-day advance purchase. Other fares dropped by as much as seventy-five percent.

13. The data to produce this chart were obtained from these companies' respective annual reports (as was the broader range of data to show Southwest's subsequent performance in figure 4.1).

14. I am grateful to Southwest Airlines for providing this information.

15. Jody Hoffer Gittell, *The Southwest Airlines Way: Using the Power of Relationships to Achieve High Performance* (New York: McGraw-Hill Companies, Inc., 2003), makes this observation, describing some of these efforts.

16. Ibid., 5. Gittell includes this statement made by an industry analyst speaking at the Massachusetts Institute of Technology.

17. Ibid., 5. Gittell goes on to refute this common misperception about Southwest's unions.
18. Trottman, "Up in the Air: Amid Crippled Rivals, Southwest Again Tries to Spread Its Wings—Low-Fare Airline Maintains Service, Mulls Expansion in Risky Bid for Traffic—Tapping $475 Million in Credit," *Wall Street Journal* (October 11, 2001). Trottman describes how the company's response to September 11th was to increase its presence. Gittell, in *The Southwest Airlines Way,* 242, indicates that Southwest stuck to its no-layoff policy.
19. This quotation is included with this overall description in Walton and Huey, *Sam Walton: Made in America* (New York: Doubleday, 1992), 194.
20. Slater, in *The Wal-Mart Decade,* 176, identifies that it was on April 15, 2002 that "Wal-Mart topped the *Fortune* 500 list of the largest American corporations for the first time." This was the same year that Kmart was in bankruptcy (57).
21. Walton and Huey, in *Sam Walton: Made in America,* 195, provide this data. Ortega, in *In Sam We Trust,* 108–10, describes the economic plight of the early 1980s, when "retailers were hit hard too—especially discounters, who were facing the toughest competition most of them had ever seen." Ortega further states that "big national chains and small regional outfits alike had been trying to expand as fast as possible . . ." They seem to have been caught off guard when demand suddenly dropped. It was during this time frame that Wal-Mart opened up ninety-one new stores and increased its sales by as much as forty-nine percent per year.
22. The data to produce this chart were obtained from Kmart and Wal-Mart annual reports. The comparisons made here with Kmart only refer to its performance prior to its restructuring due to bankruptcy; no assessment of its subsequent condition is made. Kmart's 1995 annual report states that, not including extraordinary expenses, the 1995 net loss would have been $130M vs. $571M ($130M therefore used for the calculation shown in this figure).
23. The data to produce this chart were obtained from Toyota and Ford's annual reports. *Annual Report 2002, Ford Motor Corporation* (36–37) provides data showing that the two data points outlying Ford's value curve were years marked by substantial increases in subsidized financing and leasing, cash rebates, and other incentives. In addition, the data point identified as affected by a one-time divestiture (identified in *Annual Report, 1998, Ford Motor Corporation*) was adjusted by subtracting the proceeds of this sale from the net income used in its calculation for the chart.
24. Toyota continued its record profits and in 2003 became the second-largest automobile producer, with profits greater than the Big Three combined.

Figure 3.5 also shows the effect of others' factory incentives on their value margins; Ford's huge customer incentives did seem to succeed in driving up demand—but its actions during these years also drove up loss well above its value curve. Toyota now challenges GM to become the world's largest automobile producer, an event that seems less than a surprise, as projected by Sholnn Freeman, "Toyota Expects to Be World's No. 1 Automaker Next Year," *The Washington Post* (December 23, 2006): A1 and A4.

Chapter Four

1. Peter Drucker, *Managing in a Time of Great Change* (New York: Truman Talley Books/Dutton, 1995), 21–22.
2. Deming, in *The New Economics,* 180, describes special causes. Calculation of Southwest Airlines' control limits uses the approach of "individuals control charts" as described by the *Engineering Statistics Handbook,* which can be found at: http://www.itl.nist.gov/div898/handbook/pmc/section 3/pmc322.htm.
3. Taiichi Ohno, in *Toyota Production System,* 6, refers to a key one of these initiatives, *kanban,* as "the means by which the Toyota production system moves smoothly." But Ohno goes on to state (33) that implementing this depends on the broader capabilities of the system: "Until one completely grasps this method of doing work so that things will flow, it is impossible to go right into the kanban system when the time comes." He further states, "When people have no concept of this, it is very difficult to introduce the kanban system."
4. Gittell, in *The Southwest Airlines Way,* 216, describes what happened when Continental Airline's Continental Lite cut its turnaround times from fifty minutes down to twenty minutes—with a significant impact on customer quality. The book quotes from Perry Flint, "Continental Divide," *Air Transport World* (September 1994): "On-time performance dropped precipitously and customer complaints—the old and persistent Continental bugaboo—rose."
5. Frederick Winslow Taylor, *The Principles of Scientific Management* (New York: W. W. Norton & Company, 1967, first copyrighted in 1911), 100. Taylor compares "rule of thumb management" to a well-planned and controlled operation that defines everything.
6. *The Manufacturing Affordability Development Program: A Structured Approach to Rapidly Improved Affordability,* Final Report, describes these results.
7. The analogy of police cruisers acting as pace cars was described by Ruffa and Perozziello in *Breaking the Cost Barrier.*

8. Based on a similar figure from *The Manufacturing Affordability Development Program, A Structured Approach to Rapidly Improved Affordability,* Final Report.
9. Drucker, *Managing in a Time of Great Change* (49).
10. This is the same basic analogy as is presented in "the parable of the boiled frog" in Peter M. Senge, *The Fifth Discipline: The Art & Practice of The Learning Organization* (22).

Part II: The Foundational Elements

1. Womack and Jones, in *Lean Thinking,* 15–26, describes these elements of lean manufacturing: *value, value streams, flow, pull,* and *perfection.*

Chapter Five

1. Peter Drucker makes this statement in *The Effective Executive* (New York: HarperCollins Publishers, 1966), 145.
2. These facts on Ford's growth in the 1950s, its automobile lines, and expectation of the "upper middle" segment can be found in: Peter F. Drucker, *Innovation and Entrepreneurship: Practices and Principles* (New York: Harper & Row, Publishers, Inc., 1985), 51.
3. Deming, *The New Economics* (105).
4. Drucker, *Innovation and Entrepreneurship* (51). Drucker states that, when Ford found that this segment had been overtaken by another one, the company quickly filled it with the Thunderbird, "the greatest success of any American car since Henry Ford, Sr., had introduced his Model T in 1908."
5. Thomas H. Johnson and Robert S. Kaplan, *Relevance Lost: The Rise and Fall of Management Accounting* (USA: Harvard Business School Press, 1987), 9.
6. This same accumulation of waste contributed to similar problems in the American aircraft industry in the years following World War II; as one aerospace executive noted, "As business got better, efficiency got worse." This is described in John E. Steiner, *Problems and Challenges: A Path to the Future* (paper presented to the Royal Aeronautical Society, London, England, October 10, 1974), 1.
7. Senge, *The Fifth Discipline* (325–32).
8. Senge, *The Fifth Discipline* (333), introduces this term and makes this observation.
9. Richard J. Schonberger, *Let's Fix It: Overcoming the Crisis in Manufacturing* (New York: The Free Press, 2001), 7.

10. Womack, Jones, and Roos, *The Machine that Changed the World,* 250.

11. Drucker, in *Management Challenges for the 21st Century,* 28–29, states, "Another critical implication is that the starting point for management can no longer be its own products or service, and not even its known market and its known end-users for its products and services. The starting point has to be what *customers consider value.* The starting point has to be the assumption—an assumption amply proven by all our experience—that the customer never buys what the supplier sells. What is value to the customer is always something quite different from what is value or quality to the supplier."

12. Womack, Jones, and Roos, *The Machine that Changed the World,* 30, describes some of the maintenance that drivers could do themselves.

13. Kevin and Jackie Freiberg, in *Nuts,* 51, make the statement that "The hub-and-spoke system is an efficient way to fill an airplane, but it usually doesn't offer efficient aircraft utilization." Charles A. O'Reilly and Jeffrey Pfeffer—in *Hidden Value: How Great Companies Achieve Extraordinary Results with Ordinary People* (USA: Harvard Business School Press, 2000), 31—recognized that "Southwest thus needs a much lower load factor to break even."

14. Keith L. Alexander, "Legacy' Airlines Get No Lift: Despite Passenger Numbers, Established Carriers Struggle Mightily," *The Washington Post* (July 16, 2004): E1. Alexander describes that Delta, United, US Airways, and Northwest "are filling more than 80% of their seats on many routes—the highest percentage since the attacks." The article then quotes John Heimlich, chief economist with the Air Transport Association, as saying, "If airlines are still losing money in the summer, then when can they make money?"

15. Kevin and Jackie Freiberg include this quote by Herb Kelleher in *Nuts,* 62.

16. Southwest Airlines provided this statement to this author.

17. This statement was provided by Southwest Airlines to this author.

18. This statement was provided by Southwest Airlines to this author.

19. The U.S. Department of Transportation seems to have coined the term, "the Southwest effect" in its report: Randall D. Bennett and James M. Craun, *The Airline Deregulation Evolution Continues: The Southwest Effect* (Washington, DC: U.S. Department of Transportation, Office of Aviation Analysis.

20. Sholnn Freeman, "Toyota Expects to Be World's No. 1 Automaker Next Year," *The Washington Post* (December 23, 2006): A1 and A4. Freeman quotes Jim Press, Toyota's U.S. chief executive: "We had the foresight to

start hybrid development earlier than other companies. This year we will sell more hybrids than Cadillac will sell cars."

21. Southwest won the industry's "Triple Crown"—a measure of the least delays, complaints, and mishandled bags—while earning its reputation for its low fares and operating efficiency. Gittell, in *The Southwest Airlines Way*, 7, states that it held this honor for *entire years*—from 1992 through 1996—a tremendous feat since no other airline has held it for more than a month at a time.

22. Jeffrey K. Liker, *The Toyota Way: 14 Management Principles from the World's Greatest Manufacturer* (USA: McGraw-Hill, 2003), 5.

23. Ibid., 5.: "According to a 2003 study in Consumer Reports, one of the most widely read magazines for auto-buying customers, 15 of the 38 most reliable models from any manufacturer over the last seven years were made by Toyota/Lexus. No other manufacturer comes close."

24. "Airlines Reward Passengers for Late Departures," Business Class, *The Washington Post* (October 2, 2002): E1. Keith L. Alexander reports that "US Airways and Delta said they will give 1,500 bonus miles to passengers on flights between Reagan National and New York's LaGuardia Airport that leave more than five minutes late."

25. Bill Brubaker, "Low-Fare and Hoping: Delta's Pricing Move Simplifies Rates but Leads Carriers in a Risky Direction," *The Washington Post* (January 9, 2005): F1 and F8.

26. Bob Ortega, in *In Sam We Trust*, 134, contrasts Wal-Mart with others, stating "By holding constant sales and promotions, many stores in effect train shoppers to wait until there's a sale to buy anything. Everyday low-pricing was supposed to do the opposite, and at Wal-Mart, it worked." It describes various forms of savings by not having to hold special promotions.

27. Walton and Huey, *Sam Walton: Made in America*, 128.

28. I am grateful to Ms. Joy McCord, Hibbett VP for Marketing, for describing the importance of Hibbett's up-front value assessment. Lawrence Rothman—in "Fool on the Street: Hibbett Sports' Home Run?", *The Motley Fool* (July 19, 2007): www.fool.com/investing/value/2007/07/19/fool-on-the-street-hibbett-sports-home-run.aspx)—describes Hibbett's successful strategy, citing the company's statistics that its operating margins were 12.1% in 2006—the highest in its industry. Kayleen Schaefer—in "Hibbett Thinks Small to Think Big," *Footwear News* (June 24, 2002): 10—supports the point that Hibbett is aggressively opening stores while others have been trimming their activities. A description of Hibbett's history and market evaluation is contained in *International Directory of Company Histories*, vol. 70 (St. James Press, 2005).

29. Don Garrity made this statement to this author about the nature of his business.
30. Johnson and Kaplan, *Relevance Lost,* 4.
31. Johnson and Kaplan, *Relevance Lost,* 128. They provide some history on this, describing how "the high cost of processing information" apparently doomed one approach around the turn of the twentieth century that sought to link "every effort of analysis . . . to the purpose for which the business is being run." The book speculates that their "high cost-to-benefit ratio" was "perhaps the main reason for [their] disapperance . . ."
32. Southwest Airlines provided information to this author regarding its actions to keep employees focused on its revenue and profitability, including its large employee education program called "Knowing the Score."
33. Gittell, *The Southwest Airlines Way,* 31–32, contains this typical description by Southwest employees. This book coins the term, *relational coordination,* describing it as particularly useful in environments high in uncertainty, 50. Southwest's use of positions designed for "boundary spanning" appears to be a powerful means of giving its people a broad span of insight.
34. This term is used and the approach is described in Walton and Huey, *Sam Walton: Made in America,* 227.

Chapter Six

1. Womack, and Jones, *Lean Thinking,* 282.
2. Ruffa and Perozziello, in *Breaking the Cost Barrier,* 209, describe the case of a factory that directly targeted the outcome of slashing its inventories without first addressing its underlying drivers. The result was "stock-outs and workarounds mounting to the point that operations were nearly crippled." The authors go on to state that "Only once inventories were increased was order restored."
3. Charles H. Fine, *Clock Speed: Winning Industry Control in the Age of Temporary Advantage* (New York: Perseus Books, 1998), 90–91. Fine discusses this *bullwhip effect.* Jones, Daniel, and Womack—in *Seeing the Whole: Mapping the Extended Value Stream,* (Brookline, MA: The Lean Enterprise Institute, Inc., 2002)—term this "the Forrester Effect," documented by MIT's Jay Forrester in the 1960s.
4. This figure is intended to show how inventories are used to buffer factories from actual demands. This approach is widely described in works on production and inventory control, such as Thomas E. Vollman, William L. Berry, and D. Clay Whybark, *Manufacturing Planning and Control Systems* (New York: Irwin Professional Publishing, 1992), figures 17.3 and 17.7.

5. Peter M. Senge, *The Fifth Discipline*, 49, gives an in-depth description of "the beer game," and an assessment of the dynamic effect it depicts.

6. There are many examples of this; for instance, Charles Fine describes in *Clock Speed* (99) how Ford and Xerox restructured their supply chains. A description of the problems faced in downsizing supply chains can be found in: Richard Foster and Sara Kaplan, *Creative Destruction: Why Companies that Are Built to Last Underperform the Market—And How to Successfully Transform Them* (Doubleday, USA, 2001), 1. The authors state: "Although GE led the way, many U.S. companies downsized during the 1980s. Most saw short-term improvement in their financial performance as a result of their reductions. But far fewer know what to do after the cuts to refocus or revitalize their companies. As a result, some disappeared. Some, like IBM, went through real crisis before they turned around."

7. Charles Fine identifies in *Clock Speed* (99) this example. Michael Dell, *Direct from Dell: Strategies that Revolutionized an Industry* (USA: Harper-Collins, 1999), 78–79. Dell describes the benefits of compressing the "long chain of partners" that are typically in the middle of delivering a product to the customer, which gained widespread attention.

8. Timothy M. Lasseter, *Balanced Sourcing: Cooperation and Competition in Supplier Relationships* (USA: Jossey-Bass, 1998), 61, uses an example of a firm whose supply chain consolidation actually *increased* its costs by thirty percent to show that more is needed than simply reducing the number of suppliers as is too often done. In *The Toyota Way* (205), Jeffrey Liker relates a similar result, describing how Ford put in place a contract with a logistics provider to create a just-in-time system delivering "every part, every day" to its assembly lines. This ultimately failed, costing logistics $100 million more a year and taking around a year to undo.

9. Womack and Jones, *Lean Thinking* (19), describe the concept of the *value stream.*

10. This is based on the chart illustrating aircraft spares lead times, contained in: *Supplier Utilization Through Responsive Grouped Enterprises*, Submission to the Supply Chain Council Awards for Excellence in Supply Chain Operations and Management (http://www.acq.osd.mil/log/sci/awards/2002_sci_award/submissions/SupplyChainAward_DLA.pdf). The subsequent description of lag in producing a spare part is based on a sampling of typical airframe parts studied by the author and presented at Aviation Week's Air Expo conference in 2001.

11. It is important to note that enormous lead times are only part of the wasteful activities that occur at each step along the way. Womack and Jones, in *Lean Thinking*, 37, describe the "value stream map." A true value stream

map depicts not only the time that separates these activities, but also excess motion, processing time, and stores of inventory that must be staged at each interface. The latter has far-reaching effects, not only tying up the firm's capital, but causing the additional waste of stocking, tracking, and reissuing at each step along the way—activities that add to costs while creating no value for the customer.

12. Hammer, Michael, and Champy, *Reengineering the Corporation: A Manifesto for Business Revolution* (New York: HarperBusiness, 1993), 124.
13. James M. Morgan, and Jeffrey K. Liker, in *The Toyota Product Development System*, 183–97, describe Toyota's rigorous program for developing and certifying suppliers.
14. Liker, in *The Toyota Way*, 120–21 and 217, describes Toyota's relationship with Trim Masters, a US supplier of seats for the Camry and Avalon vehicles produced in Toyota's Georgetown, Kentucky plant.
15. A description of Hibbett's store-level training is contained in *International Directory of Company Histories*, vol. 70 (St. James Press, 2005).
16. Walton and Huey, *Sam Walton: Made in America*, 186, make this statement. Elliott, Dorinda, and Powell, in "Wal-Mart Nation," *Time*, (June 19, 2005), describe Wal-Mart's oversight of suppliers, quoting a factory manager who states, "Wal-Mart's requirements are very tight—on quality, ethical standards, production lead times. They've pushed us to achiever better in all ways."
17. This statement and the information concerning Wal-Mart's inventory levels in the prior paragraph can be found in Lasseter, *Balanced Sourcing*, 113–14.
18. Lasseter, *Balanced Sourcing: Cooperation and Competition in Supplier Relationships*, 91.
19. Ibid., 93.
20. Gittell, in *The Southwest Airlines Way*, 132–36, provides examples of the boundary spanning activities performed by Southwest's operations agents.
21. Andrew Raskin, "Who's Minding the Store?" *CNN Money.com, Business 2.0 Magazine* (February 1, 2003).
22. Walton and Huey, *Sam Walton: Made in America*, 213–14.
23. Charlie S. Field and Donna B. Stoddard—in "Getting IT Right," *Harvard Business Review* (February 2004): 72–73—indicate that many Information Technology programs run into problems. Statistics derived from Gartner Research give a measure of the loss, indicating that companies worldwide waste about $500 billion. The article describes poorly implemented systems ranging from ERP and CRM to data warehouses that are not implemented well.
24. Walton and Huey, *Sam Walton: Made in America*, 206.

25. Schonberger, in *Let's Fix It!*, 12, describes that many manufacturers "have large sums tied up in still capable supermachines bought years ago. Continued use of such equipment holds the manufacturer hostage to the batch-and-queue system."

26. Liker, in *The Toyota Way*, 162, describes a meeting with Mikio Kitano who was in charge of Toyota's largest industrial complex—the Motomachi complex. During this encounter with an IT person who presented a classic system design flowchart he stated, "At Toyota we do not make information systems. We make cars. Show me the process of making cars and how the information system supports that."

27. Robert Slater, *The Wal-Mart Decade: How a New Generation of Leaders Turned Sam Walton's Legacy into the Worlds #1 Company* (USA: Penguin, 2003), 62.

28. Ortega, in *In Sam We Trust*, 128–29, contains this statement and describes how important it was to Wal-Mart's success that it jumped to the forefront of this "just-in-time distribution." Richard Schonberger, "Supply Chains: Tightening the Links," *Manufacturing Engineering* (Society of Manufacturing Engineers, September, 2006, Volume 137 No. 3), states that: "For its own distribution centers, Wal-Mart pioneered cross-docking . . . reportedly delivers 85% of its merchandise using cross-docking." Liker, in *The Toyota Way*, 203, points out that cross-docking is also central to Toyota's ability to maintain smooth flow, synchronizing materiel flow with different replenishment time needs from suppliers that are geographically dispersed. The author compares Toyota's success with another automotive manufacturer who unsuccessfully attempted this, seemingly (though not specified in his conclusion) because it was not done in a way that coordinated all forms of flow throughout the value stream.

29. Toyota also has methods in place to communicate its requirements to its network of suppliers. Liker, in *The Toyota Way*, 122, describes the iterative way in which this is done—coordinating the complex array of changes with its suppliers that result when a customer makes a change to a car's configuration.

30. Ortega, *In Sam We Trust*, 130, contains the information used in this paragraph; Ortega also indicates that Wal-Mart's distribution costs of less than two cents per dollar represented the lowest figure in the industry.

31. This statement along with the information concerning its schedule optimizing software was provided by Southwest Airlines to this author.

32. This information was provided by Southwest Airlines to this author.

33. Dertouzos, Lester, and Solow, in *Made in America*, 67, describe America's shortfall in translating new discoveries into products and services.

34. Ruffa and Perozziello, in *Breaking the Cost Barrier*, 33, describe how in aerospace, "Coordination of work became a formal process largely accomplished through bureaucratic channels. No longer could an engineer make changes to a design by simply walking out to the production shop to discuss it with the chief builder, as Wilbur and Orville could with their mechanic, Charlie Taylor."

35. Womack, Jones, and Roos, in *The Machine that Changed the World*, 129, point out that Alfred Sloan grouped together scientists and engineers for this purpose.

36. Ruffa and Perozziello, *Breaking the Cost Barrier*, 163.

37. Womack, Jones, and Roos, *The Machine that Changed the World*, 118. Figure 5.1 shows the strikingly faster recovery time for lean producers from product introduction.

38. Over the last decade it has become widely accepted that good product development can mitigate seventy to eighty percent of product cost, as pointed out in: Lasseter, *Balanced Sourcing: Cooperation and Competition in Supplier Relationships*, 133. Moreover, early coordination is critical to making products more producible and affordable, as described in: Ruffa and Perozziello, *Breaking the Cost Barrier*, 164.

39. Morgan, James, and Liker, Jeffrey. *The Toyota Product Development System*, 45, contains this statement. It also describes, 153, the concept of the *obeya* room (noted in the prior paragraph).

40. Morgan and Liker, *The Toyota Product Development System*, 170–71.

41. Womack, Jones, and Roos, *The Machine that Changed the World*, 131–32.

42. *Profiting from Uncertainty*, 128–30, describes alternatives to such all-or-nothing decisions, using a decision-tree process.

Chapter Seven

1. Senge, *The Dance of Change*, 296, quotes this statement made by H. Thomas Johnson.

2. Womack, Jones, and Roos, in *The Machine that Changed the World*, 48, identify these facts, stating also that Toyota had produced few automobiles to this point, mostly relegated to making trucks for the war effort by Japan's military government.

3. Ibid., 53–54. The authors describe this labor settlement leading to substantial management concessions—and setting the stage for Toyota's system of management.

4. Walton and Huey, in *Sam Walton: Made in America*, 49, describe that this

constant need to overcome tremendous barriers as he grew his company was perhaps the greatest contributor to the success of Wal-Mart.

5. Ibid., 87.

6. Womack, Jones, and Roos, in *The Machine that Changed the World*, 51, make this point.

7. Kiyoshi Suzaki *The New Manufacturing Challenge: Techniques for Continuous Improvement* (New York: The Free Press, 1987), 124. Suzaki provides an overview of Toyota's "production leveling."

8. Womack and Jones, *Lean Thinking*, 70.

9. Jones, Dan, and Womack, *Seeing the Whole: Mapping the Extended Value Stream* (Brookline, MA: The Lean Enterprise Institute, 2002), 45. The authors describe Toyota's use of "standard inventory." Dennis, Pascal, and Shook—in *Lean Production Simplified: A Plain-Language Guide to the World's Most Powerful Production System* (New York: Productivity Press, 2002), 25—describe *muri* as "unevenness or fluctuations in work . . ." They further describe *mura* as the disruption caused by this. This book (73) refers to a supermarket as "a controlled inventory of parts that is used to schedule an upstream process through some sort of kanban." It further describes this as a means for mitigating some sort of disconnect in flow, such as mismatches in cycle times, unreliable processes, or long lead times.

10. Shigeo Shingo, *A Study of the Toyota Production System: From an Industrial Engineering Viewpoint* (Portland, OR: Productivity Press, 1989), 139.

11. Similar to a figure published on the web site www.dscr.dla.mil as of May 23, 1998, related to the SURGE (Supplier Utilization of Responsive Grouped Enterprises) program.

12. Richard J. Schonberger, *World Class Manufacturing* (New York: Free Press, 1986), 111.

13. This calculation can be found in Ruffa and Perozziello, *Breaking the Cost Barrier,* 151–54.

14. Kevin and Jackie Freiberg, in *Nuts!* 197, describe the firms' flexibility, stating that Southwest's Top Wrench award is given to mechanics that become qualified to service the entire fleet. *The Secret Behind High Profits at Low Fare Airlines: A Majority Fly the Boeing 737 Exclusively* (The Boeing Company, Seattle, June 14, 2002, found at www.boeing.com/commercial/news/feature/profit.html) provides facts on efficiencies that Southwest gains using only the 737 aircraft.

15. Kevin and Jackie Freiberg, in *Nuts!* 134–35, include this statement as part of a description of the impact of flight delays by Jim Wimberly, vice president of ground operations at Southwest Airlines.

16. Micheline Maynard, "Survival of the Fittest and Leanest Becomes Strategy for the Airlines," *The New York Times* (October 30, 2004; A1, C3) states that Southwest uses seventy-five people per plane while the industry average is one hundred (twenty-five percent fewer). Southwest reported to the present author that it has further improved—dropping down from 86 to 68 employees per plane from 2003 to 2006. Moreover, over five years, employee productivity improved more than twenty percent. It can therefore be shown that the company provides the better reliability and service for many fewer resources than a traditional approach would take—representing a classic "lean" result.

17. O'Reilly and Pfeffer, in *Hidden Value,* 31, indicate that, with fewer of its aircraft tied up in traffic or maintenance delays (or by the disruption caused by others), Southwest needs fewer planes. Kevin and Jackie Freiberg, in *Nuts!* 60, indicate it uses around thirty-five less than competitors with "industry-average turnaround time."

18. Andrew Raskin, "Who's Minding the Store?" *CNN Money.com, Business 2.0 Magazine* (February 1, 2003).

19. Dertouzos, Lester, and Solow, in *Made in America,* 182, discuss the difference between how work was arranged in Japanese versus American automotive industries.

20. Johnson and Kaplan, in *Relevance Lost,* 214, make the observation that "U.S. industrial engineers were directed to commit the bulk of their time to speeding up production processes to reduce cycle time." Womack, Jones, and Roos, in *The Machine that Changed the World,* 53, state that, conversely, "by the late 1950's, [Ohno] had reduced the time required to change dies from a day to an astonishing three minutes and eliminated the need for die-change specialists."

21. Kiyoshi Suzaki, *The New Manufacturing Challenge* (New York: The Free Press, 1987), 34. Suzaki describes internal and external setups.

22. Kevin and Jackie Freiberg, in *Nuts!* 81, quote Phil Condit, Boeing's president and CEO at the time, describing the work his firm does that clearly supports Southwest's setups.

23. Ibid., 51. The authors compare Southwest's average of 10.5 to the industry average of 5.0 flights per gate. They also state, "A typical Boeing 737 in the Southwest fleet is used 11.5 hours per day, compared with the average 8.6 hours a day of other carriers." (Southwest confirmed to the present author that a daily utilization of about 11 hours still applies.) With more than double the average flights per gate, it more fully utilizes its ground crews— not to mention its planes, which it keeps in the air about a third more than other carriers.

24. Womack and Jones, in *Lean Thinking,* 27, define *kaizen* in this way.

25. James Morgan and Jeffrey Liker, in *The Toyota Product Development System,* 194–95, contain this quote and identify that Toyota outsources over seventy percent of its vehicle content.

26. Ibid., 182–83.

27. Liker, *The Toyota Way,* 201.

28. "Part Grouping: Angioplasty for the Supply Chain," by Colonel Michael C. Yusi, USAF, *Air Force Journal of Logistics,* Spring 2003, 15–26.

29. Gittell, in *The Southwest Airlines Way,* 157, includes this quote.

30. Morgan and Liker, in *The Toyota Product Development System,* 42–43, describe how Toyota stands out by maximizing the number of vehicles it builds using a single platform, and "commonizing" key aspects of vehicle geometry—forms, shapes and holes in sheet metal—and standardizing subassemblies to make manufacturing more efficient.

31. Liker, *The Toyota Way,* 160.

32. This quote, by Don Garrity, is from discussions with this author.

33. This quote, by Don Garrity, was made during discussions with this author.

34. The information on Garrity Tool Company presented here was identified during the author's factory tour and subsequent discussions with Don Garrity, John Entwistle, and Ryan DeAnda. Quotes by Don Garrity are from subsequent discussions with this author. The company's web site reports that it received honors including the Indianapolis Mayor's Eagle Award, the State of Indiana Quality Improvement Award, Indiana Growth 100 Awards, Indiana Business Award, and Indiana Heartland Ernst & Young Entrepreneur of the Year (finalist).

35. Charles N. Smart, "Sweet Spot: The Relationship Between Forecasting and Optimal Stocking Levels," *APICS Magazine* (February, 2004): 55.

36. Annual Report 2004, *Cost Reduction,* Toyota Motor Corporation, 27.

Chapter Eight

1. Walton and Huey, *Sam Walton: Made in America,* 86. Abe Marks, Head of Hartfield Zody's at the time and first president of NMRI, remarked that Sam Walton's genius was in using information technology to help pull things together.

2. This is a well-known story of Khrushchev's visit to an American supermarket, depicting him as so astonished to see such a wide range of goods that he simply assumed that it had to be propaganda. The news stories at the time support the general occurrence of such an event, and make his portrayed reaction seem plausible. For instance, "The Education of Mr. K.,"

Time (October 5, 1959), described how Khrushchev shuffled his schedule, changing the location and time for his supermarket visit. Moreover, Khrushchev's speech published in *The New York Times* (September 22, 1959: 23), praised the manager of the supermarket he visited that day in a way that seemed to show he was amazed by what he saw.

3. The conflict between push and pull is described by Doug Bartholomew, "Lean vs. ERP," *Industry Week* (July 19, 1999): 24.

4. Eliyahu M. Goldratt and Jeff Cox, *The Goal: A Process of Ongoing Improvement* (Great Burrington, MA: The North River Press, 1984), 100.

5. Womack, Jones, and Roos, *The Machine that Changed the World,* 36.

6. Goldratt and Cox, *The Goal,* 104.

7. Ruffa and Perozziello, in *Breaking the Cost Barrier,* 118, contain this feedback on high automation from some aerospace manufacturers. Schonberger, in *Let's Fix It!* 12, further states, "IT applications have their place in industry. But the legacy systems that schedule, dispatch, release, track, count, and cost everything that moves are, by today's standards, largely non-value-adding wastes . . ."

8. Walton and Huey, *Sam Walton: Made in America,* 86.

9. Ortega, in *In Sam We Trust,* 43–44, makes this statement, and quotes Cullen's reference to "monstrous" stores as part of the subsequent statement. Ortega further discusses that Piggly-Wiggly had previously attempted this self-service approach, which was shut down before it had a chance to take hold. Cullen held on with this approach longer, and was successful — giving it time to show that it had caught on with customers. By enabling a store to carry such a range of items made it appealing for customers to travel to lower rent areas, which also helped reduce costs. As a result, the supermarket eventually overtook thousands of small grocers, and has become the standard for today's grocery stores.

10. Kiyoshi Suzaki, in *The New Manufacturing Challenge,* 148, provides a description of *kanban.*

11. Ohno, in *Toyota Production System,* 26–27, credited the supermarket for inspiring his creation of a new system that decades later would itself come to be viewed as the benchmark for businesses everywhere. He states that "From the supermarket we got the idea of viewing the earlier process in production as a kind of store."

12. Suzaki, in *The New Manufacturing Challenge,* 155–56, explains that making *kanban* work means also following a number of other fundamental rules. Ohno, in *Toyota Production System,* 27, describes that, "Our biggest problem with this [kanban] system was how to avoid throwing the earlier process into confusion when a later process picked up large quantities

at a time. Eventually, after trial and error, we came up with production leveling . . ."

13. Suzaki, *The New Manufacturing Challenge,* 154.
14. Ruffa and Perozziello, *Breaking the Cost Barrier,* 154.
15. Ibid., 101.
16. Gittell, in *The Southwest Airlines Way,* 126, describes these activities, which act just like external setup activities (a classic lean technique described earlier) in keeping Southwest's consistent gate times, a key to keeping flights moving on schedule and keeping customers satisfied.
17. A similar point is made in *The Toyota Way* (110–11), stating, "There are many examples of push scheduling throughout Toyota." It further states, "These days Toyota is increasingly using computer systems for scheduling. For example, when ordering parts from suppliers, Toyota is moving to electronic *kanban* rather than sorting and sending cards back. In this case, it does not have to be either/or." Also, ". . . Toyota will often use a computer system for scheduling some operations, but then use manual cues like cards or white boards to visually control the process."
18. Suzaki, in *The New Manufacturing Challenge,* 98, identifies *poka-yoke* as a Japanese word that means "foolproof mechanism."
19. Ibid., 6.
20. Ruffa and Perozziello, *Breaking the Cost Barrier,* 132.
21. Walton and Huey, *Made in America,* 213.
22. Ortega, *In Sam We Trust,* 129–30.
23. The U.S. General Accounting Office cited an example of such an item, praising key attributes of a system whose creation was led by the author to identify and address what this book describes as "hotspots" causing variation and affecting the risk of obtaining critical military spare parts during wartime surges in demand: *Defense Inventory: Improved Industrial Base Assessments for Army War Reserve Spares Could Save Money* (The United States General Accounting Office, GAO-02-650, July 2002), 9.
24. In some cases this meant investing in suppliers' surge capacity, adding to or optimizing equipment or obtaining new tooling. In others, it meant accumulating strategic stores of key materials and partially finished components at their lowest possible state of value—many times right at their source—integrating them into their ongoing production to keep supplies fresh and current.
25. Southwest Airlines' 2004 Annual Report indicated that it used fuel hedging extensively while major competitors used it less during the 2004 price spike. Since fuel prices are one of the most significant operating costs for carriers, mitigating uncertainty in this area seems to have been essential to

Southwest's success. I am grateful to Southwest for providing additional background on this, identifying that the company identified this as a significant risk after the first gulf war, when prices spiked—as did the other airlines—but Southwest's sustained profitability permitted it to maintain its hedges while many others could not afford to hold them. Since 1999, fuel hedging has saved the company almost $3 billion, and the company continues to be well hedged.

26. Walton and Huey, *Made in America*, 89.

27. In December, 2006, it was widely reported that Chrysler corporation set aside half a billion dollars for its dealers to move 2006 models—equating to thousands of dollars per vehicle. Ford identifies multibillion dollar incentives in its *2002 Annual Report.*

28. Annual Report 2006, *An Interview with the President,* Toyota Motor Corporation (Year ended March 31, 2006): 10.

29. Learning curves are notably absent in such definitive works as Yasuhiro Monden, *The Toyota Production System,* 3rd ed. (Norcross, GA: Engineering and Management Press, 1998), and Shigeo Shingo, *A Study of the Toyota Production System from an Industrial Engineering Standpoint* (Portland, OR: Productivity Press, 1989). Instead, Toyota takes care to remove waste prior to production; the company puts in place further improvements in preplanned increments to maintain synchronization—a very different approach than the constant drift (and accompanying lag) built into America's traditional management system.

30. The data used to produce this chart were obtained from Toyota's annual reports.

31. Annual Report 2004, *President's Message* (Toyota Motor Corporation, Year ended March 31, 2005): 11, makes this statement and describes how Toyota is steering through the increasing challenges presented by fluctuating economic conditions and market changes through its "globally balanced operations and a full product lineup." Annual Report 2002, *Interview with the President* (Toyota Motor Corporation, 2002) describes that Toyota's establishment of "an operating system that incorporates the most effective use of global-scale manufacturing . . . is crucial."

32. Annual Report 2003, *Taking the Initiative in Innovative Production Engineering,* (Toyota Motor Corporation, 26, describes such measures as the UMR, or Unit & Material Manufacturing Reform, aimed at "achieving unprecedented reductions in the production costs of unit components." Subsequent annual reports give strong evidence·that Toyota continues to achieve these gains.

33. Annual Report 2005, *Positioned for the Future: Cost Reduction Activities* (Toyota Motor Corporation), 33.

Chapter Nine

1. Annual Report 2006, *President's Message,* (Toyota Motor Corporation), 7.
2. Glenn Frankel, "Ireland's Highflying Mr. Low Fare," *The Washington Post* (March 5, 2004): E1, makes this statement and describes Ryanair's rise from O'Leary's trip to Dallas in 1991 to its status as the world's most profitable airline — with hopes of becoming Europe's largest by the end of the decade.
3. Hammer and Champy, in *Reengineering the Corporation,* 150, describe a "case for action," stating that the information that makes it up probably will not be new, but pulling it together will help show the need for taking action. Much like reengineering, lean dynamics is transformational and far-reaching; as such, it requires a similar broad-based approach for convincing people that what they are about to do is critical to their future.
4. Ralston, Bill, and Wilson, *The Scenario Planning Handbook: Developing Strategies in Uncertain Times* (USA: Thomson South-western, 2006), 4.
5. *Annual Report 2002, Ford Motor Company,* makes this statement.
6. The data to produce this chart were obtained from Toyota's and Ford's annual reports.
7. These principles are consistent with those identified by Hammer and Champy, *Reengineering the Corporation,* 156, which states that a vision should contain three basic elements: a focus on operations; measurable objectives and metrics; and it should change the basis for competition in the industry.
8. "Business in Brief," *The Washington Post* (May 12, 2004): E2. Caption under a photograph of a Toyota showroom in Tokyo provides these facts. Toyota's industry leadership is projected in: Sholnn Freeman, "Toyota Expects to Be World's No. 1 Automaker Next Year," *The Washington Post* (December 23, 2006): A1 and A4.
9. Greg Schneider, "Ford Makes Profit, but Loses Ground," *The Washington Post* (January 23, 2004): E2. A similar statement was made in this article.
10. Gittell, in *The Southwest Airlines Way,* 7, discusses the effect Southwest's low pricing has on creating passenger volume.
11. Annual Report 2002, *Chairman's Message* (Toyota Motor Company).
12. Toyota's 2002 Annual Report, for instance, foretold its current success with fuel economy vehicles.

13. Larry Bossidy and Ram Charan, *Execution: The Discipline of Getting Things Done* (New York: Crown Business, 2002).
14. Ohno, *The Toyota Production System: Beyond Large Scale Production*, 35–36.
15. Womack and Jones, in *Lean Thinking*, 256–57, describe a structure in which firms are organized by product families, with each reporting directly to the CEO. What is envisioned within this book is a variation on this description; during transformation, these product-family owners would report to the CEO along with the overall transformation lead who would assemble the overall picture of bottom-line value.
16. Corporations have demonstrated the importance of adopting guiding elements in a way generally consistent with that identified by Hammer and Champy, in *Reengineering the Corporation*, 102—identifying a transformation lead, a steering committee, and owners at the ground level. This book deviates with the latter in stating that firms must focus the efforts of those on the front lines on product families/value streams.

Chapter Ten

1. Deming, *The New Economics: For Industry, Government, Education*, 1.
2. John P. Kotter, *Leading Change* (USA: Harvard Business School Press, 1996), 68.
3. Ruffa and Perozziello, in *Breaking the Cost Barrier*, describe these results.
4. The author led the development of an information tool using this approach to identify opportunities to mitigate supplier constraints as described in *Supplier Utilization Through Responsive Grouped Enterprises*, Submission to the Supply Chain Council Awards for Excellence in Supply Chain Operations and Management. The description here appears generally consistent with the methodology for identifying product families identified in *Seeing the Whole: Mapping the Extended Value Stream* (Brookline, MA: The Lean Enterprise Institute, 2002), 3.
5. Ruffa and Perozziello, *Breaking the Cost Barrier*, 124.

Chapter Eleven

1. Michael Dell, in *Direct from Dell*, 78–79, describes the "direct model" and how it shortens the "long chain of partners" that typically deliver a product to the customer. It further states (80) that "inventory velocity has become a passion for us."

2. Jeffrey Liker and David Meier, *The Toyota Way Fieldbook: A Practical Guide for Implementing Toyota's 4Ps* (USA: McGraw-Hill, 2006), 145.
3. J. Welch and J. A. Byrne, *Jack: Straight from the Gut*, 128.
4. Ibid., 135. The authors state, "What worked before—control—is not enough for tomorrow . . ." While this comment was aimed at Welch's finance organization, his follow-on points indicated that the unthinking, command, and control organization of the past will no longer work. Instead, he wants people to question everything, to innovate—to create an organization of volunteers.
5. Deming, in *Out of the Crisis*, 78–82, discusses the problems that workers face because of problems in communication, waste in production, and problems with supplier contracts—a range of wastes that disrupt flow, drive up loss, and affect competitiveness. He indicates that workers desire to do things right; their frustration comes from their inability to take any sort of corrective action. Thus, they must come to see that this new way of doing business will give them the insight and authority to affect at least some of these situations.
6. This statement was provided to the author by John Entwistle, general manager of Garrity Tool Company.
7. Brian Hindle, "At 3M, A Struggle Between Efficiency and Creativity," *Business Week* (June 11, 2007), provides this information, and quotes 3M's CEO, who indicated that initiatives like Six Sigma bring the potential hazard of emphasizing "sameness" over creativity, undermining the real value offered by the company.

Chapter Twelve

1. Paul J. H. Schoemaker, *Profiting from Uncertainty: Strategies for Succeeding No Matter What the Future Brings* (New York: The Free Press, 2002), 7.
2. Deming, in *The New Economics*, 6, describes an exchange during one of Deming's seminars in which a man asked this question. Deming's response was in essence that a healthy firm is in the best position to increase value, whereas one that is struggling can only manage for the short term.
3. "Airbus, Boeing Envision Different Futures for Airlines," *The Washington Post* (May 29, 2004): E2. Although Boeing later improved, its future position is clearly not assured.
4. A report by the Boston Consulting Group released in May 2004 was described in: Paul Blustein, "Implored to 'Offshore' More—U.S. Firms

Are Too Reluctant to Outsource Jobs, Report Says," *The Washington Post* (July 2, 2004): E1. This article quoted this report as stating: "Successful companies ask themselves, 'What must I keep at home?' rather than 'What can I shift to LCC's?" This report purportedly indicates that many client companies' executives have low regard for American employees—from costs and erosion of skills to motivation—as compared to those overseas, and indicates that overseas facilities can quickly achieve similar or greater quality.

5. Hibbett was recognized by Forbes.com in *The 200 Best Small Companies* (www .forbes.com/free_forbes/2005/1031/187.html; year after year it climbs the list); it has subsequently been the subject of a number of articles.

6. Mike Troy, "Soft Economy Can't Stop Hibbett," *DSN Retailing Today* (May 5, 2003): 5. Hibbett's annual report describes its focus on employee development, particularly its detailed product and sales training, as well as its Hibbett Universities (HU) for store managers.

7. The data to produce figure 12.1 was obtained from Hibbett's annual reports.

8. I am grateful to Hibbett Sports for providing the information and statement in this paragraph.

9. Hibbett provided this information on merchandising's activities, as well as internal coordination methods to the author. A description of Hibbett's store-level training and other company coordination is contained in *International Directory of Company Histories*, vol. 70 (St. James Press, 2005).

10. Mike Troy, "Soft Economy Can't Stop Hibbett," *DSN Retailing Today* (May 5, 2003): 5.

11. Mike Troy, "Sporting Goods Executives Share Outlook at NSGA Show," *Discount Store News* (August 4, 1997).

12. Chris Isidore, in "GM Moves Back Ahead of Toyota," *CNNMoney.com* (October, 22, 2007), describes Toyota's challenges with declining quality ratings and its prospects for growth in the U.S. market.

Appendix

1. Sloan, in *My Years with General Motors*, 214–15, provides a table titled "Historical Summary of Sales, Net Income Before and after Taxes, and Dividends" for General Motors Corporation for the years 1917 to 1962.

2. Ibid., 200–1; describes the conditions that led in 1935 to authorizing "expenditures to reorganize, readjust, and expand the manufacturing facilities." Since this investment was for creating new value (as opposed to an

expense tied to sustaining the firm's activities), it has been added back into the net income number so that it will not result in a misleadingly high calculation of "value required."

3. Michael Baye, *Managerial Economics and Business Strategy*. New York: McGraw Hill/Irwin, 2002), 274.

4. Ibid., 187. The LRAC curves can be seen in figure 5.15(b).

Index

About the Author

STEPHEN A. RUFFA is an aerospace engineer, a researcher, and the originator of the concept of lean dynamics. His distinctive observations are framed by a quarter-century of background engaged in supporting many of the Defense Department's dynamic needs—from the design, manufacture, test, and repair of cutting-edge aircraft, to projects ensuring the availability of critical supplies for wartime demand surges. His joint government-industry study of lean manufacturing tools and practices across seventeen aerospace producers, together with his experience with implementing business improvement initiatives and his research on today's leading firms gives him the unique perspective that made this project possible. His works have been widely cited and recognized; his previous book, *Breaking the Cost Barrier: A Proven Approach to Managing and Implementing Lean Manufacturing* (John Wiley & Sons, 2000) was awarded the 2001 Shingo Prize for Excellence in Manufacturing Research. He can be contacted at sruffa@goinglean.net.

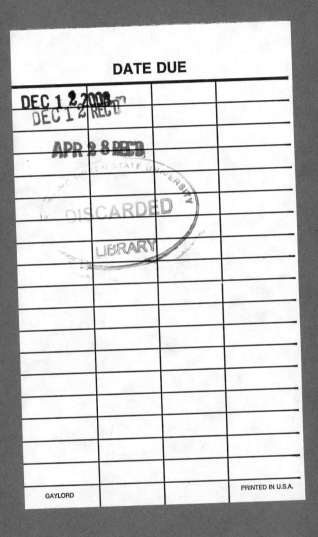